KYM MARSH

from the Heart

HODDER &
STOUGHTON

First published in Great Britain in 2011 by Hodder & Stoughton
An Hachette UK company

1

Copyright © Kym Marsh 2011

The right of Kym Marsh to be identified as the Author
of the Work has been asserted by her in accordance with
the Copyright, Designs and Patents Act 1988.

A CIP catalogue record for this title
is available from the British Library.

Hardback ISBN 978 1 444 70594 2
Trade Paperback ISBN 978 1 444 70595 9
eBook ISBN 978 1 848 94970 6

Typeset in Monotype Sabon by Ellipsis Digital Limited, Glasgow

Printed and bound by CPI Mackays, Chatham ME5 8TD

Hodder & Stoughton policy is to use papers that are natural,
renewable and recyclable products and made from wood grown
in sustainable forests. The logging and manufacturing processes
are expected to conform to the environmental regulations
of the country of origin.

Hodder & Stoughton Ltd
338 Euston Road
London NW1 3BH

www.hodder.co.uk

For David, Emily, Archie and Polly

CONTENTS

1
KIMBERLEY WITH AN 'I'

....

Kimberley Gail Marsh. That's what they called me. Gail!!

Back in those days I was Kim with an 'i'. The 'y' crept in halfway through my teens when I decided an 'i' was just way too uncool for a wannabe popstar! It makes me smile.

I was Mum and Dad's fourth child and by the time they got to me they were probably exhausted and way beyond worrying about little things like middle names.

'Where on earth did you get Gail from?' I asked Mum once.

'Oh, it was the name of the little girl who'd been living next door,' she replied. By that point there was no faffing around with baby-name books.

It was the same with the cine camera. We've got hours and hours of film footage of my oldest brother David, then plenty more of my sister Tracey and other brother Jonathan, but when it comes to me all you get is one shot of Mum carrying a baby – me – down my Grandma's garden path, stopping to smile at the camera. Then it just cuts out. I had quite a while to wait before I was in the spotlight again!

Being the youngest of four kids definitely teaches you from an early age that if you want to get attention you have to shout pretty loud. Thankfully I could always do that!

I was born on 13th June 1976 at Whiston Hospital in Knowsley, right at the beginning of one of the longest, hottest summers on record. David was ten, Tracey was seven and Jonathan five and just starting school.

My parents were made up at having a new baby. Mum had lost a baby after David and that had been really hard for them. She had been about five and a half months pregnant and no one could understand why she seemed to be losing weight rather than putting it on. It was in the days before scans and so it took a couple of weeks for the doctors to realise that the baby had died inside her and was poisoning her. It was a really tough time for the family. So when I turned up, Mum and Dad were just delighted to have another healthy little baby.

Back then we were all living in a cosy three-bedroom house in Avondale Road in Haydock. If you've not been to Haydock, it's a small town, halfway between Wigan and Warrington. There's not much there but for me it was home. I was two when we moved just down the road to a slightly larger end of terrace house in Kenyon's Lane, just next to the East Lancs Road. It had been a shop years earlier and on the side of the house you could still see the faded painted sign: 'Lemonade 1d' – what a bargain!

We lived in Kenyon's Lane until I was almost four, when Dad took us up in the world to a slightly bigger semi, ten minutes away in a village called Garswood. The village was thought to be a bit posher than Haydock. We loved it there.

Dad had worked his arse off to afford that house. He was a joiner and always out grafting. He ran a business with Mum's sister, my auntie Dilys. But running your own firm is never easy. When I was still tiny the business went under because a guy who owed them loads of money went bust, leaving them with nothing. It was a disaster. But gradually Dad built things up again on a smaller scale. But Dad was constantly working, if you're self-employed you don't have a choice, because if you're not working then you're not earning. I can't ever remember seeing Dad in those days without a pencil behind his ear, just in case it was needed at a moment's notice to jot down measurements or mark a spot on some timber. And every fag packet he ever had was covered in measurements scrawled in pencil. Dad smoked a lot in those days and for years I hardly saw him without a cigarette hanging out of his mouth. There wasn't as much press about the dangers of smoking back then, and Dad loved his fags.

I remember that there was always that warm rich smell of sawdust everywhere Dad went. He used to work a lot in the garage next to our house and if I was playing outside I'd go up to the door and listen to him sawing and breathe in the smell of wood shavings. And every time I opened the door of his beaten up old Ford Granada, a whirlwind of wood shavings would come flying out.

Dad still had his Kevin Keegan perm in those days. It seems crazy now that normal blokes like my dad would go out and get their hair permed, but they did. Despite the hairstyle Dad wasn't much of a one for fashion or bling. Looking back, he seemed to spend the whole time in work clothes, which meant a well-worn pair of jeans and a paint-splattered jumper.

My dad was my hero. I followed him everywhere from the moment I learnt to walk. When he saw me wandering up behind him, Dad would say: 'Here comes my shadow.' But I know he loved having me around too. We had a very special bond.

Whatever he was interested in, I was into too. We both loved music and from my earliest days he was always there, encouraging me to sing.

We also share pretty fiery tempers too. While Mum and my brother Jon are both placid and quite laid-back, me, Dad, David and Tracey are the total opposite. We're the more volatile ones in the family and we've all got terrible tempers if we're pushed.

Mum and Dad were very traditional in their outlook: Mum had a couple of short-term jobs in a factory but mostly she stayed at home looking after us kids and Dad was the bread-winner. With Dad working almost every hour God sends it was left to Mum to look after the four of us kids. It can't have been easy but she didn't complain. My mum is only five foot tall and when I was little she was quite tubby – not surprising, considering she'd had four kids. She went up to 10 st 7 lbs which was loads for her and she hated it but after a while she lost it all again and has never been more than a size 8 ever since.

Mum and Dad were joined at the hip, and they still are to this day. They met when Dad was playing in a band called Ricky and the Dominant Four. His name's not Ricky – it's Dave – so I guess he must have been one of the Dominant Four! He played lead guitar and used to sing a bit too. The band did really well for a time. They actually played alongside the Beatles at the Cavern Club in Liverpool; their name is even on one of the bricks in the club's wall.

One night they were playing at the Wings Club in Widnes and Dad saw this girl in the crowd that he really fancied. He couldn't take his eyes off her. When the band finished their set Dad decided to chat her up. He can't have been that rock 'n' roll though, because he had to get his mate to ask her out for him. Good job his mate agreed to help him out, because that bird was my mum.

She said yes straight away and they started dating. I like to think it was love at first sight. At least, that's the way it went down in family history.

Sadly things didn't go so well for Ricky and the Dominant Four. They had record company bosses coming to watch their gigs and were about to get signed when they had a falling out and broke up. So that was that. The Beatles went on to conquer the world and my dad went back to being a joiner.

My mum's mum was not at all happy about her going out with some fella who'd been in a band. One night they went out on a date together and Mum was just a few minutes late home. When she got back my grandma was already stood at the top of the road, fuming. 'You're not seeing him again,' she shouted, when my mum tried to make excuses.

Funnily enough, Dad's family didn't think my mum was good enough for their golden boy either. Both families were working class but maybe, just maybe, Dad's lot looked down on Mum's a little bit. So there was quite a bit of resistance from both sides to start off with. But in the end there was nothing anyone could do to stop the pair – they were meant to be together.

In a way, fate stepped in. They'd only been together six months when Mum fell pregnant with my brother, David. They were married just a couple of months after that. Mum was only eighteen and Dad was twenty. Everyone said it wouldn't last, but forty-five years later they're still together.

It can't have been easy for them at first though, because their families were dead set against the marriage. After they married they also had more problems when a fella conned them into buying a house which wasn't his to sell. They lost all their savings and had to move in with my Grandma and Granddad Marsh for a while but there were definitely tensions.

May Marsh was a very strong-willed woman with a heart of gold. She was tiny, but apparently she had a huge voice and a big personality. She went blind from diabetes when Dad, her youngest child, was just five years old. Even when he was an adult she still looked down when she spoke to him because I suppose the last time she'd seen him he was only three foot tall. When my parents got together she was so worried because Mum and Dad were just kids.

One day Grandma Marsh came home just as Mum was stacking up some dining chairs to lend to her sister and brother-in-law. Grandma Marsh couldn't see but Mum explained what she was doing.

'I'm lending our chairs to Norman for a party,' she said.

'I bought those chairs,' Grandma Marsh snapped.

'But they were a wedding present,' my poor mum protested.

'Yes, for my son.'

And that was it. It all kicked off and ended up with Grandma slapping Mum across the face with a wet dishcloth and saying she was a no-good piece of rubbish and it was all her fault that she'd got pregnant and made her son marry her.

And that wasn't the end of it either.

Mum got little David and went straight back to her mum's house and told her everything that had happened.

'You just stay here and have a cup of tea, Pauline,' Grandma Bousefield said. 'I need to pop out.'

Grandma Bousefield was so furious about the way her daughter had been treated that she marched all the way back to Grandma Marsh's house. When she got there she was so wound up that Granddad Marsh wouldn't let her anywhere near his wife. I think he thought she'd hit her and then it'd all end up in court. And it probably would have done. What a pair!

Mum didn't speak to Dad's family for two years after that. But by the time I was born it had all blown over and everyone was friends again.

Mum and Dad were never really a lovey-dovey couple in public, but they were obviously utterly besotted with each other. It wasn't all hearts and flowers, but they were always very much a team. If Dad wasn't working they would be together all the time. Dad was never one for going to the pub with his mates. He'd prefer to be at home helping Mum out. It was always clear to me that they truly loved being in each other's company. I've always thought that's the best thing you could ask for in a marriage – that kind of solid companionship.

Mum and Dad were delighted with our new home in Garswood. It was what they'd been working towards all their married life. Shame I put the dampeners on moving-in day. What happened was that I was lying behind a door, and when someone walked in I somehow twisted my neck. We should have been getting settled in, but instead we spent the evening in the local casualty department.

It was the 1980s when we moved into that house and after being firmly locked in seventies' style for years in the old place, the new place was a great opportunity to get all new furniture and decorations. In the old place, there was pampas grass in the garden and one of those front rooms that you see on the front of retro birthday cards now, with a red and brown stripy knitted throw on the sofa, swirly wallpaper and big pots with feathers in them. What a look!

But that was nothing on Auntie Joan and Uncle Fred's house. Fred is Dad's brother, and we saw a lot of him and Auntie Joan growing up. They had one of those pictures on the wall of a swan unfurling its wings over a naked couple. I think it's called *Wings of Love* and it's just so 1970s it hurts!

Our house was a semi-detached dormer bungalow and I loved everything about it. Me and Tracey shared a room, which can't have been great for her because there was seven years between us, but she never complained. We had bunk beds and I was on the bottom one, so I was forever getting my long, blond hair caught up in the mattress springs of the bunk above. Luckily Tracey was always there to untangle it for me, or it could have ended in tears.

Tracey was brilliant with me . . . and still is. She would take me into town on a Saturday and buy me little treats with her pocket money. She really is an amazing big sister. I'm sure I used to do her head in at times though.

One night I got out of bed screaming and was banging on the wardrobe door: 'I've gone blind, I've gone blind.'

'No Kim,' she snapped. 'I've just turned off the light. Now get back into bed you silly little cow.' Sisters, eh!

It must have been even worse for Tracey when she hit her teens and I was still hanging around her all the time, cramping her style.

At fifteen, Tracey and her best mate Jill Casson decided to become punks. They really went for it and Tracey had the whole look: leopard-print skirts and vests, dog collars, bleached-blond spiky hair, black lipstick, one lime green sock, one fluorescent pink one.

I was still playing with dolls and dressing up in fairy costumes so I thought it was all a bit weird. But it was cool too, because everything Tracey did back then seemed the height of cool to me.

She might have looked pretty terrifying to strangers in the street but Tracey was still a great laugh at home. She was very funny with a really sarcastic sense of humour. She had a terrible temper at times though, and I wouldn't want to cross her. Once I must have been really winding her up because she locked me outside the house in my underskirt. I probably behaved myself a bit more after that.

Like a lot of teenagers, Tracey did go a bit off the rails for a while and I'm sure Mum and Dad were tearing their hair out about her. One night she and some mates were messing about with a Ouija board and she claimed Sid Vicious had appeared to her and punched her in the face.

Another time Dad found her drunk over the back of the school field and went absolutely mad. He dragged her home and I held her hair back as she threw up into a washing-up bowl. 'You're silly,' I said to her, with all the seriousness an eight-year-old can muster. That probably didn't help much at the time. Next thing we knew, she got 'Sid' tattooed in India ink on her arm when she was drunk, in tribute to Sid Vicious. You can imagine what Mum and Dad thought about that!

Our bedroom must have looked bizarre. On one side were all my dolls and pink girly stuff and on the other side were posters of the Sex Pistols and Public Image Ltd.

I was too young to understand then, but I think Tracey must have been quite unhappy for a while. Beneath her sarky humour she was actually becoming quite a troubled person. She left school at sixteen but struggled to find a job and that was tough for her. She was still a punk and hanging around with what Dad called 'unsavoury characters'. Mum and Dad were really worried about her, but the more they made it obvious that they didn't approve of her friends, the more Tracey wanted to hang out with them. At first it seemed like the usual teen rebellion. Then one evening Mum was watching the telly and Tracey walked into the room and said: 'I've taken an overdose.'

I was in the room when Tracey came in and I heard what she said but I didn't really understand it – I was still only nine years old. Then there was this flurry of activity and Mum and Dad raced off to hospital with Tracey to get her stomach pumped. I was on the periphery of it all but I realised that something very bad had happened, and I didn't know what to do.

Looking back, it was clearly a cry for help from Tracey rather than a serious attempt to kill herself. Why else would she have told Mum straight away after taking the tablets? Thank God she did, and they were able to get her the treatment she needed.

Afterwards things just went back to normal. Or, at least, that's how it felt to me. Looking back, it must have been the most awful time for Mum, Dad and Tracey and there must have been loads of stuff going on in our family, but it all went pretty much over my head. Certainly Mum and Dad were very good at hiding things they thought might upset us.

Although she was physically better within a couple of days, it must have taken months and months for both Tracey and my parents to recover emotionally. She told them that she'd done it because she didn't think anyone would mind because nobody loved her. I still don't understand that because Mum and Dad made all of us kids feel very loved all the time. I can only imagine she must have gone to a very dark place in her mind.

It's only now I've got teenage kids of my own that I can imagine the terror of having a child try to commit suicide. I don't know how my parents coped as well as they did.

When I was really little my brothers David and Jon used to shared a bedroom upstairs. Since David was ten years older than me, by the time I was eight he'd moved out and Jon had the room to himself.

David had been a right handful when he was little. He was beautiful-looking with a head of blonde curls, but he was forever swearing at people. Old ladies would see him on the bus and say, 'Aren't you sweet?' and he'd shout back, 'Bugger off you silly old bugger,' then kick them in the leg. Charming!

According to my parents, he was a real horror of a child. He stuck a knitting needle in my auntie Joan's electric fire and blew it up, set fire to the kitchen bin, and had to go to hospital for shoving a stone up his nose. As the poor doctors were trying to get it out he was yelling: 'My granddad's going to kill you buggers for hurting me!'

Things didn't get much better when he got older. In his teens David became a Mod and would wear a long parka coat, Dr Martens boots and ride a scooter. The police were always bringing him home after he'd been caught fighting in the street.

But then he met his girlfriend, Sheila, and calmed down a bit, much to everyone's relief.

Mum says Jon was 'the only one who never caused me any trouble'. And she's right, really. Having said that, he caused me plenty when I was little. I don't think he ever really forgave me for turning up five years after him and snatching the role of baby of the family.

Jon couldn't bear me going into his bedroom so he would measure the turn-over of his bedcover to see if I'd been in there. And he'd never let me play with his Linka building set. The only game I was allowed to play with him was one where I laid on the floor and he jumped over me. It's funny how many times he managed to 'accidentally' kick me in the head while he was doing it. Maybe that was why I was allowed to play!

To be fair, to everyone else Jon was gentle, kind and thoughtful. And once I hit five years old we both started getting on a lot better too. Maybe I was old enough to be more of a playmate and less of an annoyance.

Gradually Jon and I became best mates. We both got BMX bikes and he could do bunny hops on his on the kerb outside our house. That was dead cool! I was in awe of my little big brother.

Mum and Dad were always pretty strict with us. There were set times that we were supposed to be in by and house rules we had to stick to. And maybe because David and Tracey had rebelled a bit in their teens, Jon and I couldn't get away with anything.

My dad wouldn't stand any messing at all. We might be able to get away with some things with Mum but if Dad found out we'd done something wrong then we'd know about it. In those days everyone used to give their kids a quick slap round the back of the legs if they'd been playing up and we were all used to it.

One night me and Jon had got out of the bath and were having a pillow fight when the pillow burst open and tiny bits of foam went flying all over the landing. Dad came storming up the stairs, saw the mess and slapped me, right on my bum. I hadn't got my pyjamas on and so there was this massive hand mark right across my bottom. That was the last pillow fight for a while.

I think Mum and Dad got it right though. There's a lot to be said for discipline. People think they're being kind to their kids by letting them have whatever they want and do whatever they want, but that doesn't make for well-adjusted adults. You don't do your kids any favours by spoiling them.

My best friend in Garswood was Trisha Dawson, who lived in the house diagonally opposite to us. Then Cheryl and Julia

Roberts (not *the* Julia Roberts) moved in next door to Trisha and we all hung around together.

Most of the time we got on brilliantly, but we did have our moments! One day we were playing Throw the Shoe (you can probably guess the rules). When it was my turn I lobbed the shoe as hard as I could, but Cheryl chose that moment to jump in front of me. The shoe smashed into her face and blood started pouring out of her nose. Cheryl ran off into her house crying.

Now everyone was terrified of Cheryl's dad, Alan. I knew he'd be out within moments so I went sprinting home and hid behind a chair in the front room.

Sure enough a couple of seconds later the doorbell went.

'Look what your daughter has done to our Cheryl,' Alan snarled at my mum.

He was a really big bloke and Mum was tiny next to him, but when it came to defending her kids she was like a giant. In no time at all Cheryl's dad had been sent packing up the path with a right flea in his ear.

And sure enough, by the following day me and Cheryl were mates again. We'd do handstands for hours and play What's the Time Mr Wolf? and Kerby with an old football. Mum would let me out in the morning and then she wouldn't see us again until six in the evening.

When I got a bit older, me and Trisha were allowed to go into St Helen's on the bus. Usually it was to go shopping for a 'big occasion' like Father's Day or one of my brothers' birthdays. I'd arrive home with a pair of psychedelic Y-fronts or a bottle of Hai Karate aftershave – classy presents, back then.

Once me and Trisha found a stray dog. I was desperate to

keep it but Mum was having none of that so we pretended it had run away and kept it in Trisha's garage. We fed it on cat food because that was all that we had but then Mum worked out what we were doing and rang the RSPCA. They came and took him away. I didn't forgive my mum for ages for that.

Even without that dog, our house was full of animals. There was a rabbit and Tracey's mice, Sugar and Sooty, various hamsters came and went, Jon's budgie Bluey and an aviary of little birds in the back garden. When Bluey died Jon was so upset he had to have a day off school. Dad made him a proper coffin out of wood and then we buried old Bluey in the front garden.

If I wasn't at home or out playing with Trisha we'd be round at one of my grandparents' houses.

Dad's mum, Grandma Marsh, died when I was one so I don't remember her, but it sounds like she was an amazing woman. She never let her blindness stop her doing anything. She had Braille on the cooker so she knew what temperature to put the hob on at. And she kept food in a strict order in the kitchen cupboards so she could always find what she needed. It worked brilliantly until one day someone decided to rearrange the cupboards and Grandma made a rice pudding out of birdseed.

They were all sat around eating it until they realised it didn't taste quite right. Apparently Grandma thought it was hilarious.

Dad has a brother, Uncle Fred, and sister, Auntie Jean, but sadly they both inherited their mum's diabetes and now they too are losing their sight.

My dad's dad was called Wally Marsh. Jon was named after

him – Jonathan Walter Stephen Marsh. And I thought Gail was bad!

I was very close to Granddad Marsh. I adored him and he was so proud of me, particularly when I started singing. After Grandma died he married a lady who we called Auntie Liz. When we went to visit their bungalow in Widnes, Granddad would always have saved me the green triangles from his box of Quality Street.

Granddad and Auntie Liz's house was full of strange ornaments and smells; there were smelling salts in a brown bottle that he kept on the mantelpiece and lavender bags which he made from lavender grown in his garden. Outside there was a greenhouse full of little red tomatoes in the summertime.

As I got a bit older and I started singing in public, Granddad Marsh's house became like a shrine to me, with pictures of me performing all over the walls. Maybe it was because Grandma used to sing and it reminded him of her. Or maybe just because at that age I came across as very confident – maybe even a bit of a show-off. I was always, 'look at me, look at me'. I think he liked that.

Before I'd even started primary school I was obsessed with singing. At three years old I was prancing around the front room crooning into one of my mum's candlesticks.

'Look at me, Mummy,' I'd say. 'I'm going to be on the TV one day. I'm going to be a singer when I'm a big lady.'

I don't remember watching anything particular on television that sparked that thought in me. It was like it had been there from the moment I was born. All I'd ever wanted to do was perform.

I begged Mum and Dad to send me to dancing lessons, so when I was five they enrolled me in ballet and tap classes. From then on they couldn't stop me pirouetting and clip-clopping my way up and down the hall.

But even the dancing didn't distract me from my first love: singing. There had always been music in our house and it just felt really natural for me to sing along to it. Mum and Dad were into all sorts of music. They had a big old record deck and a massive vinyl collection, but their favourites were the Beatles and the Carpenters. I loved Karen Carpenter's voice – she was a real inspiration for me.

Although he was never in a band again after Ricky and the Dominant Four broke up, Dad still played his guitar. He thought Hank Marvin was a legend and he'd sit in the front room and play The Shadows' songs for hours. He would play 'Walking Back to Happiness' or 'Bye Bye Love', and Mum would sing along. Both she and my sister Tracey had lovely voices.

While the Carpenters would be on the record player downstairs, in the bedroom I shared with Tracey she'd be listening to the Sex Pistols and upstairs David would have on the Specials or Bad Manners. Then when Jon got into his teens he was into a lot of dance music. So there were plenty of musical influences in our house and I lapped them all up.

I would have loved to have been able to make music like my dad, but the only instrument I really got to grips with was the triangle! Dad tried to teach me the guitar but I got as far as the theme tune to *Postman Pat* then gave up. But even if I couldn't play a musical instrument I found singing came totally naturally to me – performing, too.

Sometimes on Sunday afternoons I'd go with Mum and Dad when they went to the local Labour Club for a drink. I guess it was quite old-fashioned really with a guy on the piano playing like Les Dawson. Often they'd have what was called a 'Free and Easy Afternoon' when anyone could get up and sing. One afternoon when I was about ten, I went on and on at Mum about going up to do a song but she kept putting me off. I think she thought I was too young to get up in front of all those people. But I wouldn't give up and the next afternoon I mithered her for ages until she let me have a go. When she finally caved in, I went up and sang 'Living Doll'. I didn't fell nervous one little bit. In fact, I loved it. And the audience seemed to like it too. Mum and Dad were amazed. Next time we went in there they asked me to sing again and it became a regular thing. Mum even got me a little outfit to wear – fake leather trousers, fake red hair, a bright cerise belt and a pink shirt. At the time it was very fashionable, I'll have you know!

It was around this time that Granddad Marsh bought me my first proper microphone. It was a Shure SM58, a legendary microphone for singers, and I used it onstage for years – it's the one I still use now if I have to sing live somewhere. After that there was no stopping me: I was singing everywhere I possibly could.

Me and Granddad had a really strong bond. My daughter Emily now has the same kind of relationship with my dad, and it's lovely to see. A bond like that is just something special.

Granddad's house was such a cosy, calm place and I think he liked it that way. During the war he'd had a rough time and I think when he got home to England all he wanted was peace and quiet. He'd been a paratrooper and was dropped behind enemy lines in the Netherlands to take part in the Battle of Arnhem in September 1944. The incredibly brave attempt to gain control of key bridges and towns was later made into the film *A Bridge Too Far*. Hundreds of British soldiers were captured soon after landing on the ground and Granddad Marsh was one of them. He was sent to a Nazi prison camp where they took all his belongings, including his watch. Then he was kept there until the end of the war, working in the kitchens and surviving on potato peelings and black coffee (apart from the days when he was able to nick milk off the Germans).

On the day the camp was liberated Granddad went up to one of the German officers and demanded his watch to replace the one he'd had taken. My dad still has that watch which once belonged to an unknown Nazi prison guard.

Granddad was very proud of being in the Paras and later became president of the local British Legion. He'd lost a lot of friends during the war, so things like Remembrance Day really meant a lot to him and he would join the parade into town.

Granddad rarely talked about what had happened to him during the war. He preferred to talk about what I was up to at school or which new songs I had learnt. Sometimes he'd just listen while I sang to him in the front room. 'The Wind Beneath my Wings' was his favourite. When I got older I sang at his British Legion club too. You could tell he was as proud as punch.

*

Mum's parents lived on the other end of the Widnes Bridge in Runcorn. Granddad Bousefield had died when I was very little and I can't remember much about him, except for a long, wobbly wart on his hand that he'd wave at me and go 'Whoooooh!' The other strong memory I have of Granddad Bousefield is of him standing in pyjamas in a hospital ward, which must have been when we were visiting him after he fell ill with lung cancer. He'd worked with asbestos when he was younger and Mum was convinced that was what killed him.

After he died, Grandma Bousefield lived on her own in a flat in Runcorn. Sometimes we'd go round for our tea on a Sunday.

Gran's name was Regina Emily. Very posh! She'd been born on the Queen's birthday so that was where the name came from. She wasn't much like the Queen though, even if she liked to think she was. In fact, she was a total nutter, but in the best possible way.

She'd had nine kids and my mum was the last. Only just though. Mum and Auntie Pam are twins, and Mum was born just twenty minutes after her sister, but she still insisted on being known as the youngest.

Incredibly Grandma had already given birth to twins on two earlier occasions. But both times one of the twins had died. Even when Mum and Auntie Pam were born it was feared Mum wouldn't pull through as she was so tiny and in those days there wasn't any specialist equipment for keeping such vulnerable babies alive.

When Granddad Bousefield found out they were expecting Mum and Auntie Pam he wrote to their eldest son, Uncle Bill, who was then in the army. 'I'm so sorry,' Granddad wrote, apologising for the fact that he was going to have sisters more than twenty years younger than him!

Gran was hilarious. She had all these rhymes that she'd say which were either total nonsense or just rude!

'An empty sack can't stand up,' she'd say, handing round another plate of sandwiches.

When Grandma Bousefield's kids were little she'd make them sit behind the sofa covered in newspapers if there was a thunderstorm. And on wet miserable days when there was nothing else to do, she'd put them in different corners of the living room then let them fight each other!

Like I say, she was a nutter – but so funny.

She was a bonny-looking lady with curly hair, soft skin and pink plastic-rimmed glasses. When she was younger, if she was going out she'd lick her finger, rub it on the red-patterned wallpaper then dab it on her lips instead of lipstick.

But although she might have looked very sweet and gentle, her favourite things on the television were the boxing and wrestling. 'Go on. Gooooo on,' she'd shout at the telly as the fighters got stuck into each other. She loved snooker too. 'Oh here's little Rabbit Arse!' she'd laugh every time Steve Davis was on.

My early childhood now seems like a stream of happy memories. Family meant everything to us then – and it still does today. But I had great friends too and a home that we loved.

When I was ten I started performing in the Starlight Roadshow, which was a group of kids who would get together to put on shows with lots of singing and dancing. It was my first taste of performing and I absolutely loved it from the start.

Looking back, the first ten years of my life were such a happy time. I was doted on by everyone and even though we weren't rich by any standards, we were truly happy.

Maybe that's why when things started to go wrong it hit me like a truck.

2
DOUBLE LIFE

....

It was the summer before starting secondary school that every-thing started to go tits up.

Up until then my childhood had been pretty idyllic. I had brothers and a sister who adored me – well, most of the time – a fab mum and dad, a lovely house and friends up and down our road.

And school was fun. I had a classful of friends and everyone played together. There were no little cliques and everyone seemed to get along. At Garswood County Primary School I was always in the school plays and was selected for the choir too. My finest moment was playing an Indian lady in one of the shows. I told the man who ran the corner shop at the end of our road all about it and he lent me some beautiful bangles and a bindi so I really looked the part. I remember at the time thinking it was pretty fab.

I think the worst thing that ever happened to me in my entire time at Garswood Primary was when I was four, and I wet myself in PE. I was wearing pink shorts with a 'K' embroidered on them and I had to take them off and change into the old grey knickers they kept in the spare clothes box. At the time it was dead embarrassing, but in the grand scheme of things not that much of a disaster! Back then I never thought school could be a place of fear and unhappiness. That was still to come.

I was in my final year at primary school when Tracey sprung a surprise on the whole family – she was pregnant.

Tracey had just come out of her punk stage but she still hung around with slightly weird people. As for blokes, she always went for quirky, odd-looking guys with troubled pasts. She was never going to bring home some clean-cut hunk who worked in a bank! Malc was lovely, but he was definitely Tracey's usual type. He had the biggest mop of unkempt hair you've ever seen. It looked like it'd never been washed.

Malc and Tracey had been together about six months when she fell pregnant.

She was still only seventeen and me and Tracey were still sharing the bunk beds at the time. I remember thinking that her tummy was becoming quite swollen but she blamed it on an infection. I was too young to think much more about it.

Then one day Tracey started suffering terrible pains in her stomach. They got worse and worse until she was literally sliding down the walls in agony.

Mum called a doctor who came out straight away and examined Tracey. He diagnosed that yes, she did have a bladder infection but confirmed that she was also pregnant. This came as a complete shock to Tracey and of course the rest of the family. I was nine and I remember being so excited when she told me I was going to be an auntie.

Mum and Dad weren't best pleased about it though but there wasn't any screaming and shouting. By then the baby was only four months away and even if we thought Malc was a bit odd it was clear that Tracey was mad about him.

And what could Mum and Dad say anyway? Mum was only eighteen herself when she fell pregnant with David. I think in the end they might have thought it wasn't an ideal situation, but they tried to support her as best they could.

The plan was that Tracey would stay living at home during the pregnancy and then after the baby was born she and Malc would move in together then get married.

For me, it was a double whammy. Not only was I going to get a gorgeous new baby nephew or niece, I was also going to get my own bedroom when Tracey left home! I was made up at the idea of being an auntie and couldn't wait for the baby to come.

And so, even though there was a bit of family turmoil, from my perspective everything in my life was great until that summer I left Garswood County Primary School.

'We're going to have to move, love,' Mum told me one day. It was a bolt out of the blue.

'But I like it here,' I complained. Back then I didn't understand that however bad the prospect of moving was for me, it was far, far worse for my parents.

What Mum didn't tell me was that we were moving because Dad's business was in desperate trouble again. Work had been getting harder and harder to find over the past couple of years and the situation was really serious. We had no choice but to sell the house to pay off some of the debts or Dad would go bankrupt.

Looking back on it now I can see that my parents must have been worried sick about money for ages, but Mum and Dad managed to keep all that from me. The first I knew anything was wrong was when Dad's business shut down, he was out of a job and our house went on the market. Dad traded in his car for an old, second-hand clunker and suddenly money was very tight.

Mum has always been a terrible worrier and, from the sounds of it, Dad tried to protect her from the full reality of their financial problems for a while by hiding the bills that they couldn't pay. It meant that he was taking on more and more stress on his own shoulders and dealing with it on his own.

In the end the business couldn't continue and there was no choice but for Dad to pack it in and sell the house.

Even I could tell that the atmosphere in our family was changing over that summer. Mum was upset and Dad must have been incredibly stressed out by the whole thing but they still did an amazing job of keeping the worst of it from us kids.

During the six-week holidays we went on holiday to Lloret de Mar in Spain. It had been booked before the business went bust and so, as it was already paid for, Mum and Dad thought we might as well go.

When we got there it was teeming down with rain. It was like that for the entire week. Of course Dad had packed the tiniest case with nothing but shorts and T-shirts so we had nothing suitable to wear and nothing to do either except sit in our hotel room and look out at the puddles, or splash about in the pool. A new hotel was being built next door so, on top of everything else, all we could hear all day was the constant banging of the builders.

I was too young to realise it at the time, but years later Dad told me that he got really, really down during that holiday. With everything that had been going on at home and then the disastrous holiday, he hit rock bottom.

Apparently one day everything seemed so bleak to him that he even thought about taking his own life. It must have been horrific for him because he knew that when we got home from this crap holiday we were going to have to move out of our lovely house and start all over again, with absolutely nothing.

My dad is very old-fashioned and has always believed the man should be the provider in a family. I think because of everything that had happened he felt less of a man. He thought that somehow he had failed his family.

But, do you know what? I think it shows how amazing my dad was, that even though he was feeling that low, he was still able to keep things as normal as possible for us kids.

When we got home Dad went to the doctor's and I think they prescribed him some antidepressants to help him cope with everything that was going on.

The only good news around that time came when Tracey gave birth to a gorgeous baby boy – my nephew, Trevor.

I was eleven when Tracey came home from the hospital with baby Trevor and I was beside myself. He was a gorgeous baby and I adored him. I couldn't believe my luck – it was like having a real-life doll. But now the baby was here, Tracey was ready to move into the house she and Malc had found on a council estate in Wigan.

Tracey, Malc and Trevor weren't the only ones upping sticks. Soon afterwards we had all moved out of our lovely home in Garswood to a council house ten minutes away back in Haydock.

The day we packed up our things in the removal van and drove off in Dad's second-hand car was heartbreaking. I loved our house in Garswood so much and I hated the idea of leaving.

My best friend Trisha came over from across the road to say goodbye. She stood by the car and waved as we drove up the road and off to our new life. I hardly ever saw her again after that.

It was horrible. I may only have been eleven but I was very aware that after having had a very comfortable life, suddenly we seemed to have nothing.

Our new house was at the very end of a cul-de-sac called Wesley Avenue on what was then a fairly grotty council estate. Our neighbours were all lovely people, and I did make a few friends there, but some of the families were pretty rough. It certainly wasn't the best of neighbourhoods back then.

Our house may only have been rented but Dad worked night and day to make it as nice as possible. In our old house he'd built a huge fireplace out of brick and wood around which Mum had her collection of brasses, which she'd polish with Brasso once a week. Dad set to work building an almost identical fireplace in Wesley Avenue, although this time it had to be a bit smaller.

We still had the same sofas as in the old house but all the rest of the furnishings had to be sorted out as cheaply as possible.

Mum has always been incredibly house-proud and in our old house she was always dusting, mopping and polishing. She did just the same in Wesley Avenue too, but I could tell it wasn't the same for her.

From the moment we moved into that house, the atmosphere in our family was different. There was something in the air. Mum and Dad never rowed in front of us and on the surface things were just the same as they'd always been, but beneath that I think they were both feeling very down. It must have been so hard for them to lose everything they had worked for and start all over again. I think at that time we were all just a bit sad. It was quieter too with just me and Jon living at home then.

Then, at the beginning of September, I started secondary school at Birchall High School in Ashton-in-Makerfield. Lots of my friends had gone on to different schools and from the beginning I found the change very difficult.

At junior school all the kids had played with each other whoever they were. But at secondary school the girls seemed to fall into little cliques and if you didn't fit in with them it made life pretty miserable.

For some reason I found it really difficult to make friends at that school from the very beginning.

I had just one friend really, Joanne Williams, but I didn't even really see that much of her outside of school. And it felt like no one else really wanted to hang around with me. Back then I was definitely a geek rather than one of the popular crowd. I was well behaved, my school uniform was neat and tidy and I wouldn't have dared be cheeky to a teacher. I tried hard to fit in, but maybe the other kids in my class didn't think I was cool enough to hang around with.

Certainly my parents didn't have the money to spend on brand-name trainers and clothes, and when Dad picked me up from school it was in his beat-up old Datsun Estate rather than in some expensive company car like some of the other dads drove.

I struggled through my first year and managed to keep my head down.

But in the second year things got far, far worse. Suddenly the cool kids started noticing me, but for all the wrong reasons. That's when the bullying began

At first it was name-calling. 'Frigid!' they'd yell at me across the playground. I was twelve years old and had hardly been near a boy, and according to them that was wrong. Most of the bullying came from five or six girls in the year above me, who all hung around together in a cool crowd. They were doing all sorts with boys – if their mothers had known I bet they would have been horrified – and obviously they thought I should have been doing the same.

The other thing they were all obsessed with was who had the biggest tits. I was totally flat-chested until I was about fifteen, so that was another thing for them to have a go at me about.

To make matters worse, they seemed to sense that our family hadn't got much money. I suppose they could work that out from the estate where I lived. 'Scrubber,' they'd sneer at me as I walked down the corridor. Then they'd have a go about my dad's car or the clothes I was wearing.

By then I was also singing at weekends, and I think that made me stand out from the rest of the girls too. It was another different thing about me that the bullies could latch on to.

I was still performing in the Starlight Roadshow, and loving it. We would rehearse every week then do shows at weekends in different pubs and clubs. The group was based in Liverpool and run by a couple called Paul and Carol Edgar. Once a week after school, Dad would drive me the fifteen miles over there for rehearsals. It was the highlight of my week, especially when I'd had a tough time at school.

On performance nights I would sing solos like '99 Red Balloons', 'Girls Just Wanna Have Fun' and lots of Madonna stuff. I thought it was just brilliant being onstage in front of an audience. I did some dancing in the show too, but it was singing that I really loved.

When I was up there singing and dancing on a Saturday night it felt like I could be the real me. Up onstage I was confident and happy – an entirely different person to the bullied little girl who on Monday morning would feel like a quivering wreck again.

When Dad drove me down the East Lancs Road for a show the change would begin. As each mile ticked past I felt like I was coming out of the shell I'd been forced into during school hours. By the time we arrived at the venue I would be the real me again. I guess performing gave me a way of expressing who I really was. Maybe that's one reason why it became so important to me. The Starlight Roadshow was my escape from the grimness of my school life. It was a lifeline.

The other kids in the group all loved performing too, so we had loads in common. When I was with them there was no name-calling, no bitchiness.

Just before Tracey had given birth another really exciting thing had happened – my dad fixed up for me to go into a studio in Blackburn and record some songs. He'd met a guy who ran the studio at one of the shows I'd done.

'She's got a really nice voice,' the man told Dad. 'You should bring her along to the studio.' Of course, I was dead excited about the idea.

I sang a song called 'Do You Wanna Dance?' and it sounded dead good. But the most exciting thing for me was being in a proper recording studio and seeing all the equipment. I was still only eleven, but being there made me certain that I wanted to be a professional singer.

Once we had the track recorded on tape we then had to work out what to do with it next.

'I think we should take it to London and give it to some of the record companies,' Dad said.

Because he'd once been in a band himself, Dad understood quite a bit about the music industry and how it worked. Although he knew first hand how tough the business could be, he and Mum both knew it was my dream to be a singer and would do anything they could to help me. They weren't pushy parents at all, but they were incredibly supportive.

For the trip Mum went out and bought me a new outfit, a pair of chinos (very trendy at the time) and a reversible jumper, which had white rabbits on one side and was plain on the other (maybe not quite so trendy!)

I'm not sure where Dad had got the list of names and addresses of the record companies from – this was before we'd heard of the Internet – but he'd written them all out neatly on a sheet of paper.

We took the train down to London. I'd never been there before so turning up at Euston station and seeing all the cars and people was exciting in itself. Dad had warned me that I wasn't going to be signed up immediately and that I shouldn't go expecting miracles. But as we travelled around London on the tube, going from one record company to the other, maybe I was secretly hoping for a little miracle. Just a tiny one.

At each office block we handed the tape over to a receptionist while Dad explained what it was and who I was.

Goodness knows whether anyone ever even listened to those tapes but we never had a single response from any of the record companies. Each morning I ran downstairs to see if there was a letter from one of them, but nothing came. It didn't put me off though. No, if anything, the trip to London just made me more determined to be a singer.

When I accepted that none of the record companies were going to get back to me, I tried hard not to be disappointed but it was difficult: singing was my only way to escape the torments of school life, which was getting worse and worse for me, and I was becoming more and more miserable with every day that went by.

3

STICKS AND STONES

·········

Although I had a few friends in my class, the older kids continued to pick on me.

I desperately tried to pretend I was just the same as everyone else to avoid drawing attention to myself, but the reality was that I didn't really have a lot in common with a lot of the kids in my school. They were happy messing about at the back of the class and spending their weekends hanging around the park or the arcade in Ashton. I wasn't into that. And I didn't want to end up stuck in a job that I couldn't stand either. I wanted to be a performer. I had a goal in life and I was determined to graft as hard as I could to achieve it.

But with every week that passed at school, the bullying just got worse. The bitchy name-calling and the snide remarks were getting out of hand. It quickly felt as though it was spiralling way out of control.

Soon I was under attack every break time from the moment I arrived in the morning until the final bell of the afternoon rang. The other kids in my class weren't too bad but there was a gang of older kids that had set me in their targets. One of the toughest things was that I couldn't work out what I'd done to deserve all this abuse. I tried to keep my head down, but it didn't seem to make any difference.

OK, so I wasn't interested in snogging boys or smoking or going behind the New Block and doing things I shouldn't be doing. But even so, that didn't seem like a good enough reason for the other kids to hate me so much.

When I was about twelve, I did get a boyfriend but for me it was very innocent. But I don't think I was prepared to go far enough for him so he just stopped ringing me and one day I saw him walking down the street with another girl. After that finished there were even more shouts of 'Frigid!' when I walked into the playground. The boy had obviously spread the news that I wasn't into sleeping around. I was twelve years old for God's sake. The whole thing seems incredible.

But there is nothing as cruel as kids in situations like that. Now I look back and think those bullies must have had problems themselves to pick on a kid who was just minding her own business. But at the time I began to wonder if maybe they were right. Maybe there *was* something wrong with me. *After all*, I'd think to myself, *there must be some reason why everyone seems to have it in for me.*

I tried everything I could think of to fit in and be more like the other girls. I even started smoking, thinking that might make me more accepted. I'd go and buy 'seppys' from the shop up the road. They were cigarettes that were sold separately for 20p each. Then I'd smoke them in the alley by the side of the shops where we waited for the school bus. It was difficult though, because I had to make sure Mum and Dad never saw me at the same time as making sure that the bullies *did* see me. That way, I reckoned, they might just think I was cool enough to be left alone. It's funny to think about it now – me desperately trying to smoke my way into the popular crowd – but at the time it felt dead serious.

Smoking was just the start. One Saturday afternoon I went into Ashton market with my mate and nicked a top off one of the stalls. Loads of kids in my class were pinching stuff at that time and if you hadn't done it you were totally square. My heart was pounding when I shoved the top in my bag, but I had to do it just so that I could tell my classmates about it.

Even now, when I think about it I feel a bit sick. I can still see that top vividly in my mind. It was a white, off-the-shoulder number with long sleeves. It was actually pretty horrible. I could have at least nicked something half-decent!

I even persuaded Mum and Dad to throw me a thirteenth birthday party, just so I could invite all the kids in my year and try and win them over. My parents really couldn't afford it but in the end they agreed to a disco at the local Conservative Club.

The whole thing was a disaster. Even though we were barely in our teens, a load of kids from school gatecrashed with loads of booze and got really drunk. One of them pulled a cistern off the toilet wall, there was a massive fight outside and people were being sick everywhere. Mum and Dad were gutted.

I felt like things couldn't get any worse.

The bullies must have been able to sense blood because they kept it up day after day.

'Oi, you're so flat the walls are jealous,' they'd shout. Or, 'What's that heap of junk your dad is driving, Scrubber?' They hid my towel in PE, pulled my skirt up in the playground and called me fat and ugly over and over again.

If the teachers noticed what was going on they certainly didn't do anything about it. I was too terrified to tell anyone what was going on. I reckoned that if they thought I was a grass on top of being square, frigid, flat-chested, ugly, a scrubber and God-knows-what else, then things would get even worse. I thought they'd get bored eventually and leave me alone.

Instead, they started getting physical.

It got to the point where I was pushed and shoved in the corridor every day and randomly hit as I walked through the playground. They kept wanting to fight me but I just didn't have it in me. Despite the digs about my weight, I was physically small and slim and not a bruiser by any means. But a couple of the older girls would goad me over and over again.

'D'ya wanna fight?' they'd say, coming right up to my face, knowing they were terrifying me.

'No,' I'd stutter, backing off, and they'd laugh at me like it was the funniest thing they'd ever seen.

One day one of the bullies started picking on me again in the playground. I felt physically sick as I saw her looming towards me.

'D'ya wanna fight then?' she asked.

Yeah right! Of course I didn't want to fight. I wasn't mental. She was really stocky and was obviously going to batter me.

I tried to walk away but this girl started shoving me around. I kept thinking, *But I haven't done anything wrong.* In many ways that was the worst thing about it, I really had no idea what I'd done to deserve all this.

In the end a teacher broke it up. It was right at the end of the day and as I walked out of the school gates I thought to myself, *I'm not coming in tomorrow.*

Next morning when Mum called me down from bed I told her I felt sick and couldn't go in.

'Oh you do look a bit pale,' Mum said, and I was allowed to stay off.

And that was how it went from then on.

Whenever possible I would claim to be sick: tummy aches, headaches, whatever I could think up. A lot of the time Mum believed me and allowed me to stay off, but sometimes she'd insist that I go to school. I didn't tell her about the bullying. I reckoned she had enough to worry about after Dad's business had folded. For more than a year I kept it to myself, too embarrassed and miserable to tell anyone what was going on.

During that year I spent a lot of time alone in my bedroom, listening to music. Mum and Dad noticed I was becoming quieter and more withdrawn but they just put it down to my age and all the hormones racing around my body. Basically, they thought I was being a typical mardy teenager.

Staying home gave me a break from the bullies. But the more days I took off school, the further behind I fell on my lessons and the more I dreaded going back again.

Finally my mum refused to buy the line about feeling poorly any longer.

'What's going on?' she asked me one morning.

And that's when I told her the whole story about the name-calling, the pushing and shoving, the fights in the playground.

By then the bullying had been going on for over a year and I was so frightened I couldn't face going to school at all. The thought of walking up our garden path in the morning in my brown school skirt and jumper made me feel physically sick.

'Please don't make me go back there,' I begged her.

Mum made an appointment with the head teacher in the hope of sorting it all out.

'Well, Kim,' the headmaster said to me, 'why didn't you come to us about this before?'

Suddenly it was as if I was to blame for everything. *Maybe they were right*, I thought. *Maybe it* was *my fault*.

Afterwards Mum and Dad talked to the head teacher alone and were assured that the bullying would stop immediately. Predictably, that didn't happen and so things rumbled on the same.

The name-calling, pushing and shoving – and worse – continued day after day whenever I ventured into school. So more often than not I stayed at home.

Everything in my life had changed so much in such a short space of time.

Just two years earlier I had been at a school that I loved, lived in a home I adored and had friends up and down the street. Not only that, but I was excited about becoming an auntie and my mum and dad were happy.

But now I was too frightened to go to school, I barely had any friends, I had a tiny little box room in a council house in a pretty rough area, my dad was working every hour God sent to try to get us back on our feet and still my parents were struggling.

Things were pretty bad.

At school I'd almost finished my second miserable year. The teachers hadn't done much to stop the bullying and I had reached a point where I was barely attending classes because I was so scared.

'You don't have to go back any more,' Dad told me one day. 'We've got you into a new school.'

I'd like to say that when I heard that I was dancing up and down with happiness, but that wouldn't be quite true. I was pleased that I would never be going back to Birchall High, but by then the damage had already been done. I'd become so convinced that I was fat and ugly and that I didn't fit in that I was worried that all the problems would just start all over again at my next school.

I mean, if the cool kids had hated me at the last school, then surely the cool kids at the new school would hate me just as much? That's all I could think back then.

In a way, my sister Tracey's method of dealing with the problem was probably more effective than anyone else's. One day soon after I'd left Birchall, me and Tracey had gone out window shopping while Mum looked after baby Trevor. We were walking through town when I saw one of the bullies.

She was walking towards us along the pavement and just seeing her started me shaking. My heart was racing and I could feel sweat start to prickle at the back of my neck. It sounds incredible now that a fifteen-year-old girl walking down a street could make anyone feel like that, but by then I was utterly terrified of those bullies. It wasn't so much that they had pushed and shoved me every day. It was more that they'd succeeded in humiliating me so often that I was terrified of them.

'What's up?' Tracey asked, when she saw the state of me.

'Over there, that's one of them,' I admitted.

Tracey looked up and down the street then clocked who I was talking about. She marched over and grabbed the girl by the throat. The bully must have wondered what the hell was going on until she saw me in the background.

Tracey was out of her punk stage by then but she was still pretty tough.

She pushed the girl up against a wall and put her face right up close.

'You touch her,' Tracey said, pointing at me, 'you talk to her, you even look at her again and I'll kill you.'

The girl looked petrified. I'd never seen her look like that and it was strange – a complete role reversal. Finally she must have realised what it was like to have an older girl have a real go at her. For me, I think the best thing about it was that it made me see that the bully was human too and could also get scared. But despite that the damage for me had been done.

Even now, I could name every single one of those girls, the ones who made my life a misery at Birchall High School. I could tell you which form they were in, what colour their eyes were, how they wore their hair and the style of their winter coat. But what would be the point of that now? It might make me feel better to shame them publicly for what they did, but if they are reading this they will already know who they are and hopefully they will already feel a bit ashamed. And if they're sitting reading a book about a girl they once bullied, then well, they'll know I did pretty good despite their bitchiness and their slaps and their nasty little nicknames.

I just wish I could have told that to my thirteen-year-old self.

4

NEW SCHOOL, OLD PROBLEMS

....

I stood taking a drag on a fag with a couple of the girls from my class. We were standing around in 'Smokers', which was what they called the scruffy area round the back of Cansfield High School. It was where the cool kids congregated every break time, armed with their Regal and Silk Cut and well out of view of the staff room.

My navy blue skirt was rolled up around my waist to make it as short as possible. My fingernails were painted burgundy and I was wearing thick black mascara.

As far as I was concerned, I was looking pretty cool.

Ever since I arrived at Cansfield I was desperate to be accepted by the other kids. I couldn't bear the thought that some of the girls would think I was a geek again and carry on where the Birchall High girls left off. So I changed my attitude – I decided to pretend to be hard.

My plan kind of worked at first. I certainly wasn't in the cool crowd but at least I made a couple of mates. The problem was that starting a new school two years after everyone else wasn't easy. Other kids had already settled into friendships and because my self-confidence was so low I found it hard to break into those cliques.

But at least everyone was OK to me. There was no pushing and shoving and no one shouted 'Scrubber' when I walked down the corridor.

It was around that time that we moved out of the house in Wesley Avenue. Mum and Dad had been desperate to get out of there. It wasn't that there was anything particularly wrong with the house – it was more what it represented. I think Dad felt like a failure because he'd lost his own home and we'd had to rent off the council.

But it wasn't easy to get out of that council house because even though Dad was working again he still couldn't get a mortgage. Dad had been determined though to make sure he didn't go bankrupt but it was still a struggle.

In the end my brother Jon bought a house in his name, and Mum and Dad paid the mortgage. Before moving in we went to stay for a bit with Tracey, Malc and Trevor. My sister had married Malc when the baby was five months old and they moved into a council house in Wigan. They later saved enough money to buy a house in Ashton and that's where we moved in with them. By the time we moved in with them Trevor was two and toddling around. I doted on him. He was just fab – a real little personality already.

The house Jon bought was a terraced house next to a pub in Bamfurlong, towards Wigan. It wasn't a palace by any means, but it was ours and we all felt a lot more settled there.

So on the surface things appeared to be picking up.

But deep down I still felt vulnerable. The bullies had shattered my self-confidence and in my head I could still hear them slagging me off, calling me fat and ugly. When you've had those things said to you day after day after day it's pretty hard not to start believing they must be true. I was constantly terrified it was all about to start again.

I believed the only way I could make kids at the new school like me was if I pretended to be cooler and tougher than I really was. But what started out as an act to impress the other kids gradually became the real deal. Looking back, I was changing and becoming much more rebellious. I guess I'd worked out that was the safest way to avoid being picked on.

I was smoking every break time with some of the tougher girls and giving a bit of lip in class. I wasn't outrageously naughty or anything but I was no goody two-shoes any more. I'd found out the hard way that being nice didn't get you anywhere.

But even if I was messing about a bit in class, out of school I was still totally focused on becoming a singer. I'd spend every spare moment learning new songs and practising them in my bedroom. Mum and Dad had bought me my own karaoke machine when I was ten and we lived in Garswood.

Around about that time I left the Starlight Roadshow and started doing more of my own gigs in pubs and social clubs. Dad bought me some sound equipment and together we would drive to gigs in Runcorn, Widnes, Liverpool, Manchester and North Wales.

Even at the age of thirteen, performing on my own didn't faze me at all. The Starlight Roadshow had given me the chance to do solos in front of a big audience and it just felt like the next step from there. I never got nervous; I just loved being onstage. What better way to spend my evenings and weekends?

If a gig was on a school night I'd sit in double maths or geography not listening to a word the teacher was saying, just thinking of the moment that I'd step out on to that stage. When the last bell of the day rang, I'd be literally legging it out the school gates. As soon as Dad was back from work we'd get in the car and head off to the venue. When we arrived at the club we would unload the car together and then I'd go into the ladies' toilets to change into my stage outfit and do my make-up. It was hardly glamorous, but I loved it.

Some of the pubs and clubs I sang in were pretty, er, colourful, shall we say. One night I was singing 'The Wind Beneath my Wings' when two women started punching the crap out of each other right in front of me. I suddenly felt Dad's hand on my arm and he yanked me off the stage to safety.

Another time it was a man and a woman attacking each other. I never did work out what it was all about, but the man gave the woman a terrible slap.

Pretty often I'd be singing a Whitney Houston or Madonna number and there would be two guys slugging it out over by the bar. It was all good training though! Whatever might have been going on around me, the show had to go on.

Despite the occasional punch-up, most of the audiences in the clubs were brilliant. People always seemed surprised because I was so little and yet I had this big voice. My brother Dave used to call me 'Trio' because I was like the little girl with the huge gob in the adverts! I'd sing 'Perfect' by Fairground Attraction or a Shania Twain song and everyone would join in.

But there were a couple of times when idiots in the audience tried to make it difficult for me. I think because I was little they thought they could intimidate me. One night they were heckling me all through my first set and when I came offstage I was crying. I really didn't want to go back on for the second half

'No way, Dad,' I muttered. 'They're just going to do the same thing to me again.'

'You'll be fine, love,' said Dad, ever the optimist. 'Give 'em hell.'

I was just about to start singing again when this fat, bald bloke at the back started yelling at me. I could feel myself shaking but I knew that this time I had to fight back. I managed to muster up all my courage and shout back at him.

'Oi, you with the sunroof over there,' I yelled, gesturing to his bald head. 'Why don't you just shut it? Or if you think you can do better, get up here and give it a go.'

That shut him up. Everyone in the audience laughed, the fella slunk back down and I felt instantly more confident.

Through people we met on the local club circuit we were introduced to a guy called Pash who ran his own recording studios. He heard me sing and suggested to my dad that I should go in and record a couple of tracks.

Even though my first attempt at going to London and getting signed hadn't been a great success, I was still very excited about having another go at recording.

I recorded a couple of songs at Pash's studio and then one day he rang my dad and said he had someone coming in who might be interested in listening to me.

Dead excited, me and Dad rocked up to the recording studio

the next weekend. Shortly after we arrived this guy turned up. He was in his fifties and was a real larger-than-life cockney with hands like shovels and thick grey hair. He introduced himself as Kevin Kinsella and explained that he ran an independent record label in Manchester and also managed a few different acts. He had loads of contacts in the music industry and later went on to manage Robbie Williams for a while when he first came out of Take That.

He sat and listened while I sang a couple of songs. Then afterwards he walked straight over to my dad and said, 'Your daughter has a lot of talent. I really think she could do things.' He invited us to his house the next day where he had a contract all ready for us to sign.

Dad couldn't believe it – and neither could I! I was thirteen and I'd landed myself a manager. Bloody hell!

Kevin really thought I could have a big career ahead of me. He had faith in me and that was an incredible boost to my confidence. Kevin was amazing with me from the very beginning and I have no doubt that without him I wouldn't be where I am today. He put so much energy and trust in me and became like my second dad. I still call him 'Daddy' now and in some ways I'm like the daughter he never had. He'll always be a massive part of my life.

For months there was a really bad tension at home.

Then things started going wrong at school too. I fell out with one of the tough girls that I'd been hanging around with. It began over something really petty, but she fancied herself as quite hard – not someone you really wanted to fall out with.

Soon I was pretty isolated. After that, it didn't take long

for all those insecurities about being fat, ugly and unlikeable to rear up again.

Looking back, I can see that there doesn't even have to be a specific reason for someone to get bullied. A couple of nasty kids just see a weakness in another child and they start to attack. Then it snowballs and soon everyone is joining in.

It was nowhere near as bad as my last school, but as soon as the name-calling started up again I began retreating back into myself. Looking back I feel it's such a shame because of all the problems I had with other kids I was never able to really concentrate on my academic work. I just wish I'd had the chance to learn in an environment where I wasn't feeling anxious and scared all the time.

Going to the recording studio after school or on the weekend was about the only thing that made me happy. Kevin would often be there and he was dead easy to talk to about what was going on. 'Everything OK at school?' he asked me one evening.

'Not really,' I said, determined not to cry. 'I don't know what it is about me, but however hard I try, I always seem to be different. And girls don't like that, do they?'

'No, I'm afraid they don't,' Kevin replied.

We didn't talk more about it then, but obviously it got him thinking.

A couple of days later, Kevin rang my dad.

'I've been talking to Kim,' he said. 'Why don't we move her to a stage school?'

Dad paused for while. There was no way he and Mum could afford to send me anywhere like that, however much they might have wanted it.

Kevin must have read his mind because, before Dad could say anything, he went, 'It's OK. I'll pay.'

When Dad put down the phone and told me all about it, I was gobsmacked. Mum and Dad had always thought stage school would be the best place for me, but there was no way they could have afforded the fees themselves. We couldn't believe Kevin could be so generous.

I was crazy with excitement.

There was only really one stage school in the North of England at that time, the Elliott-Clarke Theatre School and College in Liverpool. Over the years it has produced dozens of singers, actors and actresses who have gone on to great things, so the thought of going there was just brilliant. When I started, Claire Sweeney, who went on to star in *Brookside*, was just finishing her time there.

Kevin sorted everything out for us and I joined halfway through the year, when I was thirteen.

Right from the beginning it was like a breath of fresh air to be surrounded by other kids who were just as focused as me. We were all working towards a career in performing, which gave us something in common. I didn't have to pretend to be tough any more.

One day Kevin called Dad and said he'd found a song that he wanted me to record. It was called 'One Kiss' and he thought it would make a great single. It was quite poppy and I loved it.

But the most exciting bit for me was when Kevin landed me a slot on ITV's *This Morning* to sing it. When he called Dad to say I was going on the show I started squealing with excitement. Back then, the show was filmed at Albert Dock in Liverpool so Dad drove me over there first thing in the morning.

I'd had my hair cut specially for the occasion. Up until then I'd had a really dodgy perm with a mullet, so I got that all cut out and had a long bob instead which I wore in a ponytail. I had a brand-new outfit too – a baggy T-shirt, shorts and a pair of orange Kickers. They were these chunky boots that were dead cool at the time.

When we got inside the studio and I saw all the cameras and the production crew, I was just made up. *This is really happening*, I had to keep on telling myself. *You're not imagining this*. It seemed like everything I'd ever dreamt about was coming true. I was pretty much walking on air.

Fred Talbot the weatherman and Susan Brookes were hosting the show that day because Richard and Judy were away. After I'd sung the song they were really sweet and asked me all about myself.

'So, do you sing in the bath?' joked Fred.

'Er, we haven't got a bath,' I replied. 'I sing in the shower though.' Everyone laughed.

It was an amazing day. But the next morning I was back in my uniform, back at school, and it felt like the whole thing had been a dream.

Though it was a brilliant experience, being on the telly didn't help me at school. In fact it just marked me out as different to my classmates. I felt the more successful my singing career became, the harder I had to work at fitting in at school, which meant me trying to be cool with more backchat and more smoking.

*

Around that time I also had to make a video for the single to try to increase its chances of getting airplay. Kevin drafted in a guy called Nigel Hall to shoot it, who is now one of Simon Cowell's right-hand men in his Syco organisation. They also booked a male model to be in the video with me.

We were going to film the video in the gardens at Granada TV in Manchester, next to the set of *Coronation Street* where, bizarrely, I would return to work almost twenty years later.

On the morning of the shoot Nigel and I were sitting in reception at Granada waiting for the model to turn up.

After a while this slightly strange-looking guy walked slowly towards the building.

'Well, if that's him, Kimberley, we've shit it,' said Nigel.

I have to admit, when it turned out it *was* him, my heart sort of fell.

But it was still fantastic to be making my own music video at thirteen years old, even if my co-star in the video looked like an ugly version of Neil Morrissey complete with leather jacket and shaggy hair. Looking back, the video must have been incredibly cheap-looking. I was wearing a polo-neck jumper and jeans, but was still absolutely freezing. It was so cold you could see my breath in the video when I started singing.

The video was shown a bit on local television and I got on local radio too, but Kevin's record company was still quite small and I was never going to go shooting to the top of the charts.

And even though I hadn't had a top ten hit that time, I was determined to carry on until I did, so I was soon back in the recording studio.

My next single was called 'Amor' and I was invited back on to *This Morning* to sing that too. I also did local newspaper and radio interviews and I managed to get a lot of publicity for the song. I just loved performing and recording.

Kevin was fantastic. Because he believed in me, I kept faith that one day I would get my break. As far as I was concerned, it was just a matter of time.

Kevin also fixed me up with some great gigs. One night I did a gig at the Hammersmith Palais in London, which was incredible. That was until someone threw a drink on me from the upstairs balcony. I mean, what an awful thing to do to a kid! But I just carried on singing and got a massive cheer from the audience, while the bloke that did it got thrown out.

I also performed at Discotheque Royale in Manchester on the same bill as Chesney Hawkes and Dannii Minogue. For me, that was completely unreal. These were people I'd read about in *Smash Hits* and now we were sharing a stage. I guess it was around about then that I changed myself from Kim to Kym – it just sounded a bit more cool, I reckoned.

Bizarrely, I even travelled to Poland to represent France in a song competition. Don't ask why I was representing France – it was something to do with some French songwriter that Kevin knew. I actually sang the song in English which was a relief but I did have to learn a bit of Polish so I could chat to the presenter between songs. It was pretty random, but it was also great training to go out and do something like that, which was so far outside my comfort zone.

That was a great trip. Before then I'd only ever been abroad with Mum and Dad camping and on our disastrous holiday to Lloret de Mar. So it was incredibly exciting. I went with

Kevin, his wife Norma and their son Kevin Junior, and we all stayed together in a hotel in Gdansk. People in Poland had saved up for months to be able to go to see this one show and it was a really big deal out there. I couldn't quite get my head round the fact that Curiosity Killed the Cat, Black Box, Tiffany and Transvision Vamp – all big acts at the time – were on the bill too, although they weren't in the contest. We were all staying in the same hotel, and the band members were dead lovely to me. I've even got pictures of me and Tiffany together. I used to look at all those big stars and think: 'I'm going to be like you one day.' And even back then I really believed it.

What was strange was that although I had the beginnings of a successful music career, at the same time I was still a very ordinary teenager.

After I signed with Kevin Kinsella, I didn't do as many live gigs in pubs and clubs because I was supposed to be focusing my efforts on recording. But now I didn't have to travel all over the place singing every night I had a lot more spare time on my hands. And of course, being a teenager, I chose to spend my time hanging out with mates from my new school.

I even had a couple of boyfriends although it was never anything more serious than a quick kiss or a trip to the cinema and the relationships only ever lasted a matter of weeks.

One lad I went out with was called Tony Anderton. He was such a laugh. I knew him because my sister was friends with his sister. Once he went running up and down the road in baby Trevor's bonnet and he did hilarious Frank Spencer impressions. But again after a couple of weeks we decided we didn't really want to be going out as boyfriend/girlfriend any more and we went back to just being friends.

Tony was great but Mum and Dad weren't so happy about some of the other kids I was hanging about with. We'd go round each other's houses or sit in the park and smoke. We weren't doing anything particularly bad – definitely nothing compared with what teenagers get up to nowadays – but my parents were worried I might go off the rails like Tracey had done. In fact I wasn't doing anything that bad at all really but I guess they were scared I might get in with a bad crowd and chuck away my chance of being a singer. But I was never, ever going to do that. I just wanted to have a laugh with my mates *and* carry on working towards my dream.

I was smoking before, during and after school, but I reckoned that as long as Mum and Dad didn't find out, it'd all be OK.

And how could they find out? At school if there was ever a bag search I shoved the fags down my bra, since they weren't allowed to check you around there. On the way home I chewed gum to disguise the smell on my breath and bought a roll-on perfume, which I smeared on my hands to disguise the whiff of tobacco on my fingers. I thought I was being dead clever – little did I realise these were all tactics that had been used by a million teenage smokers before me!

Then one night on the way home from school I did something really stupid. I threw my fags into a white carrier bag with my gym kit. Problem was, the bag was so thin that when I walked in the door Mum could see a packet of ten Regal as clear as day through the plastic.

'What the hell do you think you've got in there?' she yelled at me as I belted up the stairs. I ran upstairs and lobbed the packet straight out of a window into the backyard. God only knows what I thought I'd achieve by that; the damage had already been done.

'Wait till your dad gets home, Kym,' Mum shouted at me. I knew that was going to mean serious trouble.

Mum had never smoked, but Dad was on about forty a day at that time. Tracey and both my brothers smoked too, so it was hardly like I was the first person in my family to have a puff. But that wasn't likely to get me off the hook. To my folks, smoking was a sign that I was becoming a rebel, that I might throw away any hope I had of being a professional singer.

'So, what have you been up to then, Kym?' Dad asked when he got in that night.

'Nothing,' I replied. I was already well into the role of Sulky Teenager by then.

Dad was surprisingly calm, really. There was no shouting and swearing that night. Instead he tried to explain how worried him and Mum were about me. But as a typical stroppy teen, I thought they were making a big fuss about nothing.

'You're smoking, you're messing about at school and hanging around with girls who've got no ambition in life,' Dad said. 'If you really want to be a performer, you need to focus a bit more.'

'I'm fine,' I snapped.

'You're not fine,' Dad pointed out. 'You need to knuckle down and work harder at your singing.'

A couple of years earlier I'd been singing round the house morning, noon and night and I guess he couldn't understand where that little girl had gone and how she'd been replaced by this stroppy teenager.

I knew in my heart that I was still as committed as ever to becoming a singer but I couldn't make them see that I just wanted to do things that normal teenagers did too.

I guess Mum and Dad had been through so much disappointment over the past few years with losing the business and our home that they desperately didn't want me to miss out on my chance of a singing career. They weren't pushy parents by any means, but they thought I had a good opportunity in front of me and they were terrified I was going to let it slip through my fingers.

But sadly while all this was going on, we were coping with tragedy at home. Soon after my appearance on *This Morning* we were hit by another terrible blow when Granddad Marsh died.

His wife, Auntie Liz, had passed away just a couple of months earlier and he'd got sick himself after she died, but I never for one moment thought he was going to die. At first when he went into hospital I was allowed to go and visit him, but then Mum and Dad started going on their own.

'Why can't I come?' I'd ask.

'Granddad's a bit tired at the moment,' Mum would reply. 'Maybe he'll be feeling a bit better at the weekend.'

It was just before my 14th birthday and I had such a strong bond with Granddad – we both adored each other – so I really couldn't understand why I wasn't able to see him any more.

Looking back, I realise that my parents were just trying to protect me. The reality was that my granddad was dying from bowel cancer, and they didn't want me to have to deal with that.

Dad told me later that once he visited Granddad and he was rubbing the arm of the chair.

'What are you doing?' Dad asked.

'Oh,' Granddad said. 'I thought our Kym was here. I was just holding her hand.'

In his final days Granddad was allowed home but he was dosed up on loads of morphine because he was in so much pain. But still I wasn't allowed to visit him, and I had no idea how poorly he was.

Then apparently, late one night, Granddad started reliving every detail of what had happened when he was parachuted behind enemy lines near Arnhem and ended up in the German prisoner-of-war camp. He was talking to himself and drifting in and out of consciousness but he was clearly running the whole story through in his mind.

Then just a couple of hours later he died.

The first I knew about what had happened was when Mum and Dad came to pick me up from school in the car.

'How's Granddad?' I asked, the way I did every afternoon.

'You'd better get in the car, Kym,' Dad said.

'Why?' I demanded. 'What's happened?'

I got in the back seat as Dad turned around to me and took a deep breath. 'I'm afraid your granddad has died.'

'No. No,' I shouted. I was so angry. 'You're lying,' I said. 'You said he was going to be all right. You said he'd be OK.'

I started screaming like a madwoman and there was nothing Mum and Dad could do to calm me down. I was so shocked and furious that I'd never had a chance to say goodbye. I know my parents had just been trying to protect me, but it made Granddad's death all the harder to cope with.

I felt so cheated that I'd missed out on seeing Granddad Marsh for a final time that I insisted on going to visit him at the chapel of rest. Mum and Dad didn't want me to go but I was adamant. When I walked in he didn't really look like my granddad any more. He'd always been quite a chunky guy but now he was so thin. I wasn't scared, though. I just leant over and kissed him. I was glad I'd been able to do that, to say goodbye properly.

Granddad's funeral was amazing. A Union Jack was draped over his coffin, and there were people lining the streets, walking behind the procession and saluting when his hearse was driven past. They played 'The Last Post' for him. Inside the church they played a recording of me singing 'The Wind Beneath my Wings', which, in a way, was our song.

I've now got Granddad's war medals and I will always treasure them. Luckily he lived just long enough to see me sing professionally and I know he was dead proud. He knew that was what I always dreamt of.

I had just turned 14 but in the space of a couple of years I'd learnt how quickly things could change and how nothing was ever the same for ever. It was a tough lesson, but one I never forgot.

After Granddad's funeral I tried to get on with life at Elliott-Clarke and I made some good friends there. But I still carried scars from the bullying at my other schools. Those bullies had told me that I was fat and ugly so many times that beneath my confident exterior, my self-esteem was shot to pieces.

And those scars were about to reveal themselves in the most horrific of ways.

5
SECRETS

....

I slammed the toilet cubicle door closed and stood silently waiting for the last pair of school shoes to shuffle out of the girls' loos.

Only when I was convinced there was no one in hearing distance did I lift up the black plastic toilet seat and lean my head towards the bowl. The stench of industrial toilet cleaner caught at the back of my throat. I can still remember it now.

I stayed in that doubled-over position for a couple of seconds, sort of wondering what to do next. I was terrified of getting caught, but I knew I had to do it.

Come on, Kym, I said to myself. Before I had time to back out, I crammed my hand into my mouth and pushed my fingers as far down my throat as I could until I felt myself gag.

The rest was surprisingly easy. A couple of seconds later I was throwing up the school dinner I'd eaten just ten minutes earlier. It must have barely got into my stomach because the whole lot reappeared looking pretty much the same.

When I was finished, I pulled the toilet chain and it all

disappeared. Gone. Nothing to make me feel guilty. But more importantly, no calories in my body.

I walked out of the cubicle again and stood in front of the line of square mirrors above the hand basins. *Hmmm*, I thought. *Still look exactly the same. Got to keep on trying.* I hadn't really expected to lose three stone the first time I threw up but part of me was now determined to carry on throwing up until I did.

I washed my hands and face then dried them with one of the greyish hand towels from the dispenser on the wall.

Eugh, the smell of paper towels. Even now that fusty whiff of paper towels takes me straight back to those school toilets, back to the time when I thought chucking my guts up would make me lose weight and miraculously solve all my problems.

I was the very last person that should have been bulimic. I'd always hated being sick, I hated listening to other people being sick and I couldn't bear that bitter taste you're left with in your mouth afterwards. The whole thing was vile.

But within a couple of months of arriving at Elliott-Clarke School I'd got myself into a daily routine of vomiting. On some level I must have known it was wrong, because I never told any of my new friends about it.

It was my dirty little secret.

My best mates at stage school were Emily Walmsley and a girl called Nadia. We'd go to under-eighteens discos together and talk about music and dancing for hours – I'd never had that with friends I'd met at my other schools.

Most of the kids at the school were focused on working towards a career in show business and it was fantastic that for the first time in my school life I wasn't marked out as unusual because of my passion for singing and dancing.

But even though things were a million times better than at my old schools, something still wasn't right. Even for an ambitious kid like me, life at Elliott-Clarke was tough. During the day we had normal school lessons, which were fine, although to be honest by that time I wasn't interested in the academic stuff. I was going to be a singer, so why did I need to know about algebra? How was it going to help me to know how many wives Henry VIII had? There was no practical application to what I was learning, as far as I could see.

Although it was a drama school, we only had performing arts classes after we'd done a full day of normal classes. And even then, most of the emphasis was on dance. We'd have two-hour lessons of ballet, tap or modern almost every afternoon.

As a kid I'd loved dance classes, but when I got to Elliott-Clarke it became clear that although I was OK at it, dancing didn't come as naturally to me as it did to some of the other girls. I really felt I was struggling with dance there, and pretty soon it felt like all the enjoyment of it had been sucked out.

There were plenty of drama classes too – which were pretty fun – but we didn't do nearly as much singing. That was a bit frustrating, since it was such a passion for me.

More worryingly, I was developing all these problems around my weight.

I think most girls have body issues during their teens. You keep thinking, *Why have I got fat there? When are my boobs going to grow? Why am I like this?*

And of course, I'd had three years of being told I was fat and ugly by the bullies at my old schools. It was all too easy to convince myself that all that must be true. I really think that being bullied was at the root of my bulimia.

On top of that, I was spending two or three hours a day in dance classes surrounded by skinny little girls – natural ballerinas, unlike me.

I felt like a big galumphing elephant next to them. I was fourteen and beginning to develop breasts and curvy hips. I was becoming a woman, but I just felt fat. I'd stand at the barre and look at the other girls' skinny thighs and flat tummies. In hindsight, they were probably not much different to me, but in my mind I was flabby, lumpy and ugly.

When I look back at pictures of myself at fourteen, I've got the body of a typical teenager. I wasn't one of those rake-thin girls but I was certainly slim. At the time, though, I was convinced I had to get thinner if I was going to be as popular and successful as the other girls in my class.

I absolutely hated having to change out of my grey school skirt into my black leotard for dance. I felt like the whole class would be staring at my thighs and whispering about how gross they were. But it was such a strict regime at Elliott-Clarke that I would never even have considered asking to wear a tracksuit instead of a leotard. It just wasn't allowed.

I just hated the way I looked.

I would avoid all the mirrors in our house and took to wearing baggy sweatshirts and jeans to cover up my body. I'd even try to stand as much as I could to avoid sitting and seeing my thighs flatten out and my stomach crease. I'd imagine I had rolls of fat, and hate myself for it.

'Mum, do you think I've got fat legs?' I asked her one day as I stared at my thighs.

'Don't be daft, Kym,' she said. That had always been Mum's response if I mentioned anything about my weight. 'You're absolutely fine.' And that was the end of the conversation.

The funny thing is, like I said before, my mum has always had a bit of an issue with her weight too. For a while when I was quite little she hit ten and a half stone which is quite a bit for her because she is only 5 ft tall. The weight crept on after she had kids and at first it didn't bother her.

Eventually, someone told her she'd put on a bit of weight. She'd reached a size 14 – still hardly massive. She lost all the weight again but from then on her weight was a big issue. She was always trying out different diets, signing up for keep-fit classes and going on about how much she needed to lose weight. And while us kids were having our tea she often just wouldn't bother with hers.

I don't think that had a particular impact on me, but maybe it was lurking somewhere in the back of my mind that women had to worry about their weight.

When I first became really upset about the way I looked I tried dieting. I'd grab a slice of toast in the mornings at home, tell Mum I'd eat it on the train then throw it in the bin at the bottom of the street. Then I'd ban myself from sweets and chocolate and refuse to finish Mum's dinners at home. But none of it really made much difference to my weight. I guess what I was trying to fight was my body changing from a little girl into a woman, and there was no way I could stop that.

It was when that didn't work that I came up with the idea of throwing up meals.

I'm not quite sure how I ever learnt about bulimia or when

I first thought it would be a good idea to make myself sick. I suppose I'd heard about the celebrity bulimics at home and on telly. There was Princess Diana, who'd apparently tried to deal with her feelings of worthlessness through throwing up meals, and the singer Karen Carpenter, who'd died of heart failure after years of anorexia and bulimia. But I didn't think I'd be hurt by it.

I think what really pushed me to try it myself was over-hearing a conversation between two girls in my class at Elliott-Clarke School one day.

'Did you see her in dance class last night?' one of the girls asked the other.

'Oh my God, yes,' her mate replied. 'She is just sooo skinny.'

'I know she's tiny. But apparently she's been throwing up in the bogs at lunchtime. She's always in there. She's definitely got bulimia.'

I'd seen the girl in dance class too and been shocked by how tiny her legs were and how her bottom didn't even protrude in our black ballet leotards. It felt like my arse stuck out half a mile in mine.

To make matters worse, the teachers insisted on taking pictures of us when we were dancing, which they then put up on the wall. The teachers said it was so that we could check out each other's style and form, so that we could see areas where we needed improvement. But of course we used the photos to compare others' bodies with our own.

Maybe I should do that throwing up thing, I thought. *If it's working for her, it could work for me. I could just do it for a while and see what happens.*

*

Looking back, I don't think I was ever a true bulimic because I was very conscious of what I was doing all the way along. I knew people could die from bulimia, but I was convinced I wasn't like them. They were people who had no control over what they were doing and were addicted to making themselves sick. I never felt like it was out of my control. For me, almost right until the end, every time I made myself sick it was a conscious decision and I told myself I could stop it at any time.

Maybe I was kidding myself.

I never lost sight that what I was doing was wrong and knew that if anyone ever found out they'd go mad. I didn't ever feel cleansed after being sick in the way that a lot of bulimics do. No, for me, it was purely a case of getting those unwanted calories out of my stomach as quickly as possible.

But whatever way you look at it, it was a stupid, stupid thing to do.

For a while, I think I really believed that making myself sick would not only get rid of the fat around my thighs and the top of my arms, it would also make me more beautiful, a better dancer and more popular. I thought it could solve all my problems. Of course, in reality, it just gave me new ones.

Soon I was throwing up my school dinner every lunchtime in the girls' toilets. Sometimes I'd cry afterwards. I felt a horrible sense of guilt because I knew what I was doing wasn't right. And I was really scared of getting caught because that would mean big trouble. But I thought it would all be worth it so long as I could lose weight.

Throwing up meals soon became a daily habit and over

that first year I lost half a stone and dropped to below seven stone, which was quite light for my five-foot-four-and-a-half-inch frame. (Trust me, that half inch is very important!)

But even though my weight did drop, it still wasn't enough to make me feel any better. In my head I could still hear those bullies pecking away at me. Their words ran round and round my head.

'You're so fat.'

'You're dead ugly.'

'You're a scrubber.'

Around this time, I was becoming increasingly frustrated by the regime at Elliott-Clarke.

Aside from the fact that there were hardly any singing lessons, I also started to feel that any individuality was being driven out of me. I felt that it was almost as if we were all being cloned. It was such a strict regime at that school. We all had to wear exactly the same uniform: knee-length skirts, thick jumper, grey blazer and straw boater hats. The list of school rules seemed unending: no eating in the street, boaters to be worn at all times outdoors, no make-up, no chewing, on and on it went.

I was desperate to express myself, but at school it seemed we were all expected to look and act exactly the same. I felt trapped.

As time went on, I started to play the class clown a bit. One day my friend brought a musical box into class which looked like a book. We put it on to the bookcase next to my desk and every time the teacher turned away I'd set it off so the music started playing.

The teacher was going potty. 'Who's making that noise?' he kept shouting. But he never turned around in time to catch us.

Because the school was in Liverpool, I was out the front door at half seven in the morning to catch the train and I wasn't home until half seven in the evening – a long day for a kid, even a hard-working one like me.

Usually I caught the train with my friend Natalie Haydon, whose parents ran a pub down the road from our house. One winter morning we were on the train to school and this strange bald guy started staring at us.

'So, girls, off to school are you?' he asked.

'Er, yes,' we replied.

'And where do you go to school?'

We mumbled something about going to Liverpool. We didn't want to tell him anything, but it was pretty obvious from our uniforms where we were headed.

We got off the train at Liverpool Lime Street and set off on the ten-minute walk to Elliott-Clarke. But when we were about halfway there we turned around to see the weird bald guy following us. We were both terrified and ran the rest of the way to school. The police were called and Kevin came straight over to the school to check I was OK.

The whole incident really shook me up, especially as it was winter by then and I was coming home in the pitch black every night. Even though Dad nearly always collected me, I was still scared.

It was really the final straw for me. For me, the fun had already been taken out of performing. Life at Elliott-Clarke was so regimented: I had to dance when I was told, sing when

I was told and act when I was told. On top of that, the journey was a pain in the neck and now I was scared of weirdos on the train.

I wanted to leave, but as Kevin was paying the fees I didn't think I could. It would have looked really ungrateful. So I struggled on for a while longer.

At the same time I was still recording songs in the evenings and at weekends. What I really missed was all the live gigs I used to do. Without them, some of the thrill had gone.

Sometimes I felt like my life was happening without me actually having any involvement in it. Does that make sense? I was doing things because other people told me to, not because I wanted to do them.

Experts say that people often use bulimia as a way of exerting some control over their lives. The idea is that if someone feels they can't control the big things that are going on, they can at least control what food is going into their bodies.

I can see that that might well have been the case with me.

As the months went by, I was making myself sick more and more often. If the toilets were busy at lunchtime I couldn't take the risk of doing it, so I'd wait until the first class of the afternoon then put my hand up and ask to be excused to go to the loo. They'd be empty then and I'd be able to make myself throw up without anyone hearing.

It reached the point where I could be sick really quickly, mop my face with a paper towel and be back at my desk in less than five minutes. I was always so careful not to let anyone guess what I was up to and I don't think they ever did.

I started throwing up at home at weekends and in the evenings after my dinner too. I had to be really careful though, because our house was quite small and I couldn't let Mum and Dad hear me retch. With enough practice I managed to do it silently. I wasn't stupid and knew exactly how upset Mum would be if she found out, so I did everything I could to keep it secret.

The dangerous thing about bulimia was that it looked like I was eating normally because I could tuck into massive plates of food, knowing I'd be bringing it all up again ten minutes later.

If we went out for dinner to a restaurant, for a birthday or something, I would have the same portions as Mum and Dad. Mum would occasionally say, 'You're looking ever so thin, Kym.' But she'd seen how much I was eating, so when I said, 'Of course I have,' she had to believe me.

As the months went by something was gradually changing. In the beginning, after a meal I'd think, *Right, I want to be sick now,* but now it was more like, *I need to be sick now.* Bulimia was starting to take hold of my mind and that was a bit worrying.

But I was losing weight and looking slimmer and I liked that a lot. It made me feel like I really was able to control something about my life; I'd wanted to be thinner, and now I was.

Then, soon after I turned fifteen, it really hit me. I realised I was no longer as in control of what I was doing as I had been. Instead, the need to be sick after every meal was beginning to control me. A few times I walked into the toilet cubicle and found I could throw up when I wanted, without even having to put my fingers down my throat. I felt like I'd crossed into a different zone and that frightened me.

This isn't right, I thought one day. *What? I can't even control when I'm sick any more?* That for me was a big issue. There were so many areas of my life where I didn't feel in control – I didn't want food to become another of them. My mum was also asking more and more questions about how much I'd eaten and when. I don't think bulimia occurred to her, but I'm sure she wondered if I was anorexic.

This is going somewhere I don't want to be, I said to myself. *I've got to stop it now.*

And so I did. Just like that. It sounds weird, but from then on I tried never to make myself sick again. At times, I had wobbles; sometimes I had to make myself sick if I ate too much. I found that eating little and often was the key for me. I stuck to simple, bland food to start with, just toast or milky drinks, and eventually built up to proper meals.

I put a little bit of weight back on, but not masses, and it didn't even really bother me that much. It was like I'd been in this crazy phase for eight months or so but then it passed and it was over. Looking back now I realise how lucky I was; it was only a brush with a very serious illness for me, more of a cry for help. I would urge anyone going through a similar experience to speak to someone they trust and don't try to deal with it on your own.

Although I was looking and feeling healthier, I knew that something still had to change. I was so fed up of Elliott-Clarke by then that when I looked at those skinny little dancers, rather than think *I want to be like them*, I was more inclined to go, *To hell with the lot of them.* I'd had enough of people telling me what I should look like and dance like and be like. I wanted to be me.

I was still pretty unhappy, but I was beginning to get angry too. I'm not sure what caused that change in me, but I definitely felt the difference. I could still hear the taunts of all those old bullies in my head but I was sick of being a victim. I was mad that they'd ruined so many years of my life.

I'm convinced the main reason I had a brush with bulimia was because of the bullying I'd suffered. Really, I was one of the lucky ones, because ultimately I was able to stop throwing up. Thousands of other girls aren't so lucky and bulimia rules their lives for years and years and years.

There are dozens of anti-bullying charities and campaigns in this country now that do fantastic work. That said, I still don't think the bulk of people have any idea how damaging school bullying can be to its victims, and that still makes me angry. School should be a safe environment, not a place where children live in a constant state of terror.

Bullies of all types get gratification out of intimidating and humiliating other human beings. The sad thing is that day after day, all over the country, they're able to get away with it.

For me, this is extremely serious. Bullying really does ruin people's lives. And every day parents send their kids to a place which they have entrusted to care for them and where they're supposed to be having fun and learning about life, but in actual fact some children spend their time there in a constant state of terror. I support a lot of anti-bullying charities but I still don't think enough is being done in schools to stamp it out. I just thank God that somehow I managed to curb my bulimia when I did, and stopped bullying from ruining my life.

6
TEEN REBEL

....

It was while I was bulimic that I became best mates with Natalie Haydon. Getting the train together to Elliott-Clarke every day had made us really close, but even then I didn't tell her about making myself sick. That was something I couldn't share with anyone – not even my best friend.

In the evenings we'd meet up in the car park of her parents' pub, the Caledonian, or the Cally as it was known, and hang around there or go back to hers to watch telly.

Soon there was a group of us all hanging around together: me, Natalie, another girl called Sam Whitter, her brother Lyndon, their mate Paul Carroll and a couple of his mates.

Paul and his mates were older than us. They were seventeen and one of them had a car. I was fifteen years old and pretty naive, so to me they seemed much older and incredibly cool.

In particular, I thought Paul Carroll was the bee's knees and when he asked me out I was made up.

I'd had other boyfriends before but only for a couple of

weeks and nothing serious. Kids' stuff, really. Paul was my first proper boyfriend. He had blond hair, blue eyes and everyone thought he was really good-looking. I thought I was massively in love with him at the time but it was probably just infatuation. Looking back I was way too young to even know what love was. But if anyone had said that to me back then, I'd have gone off in a strop. As far as I was concerned this was the Real Deal.

The group of us would drive around Ashton-in-Makerfield in Paul's mate's car. It may not be most people's idea of a banging night out, but honestly the whole thing was exciting and I was having a right laugh.

Unfortunately my parents didn't see it quite like that. In fact, they were going out of their minds with worry. All they could see was their daughter hanging around with older boys and fooling around in cars. For them, the whole thing spelt disaster.

'Where are you off to tonight then?' Dad said, as I stood by the front door just about to go out and meet the others.

'Just out,' I said airily.

'Out where?'

'Just out,' I snapped. 'OK?'

But that just set Dad off big time.

'No, it's not bloody OK,' shouted my dad. 'I suppose you're going to just go and hang around that car park with them lads again, are you?'

No answer from me.

'Well you're a bloody fool, Kym,' he said. 'You could really make something of your life but you just seem to want to throw it all away. You just don't care any more.'

There had been a load of rows and lectures along those lines in our house over the previous couple of months. It kept coming back to the same old thing. They were convinced I was throwing away my career; I was trying to convince them that I just wanted to be a normal teenager.

Of course Mum and Dad didn't know that for the past year I'd been throwing up virtually every meal I'd eaten.

What with the bullying and the bulimia, it felt like things had been so crap for so long and finally I'd met this gorgeous bloke and was having an amazing time. And they were trying to put the blockers on it. I can understand now why Mum and Dad were so worried about me. They could see an amazing future for me but I just didn't seem to be interested in it. But at the time I just wanted to be left alone.

So the more Mum and Dad got on my case, the more I rebelled. The strict regime at Elliott-Clarke and Mum and Dad's fussing about my future made me feel like everyone was trying to control me. I didn't have the chance just to be myself.

Looking back, I think I still had a lot of repressed anger about the bullying and those years of unhappiness. And it was all about to spill out in the form of a full-on teenage rebellion.

Mum and Dad were so worried that they decided to find out for themselves what I was up to with Paul and his mates.

One night I was walking down near the Cally with Paul and some of the others when I noticed Dad's old estate car parked up on the other side of the road.

'Is that your dad over there?' one of my mates asked.

I looked across into the driver's window. It was dark but it was so obviously my dad – it was his car and he was trying to hide! But what was he doing parked up here in the middle of the evening? There was only one answer: he was checking up on me.

I went over and banged on the window. He slowly wound it down and stared at me.

'Dad, what the hell? What're you doing?'

'I'm trying to see what you're getting up to,' he snapped.

It was ridiculous. I was so embarrassed and so angry at him for spying on me that I just got in the car and told him to drive home. There wasn't any point in hanging around outside with the others if my dad was going to be sitting in his car watching us. I was mortified!

And that wasn't the only time he did it either. I caught him sitting in his car spying on me another couple of times after that. Every time I spotted him I felt like a stupid little kid who couldn't be trusted to stay out of trouble.

I was so mad about it. It was like I was being punished for all the things my sister Tracey had done when she'd been a teenager. Just because she'd got drunk and had some tattoos and dyed her hair blonde and got pregnant, it didn't mean I was going to go off the rails. The worst I was doing was snogging in the back of Paul's car, but my parents were imagining all sorts of horrors.

'You'll get a reputation for knocking around with boys,' my dad would shout at me.

'But I'm not doing anything wrong,' I'd scream back.

'Yes you are,' Dad would yell. 'You've got to start thinking about your future – otherwise it's going to be too late.'

At which point I'd stomp off out the room.

'And what are we going to tell Kevin?' he'd yell after me. 'That man has done so much to help you and here's you chucking it all away.'

'Just leave me alone,' I'd shout back, slamming the front door behind me.

The rows got worse and worse and more and more frequent. There was shouting, crying and a lot of door slamming. I was turning into a terrible teen. I must have been hell to live with.

Mum tried to talk to me, but I just wouldn't open up to her. As far as I was concerned her and Dad were just constantly getting at me. I refused to talk to her about why I was feeling so angry and rebellious all the time.

And so the rows got more and more vicious.

It reached a point where I was in a full-on teenage rebellion, constantly at loggerheads with Mum and Dad. I had toughened up a lot, but deep down I wondered if I was turning into someone that I didn't really like.

With hindsight, I can see that I was a hurt, angry teenager looking for someone to lash out at – and my parents were the obvious target. I wanted to smash everything that was good in my life. It was like I was pressing a self-destruct button. The worst thing was that I couldn't seem to stop myself.

Then one night, I crossed the line. I raised my hand to my own mother – and that remains one of the biggest regrets of my life.

Me and Mum were arguing again, and I was giving her a load of lip.

Mum had had enough. 'I'm sick of your attitude, Kym,' she shouted at me. 'It's got to stop.'

Instead of taking that on board, I just screamed at her. Suddenly she slapped me across the face. It wasn't hard, and she was probably just trying to calm me down, but I went crazy.

Without thinking I lashed out with my right hand and hit her straight back.

There was an awful moment when I realised what I'd done. I could see tears welling up in her eyes and she hit me right back. I've never felt so terrible. I just didn't know what to say.

Without another word, I ran upstairs to my bedroom and tried to crawl out of my tiny bedroom window, but it was way too small. I knew that when Dad got in and heard what I'd done he would go completely mental. I sat on my bed and bawled my eyes out. Hitting Mum was the worst thing I'd ever done. Even now it makes my stomach crawl to think of it.

When my dad got home that night and Mum told him what happened he saw red. I got a right hiding, like I was naughty little kid. I've never seen him so mad but, in retrospect, I totally deserved it.

I tried to apologise to Mum, but at first she didn't want to know. I think she was just very hurt and it took her a while to forgive me. All Mum and Dad had ever done was look out for me, encourage me and support me, and that is how I'd repaid them.

Looking back, the only thing I can say in my defence is that I'd been pushed around and picked on for so long that I'd reached breaking point and just wanted to fight back. The irony of it was that the people I was intent on fighting were the ones who'd done nothing but love me all the way through.

It wasn't just at home that things were tense.

I was still going to the recording studio occasionally and having meetings with my manager, Kevin, but my enthusiasm wasn't what it had been.

Dad and Kevin got on really well and Dad had confided in him about how I was becoming more and more rebellious and how worried he was that I was throwing away my chances of a singing career. Also, it was becoming more and more evident that it just wasn't working out for me at Elliott-Clarke.

'What's the matter, Kym?' Kevin asked me one day as I sat in his office.

'Nothing. I'm fine,' I lied, pretty unconvincingly.

'Is it school?' he persisted.

'I'm just not very happy there,' I said. Kevin was such a good listener that I found it easier to talk to him than to my parents. 'I'm sorry. I don't want you to think I'm an ungrateful little cow because I really, really appreciate everything you've done for me. But I can't help it. I just don't like it there.'

Kevin went away and had a long conversation with Mum and Dad. They told him how worried they were that I was going off the rails and between them they came up with a plan.

'We're going to pull you out of school,' Kevin said the next time I saw him.

'What do you mean?'

'It's just not working you being there, is it? The whole point is that it was supposed to help your career, not push you in completely the opposite direction.'

'OK,' I said slowly. When his words sank in, it felt like a massive weight had been taken off my shoulders. No more twelve-hour days in Liverpool. No more endless rounds of dance classes. But what on earth would I do instead?

'You're not going to sit around doing nothing,' Kevin went on. 'You can come and work for me, doing admin and helping out around the office.'

So that was it. I finished one Friday afternoon at Elliott-Clarke and never went back. I was coming up for 16 but hadn't stayed long enough to get any GCSEs. As far as I was concerned I was going to be a singer so I didn't need any. At first the plan was to get a private tutor to help me sit some exams but in the end that never happened – I'm not sure why.

I loved my job at Kevin's record company right from the start. I had a smart work suit that I'd put on every morning then take the train into Manchester where I'd type letters, prepare record orders, answer the phones and talk to the clubs about playing our releases.

I learnt so much about the entire music industry – it was just such an eye-opener for me. The pay was good for someone of my age and it was great having a bit of money of my own at last. I paid Mum some housekeeping then spent the rest on clothes and music.

Best of all, for the first time I felt like an adult with ideas and opinions of my own. At Elliott-Clarke I'd felt like a clone of all the other kids there – a bit of putty to be shaped however they wanted.

Kevin was still lining up gigs for me and I was recording songs too. Soon I regained my passion for singing and I straightened myself out. For the first time in ages I knew where I was headed – and that was into a career in singing.

Kevin had played it absolutely right by getting me out of school and throwing me into the adult world. It was exactly what I needed.

That's not to say that everything was rosy. Around the time I left Elliott-Clarke, Paul dumped me. Most of my boyfriends over the years dumped me. I was mostly the dumped, hardly ever the dumper. But although I'd been really into him, I wasn't that heartbroken. It had been a laugh but never a big serious relationship. I was a bit gutted, but I knew there were plenty more fish in the sea.

Soon after splitting with Paul, I met a guy called Greg Barker through a DJ at a gig. He was a couple of years older than me and was into things like heavy rock music which was the total opposite of me. But we got on really well and were together for about a year before sadly we just grew apart. Looking back, he was my first real proper love.

I'd just turned seventeen, when me and Kevin parted company. He had been there for me all the time over the years and given me amazing opportunities. I can never thank him enough for everything he did for me.

But we both felt that we'd come to the end of the line. There just wasn't much more we could do together. It was a mutual decision and we remained on really good terms. We still see each other regularly now.

I carried on trying to follow my dreams on my own. I auditioned for a few bands and did session singing on some records too. But for the most part I was back to singing in pubs and clubs and trying to earn a bit of a crust.

I have to tell you, it was a bit of a reality check.

Some of the pubs I played at were really grim. I wasn't a cute little kid any more, and there would be guys slobbering all over me or pissed-up blokes yelling abuse up to the stage. And then of course there would be the fights too. But some of the clubs were great and I would go back to those over and over again for regular gigs. Dad would still drive me to gigs all over the north-west and help me with all my backing music.

Because I didn't have my day job with Kevin any more either, cash was very tight. I helped out my mum delivering Betterware catalogues and even stuffed flyers into envelopes for a bit of cash in hand at one point.

Eventually I enrolled on a Job Seekers course to be a hotel receptionist. I thought maybe that might give me a steady income while I carried on trying to get noticed by a record company. By this point I was very aware of just how hard it was going to be to break into the music industry. But I wasn't a quitter. I was determined to just carry on battling away for as long as it took.

7
KNOCKED UP

....

It was a month before my eighteenth birthday and I was out to party!

Me and a few friends who lived nearby had gone to our local pub.

'Look, he's over there,' my mate said, nudging me. 'The one I was on about. Dave.'

I looked over, curious. All I knew about Dave Cunliffe was that he'd been saying to a few mates that he fancied me after seeing me out and about in Ashton-in-Makerfield.

'Oh right,' I said, turning away again. Then I didn't think any more of it.

A few weeks later I was out with a group of mates in the Light Fandango nightclub in town. It was in the 'in place' at the time, a former theatre turned into a club on three levels with seating on each of the tiers.

I was having a drink when a lad came and sat down next to me. I looked over and saw it was Dave Cunliffe.

'All right?' he asked. It was hardly a sparkling opener, but we started chatting anyway. It soon became clear that he was very, very funny and I found that very attractive. He was confident and cheeky and he made me laugh.

'So, would you like to go out one night?' he asked me towards the end of the evening.

I didn't have to think too hard about it. 'OK,' I said. 'That'd be good.' I wrote my phone number down on the back of a packet of Silk Cut. It was pretty cool.

Dave was great fun to be with. He was twenty-five, which made him six years older than me, but it never felt like there was a big age gap between us. We just had a right giggle together.

Dave and I started going out regularly. He was a wall and floor tiler and had worked really hard to get an apprenticeship and then set up his own business. He was very good at his job and had an excellent reputation, which meant he was always busy – and not just at work. Everywhere we went he knew people.

By then me, Mum and Dad had been living in a council house in Hindley for a couple of years. We'd moved out of Jon's house when he got a girlfriend so they could have the place to themselves. The house we'd found was on a decent council estate with views over a field and we were all quite happy there. Mum and Dad would still have preferred to have owned their own home but it just wasn't possible because of Dad's money problems before.

Dave and I were very committed to each other. I thought quite early on that this was going to be a really serious relationship.

And it was good. Really good.

Dave was very genuine and kind and just being with him made me feel happier in myself.

For once, everything was going really well. But then everything that I'd thought of as safe and secure was suddenly shattered.

In the space of a couple of weeks, my dad went from being someone I thought of as invincible to a frail old man fighting for his life.

It all began one tea time. I was at home with Mum, Dad and Dave, cooking something for us all to eat, when Dad started complaining of pains in his chest.

'This doesn't feel right, Pauline,' Dad said. 'It really hurts.'

'I'll call an ambulance,' Mum said. 'They can get you to hospital to get checked out.'

Dad hated anyone making a fuss over him, so he must have been in a lot of pain to agree to her calling 999. It seemed to take ages for the ambulance to turn up and it was just horrible seeing how much Dad was suffering. His face was grey and he was clutching his chest and wincing in agony.

Finally the ambulance turned up and they took him off to the Royal Albert Edward Hospital in Wigan. Me and Dave followed behind in his car and Tracey and Dave came over too. Jon joined us at the hospital and we all sat around Dad's bed as they prepared to carry out tests on him.

They hooked him up to an ECG machine to monitor his heartbeat. But after half an hour of monitoring him, the doctor came up to his bed and said: 'Mr Marsh, I'm pleased to say you have got the heart of a twenty-five-year-old. You're probably just suffering a bit of indigestion.'

'Oh, right,' said Dad. 'In fact, the pain has eased off a bit now.'

I could tell he was still in discomfort, but he looked a bit perkier. We were all just so relieved.

'Excellent,' said the doctor. 'Now get yourself home and have a bit of a rest. But don't worry; you're as fit as a fiddle.'

We went home and Dad claimed he felt a bit better – so much so that the next day he was out laying slabs on the front drive!

Everything seemed to go back to normal and we all thought Dad really must have had a bad bout of indigestion.

Then exactly one week later, on Mum and Dad's wedding anniversary, 24 July 1994, Dad woke in the night in crippling pain.

I was staying over at Dave's house and so Mum and Dad were by themselves. Dad was rolling around in agony. Mum immediately called the doctor and soon afterwards an on-call GP turned up. But when he examined Dad, he again said there was nothing wrong with him, apart from a chest infection.

But the pain was so bad that Dad couldn't get back to sleep. At one point he was in so much pain that he was leaning up against their bedroom wall, gasping for breath. He looked pale and drawn and despite everything the doctors had said, Mum just wasn't convinced.

'Come on, Dave,' she said. 'I'm taking you to hospital myself.'

Back at the Royal Albert Edward the doctors put Dad back on an ECG monitor, but once again they couldn't detect anything abnormal in his heart rate. The pain had

An early portrait of me, in the days when I was Kim with an 'i'!

Mum (left) and her twin sister as children. Mum was born only twenty minutes after Auntie Pam but she still insisted on being known as the youngest!

My hero: my Dad

Dad (far right) with his band, Ricky and the Dominant Four, in the '60s. They were successful enough to play alongside The Beatles at The Cavern in Liverpool

A beautiful photo of Mum (left) on her wedding day, with Auntie Pam

With Mum and my sister Tracey, before her punk years! We shared a room and I was always hanging around her

With my brother Jon. Although he is five years older we were like best mates

Me, aged seven

As a kid I loved dance, but it was singing that was my real passion

Me aged twelve at Wesle Avenue. Performing was b now becoming my way c escaping the misery of schoc

Me at the dinner table in Poland, holding a bottle of wine. I'm proudly wearing my 'Artist' ID badge after performing alongside big '80s stars like Tiffany, Transvision Vamp and Curiosity Killed the Cat

Me with my beloved Granddad, who loved my singing
and bought me my first microphone

Mum and Dad have always been joined at the hip!

Me aged 18, showing
off my bump

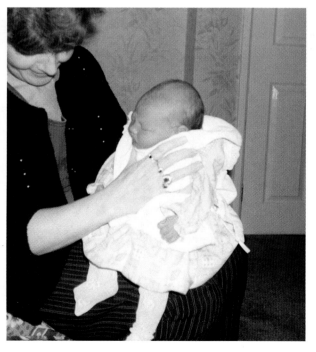

A new Granddad with baby David

Emily, pretty in pink,
with Grandma

Me with my sister Tracey's son, Jason. I love being an Auntie

With my daughter, Emily

Emily and David

The auditions for 'Popstars', summer 2000. You can see me far left of this line-up, trying to catch judge Nigel Lythgoe's eye!

Enjoying a well-earned break during the auditions process with Jessica Taylor, pre-Liberty X

subsided but because Dad was still feeling a bit dizzy and light-headed they decided to keep him in for observation anyway.

Mum and Dad walked down the ward to a bed. Dad sat on the edge of it while Mum chatted away to him and sorted out the few bits and pieces she had brought with them.

Then two minutes later Dad clutched his chest and choked, 'I'm going, Pauline, I'm going.'

He slumped backwards onto the bed, his eyes wide open and totally motionless. He'd had a massive cardiac arrest.

Mum screamed for the nurses. 'Help me, please someone help me,' she yelled down the corridor.

Nurses and doctors came sprinting into the cubicle and all hell broke loose. Dad had basically died right there in front of my mum. Now there was this incredible squad of people trying to bring him back to life.

'We need a crash team here NOW,' one of the doctors shouted. 'And get her out of here,' he hissed at a nurse, as she tried to guide Mum away from Dad's lifeless body.

Mum was hysterical. 'No, no, don't let him die,' she was pleading.

The crash team were there in seconds and began using massive electric shock pads to try to jumpstart his heart.

The nurse took Mum to a side ward and asked if she would like to call anyone. She was in such a state of shock she couldn't remember a single telephone number at first, but eventually she managed to remember Tracey's.

It was just before seven in the morning that she rang Tracey. A couple of minutes later Tracey was on the phone to me at Dave's house.

'Something's up with Dad,' she said. 'Mum's in a really bad way. We've got to get to the hospital.'

Dave drove me at breakneck speed to the Royal Albert Edward. I was clutching the seat so hard my knuckles turned white; I was that terrified at what we might find when we got there. I could tell from the way Tracey had been talking on the phone that this time it was really serious.

When we got there a nurse took us into a small room. Maybe it was because I still looked quite young, but she held my hand as she spoke.

'Now,' she said. 'Your daddy's heart stopped.'

'What?' I said.

'His heart stopped,' she repeated. 'The doctors have managed to get it going again but he is very, very poorly. He's in the coronary care unit at the moment and we're doing what we can for him. But your mum needs you right now. You need to be strong for her.'

I could barely take in what the nurse was saying. His heart had stopped beating? Did that mean he was going to die?

Dad had called me his shadow when I was a kid. He'd always been there for me. All those middle-of-the-night drives back from North Wales and God-knows-where after a gig. The time he'd taken me to London to hand out demo tapes. All those times he'd refused to give up on me, even when I was being a right little cow.

I just couldn't believe that he might not make it; that my dad might not be around any more. It was totally un-thinkable.

At that point I think I was too shocked to cry.

Then the nurse took us in to a room where Mum was sitting

on her own. She was a total wreck. She had basically seen her husband die right in front of her and she was in complete shock. She didn't even look like my mum that morning. When we walked in the room all I could see was this fragile little figure, just sobbing her heart out. I'd never, ever seen her like that before.

It was terrifying. All I could think was: this is what Mum would be like without Dad.

My brothers were there too and we all waited in that room together until finally we were allowed in to see Dad.

He was lying on a bed with tubes and who-knows-what-else sticking in him. A monitor with flashing red figures was at the side of his bed. He was going in and out of consciousness and had his eyes open. One of them was fully red because all the blood vessels in it had burst. His chest was black and blue with bruises from where they'd resuscitated him and his skin was a waxy, pale colour. It looked like my granddad lying there in the bed. Dad had aged a generation in a day.

I was shocked, but I was trying desperately not to show that.

'What've you been doing, eh, Dad?' I asked, holding his hand. 'You gave us a right fright there.' He managed a weak smile but he was so drugged up that he wasn't really with it at all.

After a while a nurse came in and said we'd better leave him to rest. I leant over and gave him a kiss. My dad. My hero.

'The next twenty-four hours are going to be critical for him,' the nurse said. We all knew exactly what that meant – Dad was clinging on to life with his fingertips.

We hung around the hospital all day, desperately hoping

for some sign of improvement. In the end the nurses said we might as well go home and try to get some rest. That night I slept with Mum in my parents' bed. Mum was in a state. She was just so scared. It was mad really, lying there on Dad's side of the bed, knowing he was alone in hospital fighting to stay alive.

Neither of us slept much that night, but it was a big comfort being together.

Us kids were all really worried about Mum. She'd always said to us: 'If anything happened to your dad I wouldn't want to be here any more.'

At the time we'd all just tell her not to be daft. But nothing was certain any more. I really couldn't think how Mum would cope without Dad. Everyone had always said they were joined at the hip. They had literally never had so much as a day apart since the day they were hitched.

With Dad so sick, I suddenly felt as if I was thrown into the role of parent and Mum became a child.

'You really ought to eat something,' I said to her as she pushed aside a plate of toast the following morning. But Mum couldn't eat or sleep or even talk really. She was making herself sick with worry.

'He's going to be OK,' I kept telling her, crossing my fingers that it was true.

When we got to the hospital the next day Dad had made a slight improvement and his condition had stabilised. I was about ready to fall down with relief – though he wasn't out of the woods yet. Not by a long shot.

Every day when we went back to visit we'd be praying that

he'd be a little better than before and gradually he did get stronger and we saw glimpses of our old dad again.

'He's a fighter,' one of the nurses on the coronary care unit told us. 'If anything is getting him through this, it's his spirit.'

My dad has always been a very positive person and that definitely helped him. But for a long while after the heart attack he seemed frightened. It had been a terrible shock for him too.

The strange thing was that while Dad was in the coronary care unit they did another ECG test on him and again they couldn't pick up any heart abnormality. It was only when one of the nurses moved a pad on his leg that it showed up. It turned out he'd had a mild heart attack the previous week, but because of the positioning of the ECG pad it was never picked up at the time.

Dad came home after a fortnight but for a long while he couldn't handle being left on his own. Even if he went to the toilet, Mum would have to wait for him outside. I think he was scared it might all happen again.

Dad remembers very little of being ill. He could remember saying to Mum, 'I'm going, Pauline,' and then he heard this massive bang, like a car door shutting. The next thing he remembers was someone sitting on his chest – that must have been when they removed a tube from his throat after they resuscitated.

The heart attack was a major turning point for Dad. He stopped smoking immediately and started taking far better care of himself. The doctors said that it was probably smoking that had blocked his artery and caused the coronary, but I'm sure all the financial stress he'd suffered over the years didn't help.

The doctors were able to treat the blocked artery with drugs, although ten years later he had to go back into hospital to have a bypass operation.

When he was recovering from his heart attack, Dad would tell us kids: 'It just shows; you've got to live each day because you never know what's around the corner.'

Dad felt he had been given a second chance and he was always conscious of making the most of life from then on.

But the medication he was on had an effect on him too. He became more irritable than he had been in the past. He started getting wound up by things that would never have bothered him before. For a while we were all treading on eggshells because we never knew what kind of mood he was going to be in. I think that was partly down to the drugs but also maybe a reaction to everything he'd been through. He'd had a difficult few years and I think all that really started to take its toll on him.

Seeing Dad so seriously ill was the thing that finally made me grow up. When I thought back to how I'd acted towards my parents when I was younger I felt sick with guilt. All they'd ever done was try to support me and I'd acted like a little madam. Now, having almost lost my dad, I was left in absolutely no doubt how important he and my mum were to me.

For a long time after his illness, Dad seemed very old. He'd always been my hero but now he had become this frightened and quite frail old man and that was shocking to me.

Dave was a fantastic support all through Dad's illness. He'd run us up to the hospital and if I was feeling down or tearful he would just sit and listen to me.

I had no doubt in my mind that this really was 'it' with Dave.

Then one day I realised my period was a couple of days late. My periods were always a bit all over the place, so at first I didn't really worry. But then I started feeling sick too, and still my period hadn't come.

After waiting a few more days I knew I had to do a pregnancy test. I bought a kit from the chemist (trying to look dead casual!) and took it home.

There wasn't much doubt in my mind what the result would be. When the blue line formed across the little plastic stick it just confirmed what I already knew.

Although we were young, Dave and I were both genuinely delighted. It might not have been the best situation – I was still a teenager, we'd only just met and we weren't even living together. But we were in love and we very much wanted this baby.

Dave was fantastic about everything. Up until that week the thought of becoming a mum had never even entered my head, but once I knew I was pregnant, I was pretty happy. After all, I was having a baby with someone I adored.

The only problem now was telling Mum and Dad.

Mum had been eighteen when she got pregnant and Tracey had been eighteen when she had baby Trevor, so it wasn't like I was breaking new ground or anything, but I still knew they'd be upset about it. Dad had only been out of hospital for a couple of weeks and they'd been through so much recently that I didn't want to give them even more aggro. Basically, I knew they'd both held out high hopes for me and my singing career and they'd think I was throwing it all away. In my mind,

I was still convinced I'd be a singer and that having a baby wouldn't affect that at all. But I knew my parents would be less convinced.

I was terrified about telling them, so decided to break the news to Tracey first. I knew she'd be great about it but I was still nervous when I dialled her number.

'Look, I've got something to tell you,' I said, after we'd had a bit of a chat. I took a deep breath. 'I'm having a baby.'

'A baby!' she screamed. 'Oh, that's fantastic. Oh my God! It's so exciting.'

Tracey clearly wasn't upset by the news and she'd been a teen mum herself, so she knew what I was letting myself in for. She'd since had two other sons, Nathan and Jason. She loved babies. It was good to have her onside.

'I know it might feel scary now,' Tracey said, 'but it'll all be OK.'

'Thanks Trace,' I said. 'But how am I going to tell Mum and Dad? Dad's not well enough to deal with this on top of everything else right now.'

'Do you want me to break it to them?' Tracey offered.

'Oh, would you? I just don't think I could do it.'

It wasn't very brave of me, I know, but I couldn't bear seeing the disappointment on their faces.

At the time I was still doing my hotel receptionist training course. One afternoon that week Tracey offered to pick me up from the training centre. When I walked out of the doors at the end of the session, Tracey's car was parked outside and she was in the driving seat. Mum was sat next to her on the passenger side.

Oh God, she knows, I thought. I could just tell by the way

Mum was sitting there. *Oh God, oh God, oh God.*

I could feel myself shaking as I walked over to the car and climbed in the back seat.

'Hi,' I said quietly.

Tracey and Mum both turned and looked at me.

'Oh Kym, you are a silly sod,' Mum said. She went on, 'I want you to know that I'll support you all the way. And it's not going to be easy, you know. Having a baby is hard work.'

'I know, I know,' I said. 'Thanks Mum.' I was so relieved that she hadn't thrown a wobbly and chucked me out of the house.

All we had to do now was tell my dad. Mum was just as worried as I was about breaking the news to him. She was scared that any sudden shock might give him another heart attack. He'd also been pretty moody since he came home from hospital and this certainly wasn't going to help matters.

'Don't worry, Kym,' Mum said. 'I'll tell him.'

But then Dad had to go back into hospital for tests. He was making good progress though and one day while she was visiting him Mum felt it was time to break the news. He was really disappointed and worried for me. After all I was his baby and he only wanted the best for me.

'So that's it then,' Dad said to Mum. 'It's all over, all her dreams, everything. She's just going to give them all up.'

Mum tried to explain to him that I was still determined to sing professionally, but he just wouldn't believe it. When Mum left him at the end of visiting time he was still really upset.

When his nurse, a lovely lady called Andrea Huyton, came to do her rounds later, Dad told her all about me being pregnant and how disappointed he was.

'Well, she could be telling you something a lot worse,' Andrea said quietly. 'She could be telling you she has got cancer or something terrible. This isn't the end of the world. A baby is great news.'

I think that gave Dad a real jolt. And having been so ill in himself he certainly knew how precious life was. I'll always be grateful to Andrea Huyton for helping Dad come to terms with me being pregnant.

When I next saw him he was sitting in the front room so I went and sat next to him on the sofa. He put his arm round me and gave me a hug. I felt the lump in my throat melt away.

'Kym, this doesn't have to be the end of your dream,' he said. 'Your mum and I are going to be here to support you all the way with the baby if you carry on pursuing your career. And now you're having a child you've got an even bigger reason to succeed. You've got to do it for your baby as well as for you.'

It was a massive relief to hear Dad say that and to know he still hadn't given up on me.

'I know, Dad,' I said. 'And I will. I am going to do it.'

And Dad was, of course, absolutely right. Now more than ever I had to succeed to my give my baby the life I'd always dreamt of.

8
TEEN MUM

....

I was eighteen years old, eight months pregnant and standing onstage in a club in Widnes belting out Whitney Houston's 'I Will Always Love You'.

I could feel the baby kicking inside me like a Premiership footballer. He always seemed to kick hardest during that song – maybe he liked the high notes! The weird thing is that when my son was two years old he was playing in the front room one day when that song came on at the end of *The Bodyguard*. He suddenly dropped his toys and just stared at the screen. It really was as though he remembered it.

He'd certainly heard it enough times! During my pregnancy I carried on working most nights in pubs and clubs around the north-west, singing Whitney Houston, Madonna or Shania Twain hits to the punters.

Each night Dad would load my amp and speakers into the back of his car and we'd drive to the gig together.

The first half of the show was usually easy-listening music, while the second half was more upbeat stuff, and everyone would be up boogieing by the end of it.

'Look at her, she brings the house down every time,' Dad would say.

When the audience had worn themselves out we'd pack up all the sound equipment again, ready for the journey home. Sometimes we'd stop off at a chippy for sausage and chips and eat it as we drove along – a habit from the old Starlight Roadshow days.

We'd talk about how the gig had gone and where we'd be going next. Occasionally we would talk about the baby. I know Dad was excited about it, particularly once he knew that I was serious about continuing with my singing.

It was hard work but I was determined to carry on following my dream, even though I was going to be a teenage mum. Of course I wanted to be a success for the baby's sake, but there was also a part of me that wanted to show other people that I hadn't given up on my career.

I was still living at home with Mum and Dad, but Dave had more or less moved in with us too.

I'd been about five months pregnant when Dave and I went to Center Parcs at Sherwood Forest for a short holiday. Before we went Dave had suggested we ought to get married and he decided he would officially propose while we were away. One evening, Dave and I were standing outside the log cabin where we were staying, when he turned to me and put something in my hand. I looked down. It was an engagement ring.

'Will you marry me?' he said.

I was just delighted. Even though I knew it was coming it was still a very special moment.

'Yes,' I said. We kissed and hugged and felt so excited about the future.

It wasn't an easy pregnancy though. Some women seem to breeze through the whole nine months looking blooming and bountiful. I felt sick all day every day for the first four months. Even when that was over I still felt pretty rough all the way up to the birth.

I was just thirty-three weeks pregnant, still seven weeks off my due date, when on Good Friday afternoon I started feeling strange pains across my stomach. I'd been into town with Mum and Tracey, buying a few bits and pieces that I needed for the baby. But there were still loads of things not ready yet. I hadn't got a cot, a pram or hardly any clothes. Emotionally, I certainly wasn't ready for the birth – not yet!

We'd just got home from the shops when the pains started.

'Mum, my tummy feels a bit tight,' I said. 'Do you think everything's OK?'

'It's probably just Braxton Hicks,' Mum said. 'It's like fake contractions – some people get them for ages before the birth.'

'Oh, OK,' I said. I really was pretty clueless about pregnancy and labour and thought I must just be making a fuss about nothing.

Dave came round after work and we all sat chatting, but the pains were getting stronger and stronger and coming more and more frequently.

'It's quite bad now, Mum,' I said after a while.

'It's probably nothing, love,' she said, 'but maybe we should get you to hospital to get you checked out anyway.'

Me, Mum and Dave set off to hospital where a midwife in the maternity ward looked me over.

First she measured how frequently the pains were coming and then she examined my cervix. When she had finished she looked worried.

'You appear to have gone into labour,' the midwife said. 'You are two centimetres dilated, which means the baby is on its way. But we would really want to try and keep the baby in a little longer if we can. We need to try and stop the labour.'

All the colour drained from my face. It all sounded so scary. Not only did I not feel ready to have the baby yet, I also knew that having a premature birth was risky for the baby.

I clung on to Mum's hand as the nurse told us that they were going to put me on a drip, which would hopefully stop the labour. They were also going to give me steroid injections to build up the baby's lungs in case labour couldn't be stopped and it was born seven weeks early.

'If the baby is born now its lungs probably won't be mature enough to work properly on their own,' the midwife explained. 'Preemies' lungs can stick together. But the steroids will help the lungs develop so hopefully there'd be less need for the baby to be put on a ventilator after birth.'

When the nurse finished speaking my heart was pounding. My baby was obviously in danger. I felt totally terrified.

I was to be given four steroid injections, one every twelve hours, and was hooked up to a drip. Everything was being done to keep the baby inside me, to give it the best chance of survival.

I was still only eighteen and as I lay in that labour ward I felt very young. I could hear women screaming in pain all night long. It was a scary place to be.

The next morning the midwife tried to take me off the drip, hoping that enough had been done to stop the labour. But no sooner was I off the drip than my contractions started again. This baby seemed desperate to come out right now, whatever danger it might be in. The midwife put me straight back on the drip again.

I lay there for another day and another night, unable to sleep and totally terrified. Mum, Dad and Dave hardly ever left my side.

Next day, Easter Sunday, the doctors tried to take me off the drip again but an hour later I was back in labour. It was a nightmare.

Later that day, Mum and Dave were with me when a consultant came round to the bed.

'We've got two options,' he said. 'We either try to hold the labour off for another two weeks until you're at a reasonable gestation and there is less chance of anything being wrong with the baby, but to be honest the labour is progressing now and you are more dilated so if we leave it for another couple of weeks the baby is at risk of infection and distress. So we could allow the labour to come now, without intervening any further, which is obviously what it wants to do. I have to warn you though, that if the baby is born now it's probably going to be very small and will probably have to be kept in special care for a while. I don't know how long for at this stage but it will probably be a few weeks, it depends on the baby.'

'I don't know what to do, I'm so scared for the baby,' I said. I felt so knackered after two nights of not sleeping and having all those contractions that I couldn't think straight.

'Listen to the doctor, love,' Mum said. 'They know what they're talking about and you've got to trust them. No drug will hold off the inevitable; the baby wants to come now.'

The labour continued so we took the doctor's advice and went ahead with the delivery through the night. The baby was so small that he really couldn't do much work himself, so it was mostly down to me to push him out. The pain was the worst thing I'd ever experienced. Totally horrendous. I'd had no bloody clue what I'd been letting myself in for. Poor Dad was so nervous for me that he managed to eat his way through all my Easter eggs without even realising he was doing it.

The contractions came in wave after wave but still it felt like the baby was no nearer to being born. In the end the midwife had to break my waters but there were still hours more contractions before the baby was born.

Finally, at 4.47 a.m. on Easter Monday, 17 April 1995, I gave birth to a tiny baby boy. He was just 4 lb 14 oz but absolutely perfect.

Everyone was delighted with him.

The baby was crying when he was born and when the nurse lifted him up onto my chest I just knew instinctively that he was healthy, small as he was. He was beautiful, even though he was covered in blood and goo and all a bit yucky. I held him for a while then handed him to Dave.

I was absolutely exhausted because I hadn't slept for three nights by then, but I was euphoric to have my baby at last. I just couldn't stop grinning.

But my happiness was cut short. Just a couple of minutes after his birth, it suddenly felt that everything was going wrong.

My baby stopped breathing and within seconds he had gone from being a healthy shade of pink to a horrible bluey-grey colour.

'What's going on?' I screamed.

One of the nurses snatched the baby away and ran down the corridor with him.

I stayed on the bed unable to move and physically shaking. After everything that had happened I couldn't be losing my baby, could I?

Poor Dad was standing in the corridor and could only watch as the nurse sprinted down the ward with her fingers down the throat of his brand-new grandson. A couple of minutes later she was back, the baby was breathing normally and he had regained his pink complexion.

Apparently he had stopped breathing but the nurse had got him breathing again and took him straight to the special care unit. My baby was alive. I was so relieved.

I wanted to call the baby Ryan because my favourite Manchester United footballer is Ryan Giggs. But in the end we decided to call him David after his father so he was David Ryan. But that made things ever so complicated because not only did we now have baby David and his dad Dave, we also had my dad David and my brother David. Got all that?

He was still very tiny and had to be placed in an incubator in the special-care baby unit. He was also slightly jaundiced, which is apparently quite common with premature babies, so he was kept under a light to get rid of that. And because he was too young to be able to suck milk properly he was tube-fed up his nose.

After two days I was discharged from hospital. It was horrible to go home without my baby but by then I knew he was going to be all right and that was all that really mattered. At that point he was still just skin and bone without an ounce of fat on him. It almost seemed like there was too much skin on his body and it fell in folds like an old lady's wrinkly tights. He had hardly any hair on his head but had like a soft, fuzzy down over the rest of his body. He looked a bit like a wizened old man. And I adored him.

Either Dad or Dave took me up to see him twice a day and I would sit and hold him or just stroke his hand for hours. In the mornings I would go in and get him dressed then try to help him learn to suck properly so that he'd be able to drink milk from a bottle.

I'd sit with him for a couple of hours then go home for a bit then return in the afternoon and sit and stroke his arm, bath him or try to get him to feed again and then get him ready for bed.

Each day he seemed to be getting stronger, although there were still some terrifying moments. He was hooked up to a breathing monitor which is called an apnea alarm, which would bleep if his breathing stopped. But for a few days his breathing seemed really irregular and the alarm went off quite a few times. Each time it was awful – I would feel like I couldn't breathe either.

After a week the doctors said David was strong enough to be allowed out of the incubator although he still had to stay in the special-care baby unit.

They had a system on the ward that as the babies got stronger they were moved to a different room, the idea being that they were getting closer to going home.

One day Dave and I got to the hospital and were just walking onto the ward when we saw six doctors and nurses standing around the cot where little David had been. They were pulling the curtains around them. Obviously something very bad was happening.

'Oh my God,' I said to Dave as we ran towards the cot. But when we got there, we saw that it wasn't David; he'd been moved to the next room. I felt such a rush of relief, but then I felt guilty – after all, someone else's baby was struggling.

David was kept in the special-care baby unit for another week and a half after coming out of the incubator. Finally he got the hang of sucking milk from a bottle and we were allowed to take him home.

The day we took him home was just wonderful. Finally I had my little baby. One of the doctors told me that after such a tough start in life David would most likely always be tiny. If only he could see my strapping 6 ft son now!

I had a tiny Moses basket in my bedroom so David could sleep next to me and Dave all night. Because he'd been so little when he was born, I'd lie awake for hours checking that he was still breathing. I was terrified something might happen to him.

David slept well right from the beginning and Dave and I shared the night feeds, so it wasn't too tiring. Even the early mornings didn't really bother me. I'd always been an early riser myself.

Once David got the hang of feeding, he never really stopped and he became quite a little chubber.

Even though I was young I found being a mum came to me quite naturally. David was a fab baby and I really enjoyed looking after him. I'd helped out with my nephews Trevor and Nathan when they were babies, so I did know a bit about making up bottles and changing nappies. All in all, I loved it.

The only difficult time was when he developed colic, which is when babies get trapped air in their stomach. He cried for day after day, which was knackering. Dave was a very hands-on dad and if I was feeling worn out he'd just take over, or my Mum and Dad would help if Dave was working.

It was fine living with Mum and Dad, but Dave and I wanted to get a place of our own. We wanted to feel like a proper family.

Dave had been looking for a place all through my pregnancy and soon after David was born he found what he thought was the perfect home for us all. It was a two-bedroom semi in Princess Avenue in Ashton-in-Makerfield. An old man had been living in the house and it was in a terrible state. It looked to me like it was about to fall down, but Dave was convinced once he'd done it up a bit it would be ideal.

'I'll soon get this place sorted,' he promised. We really did think that house was going to be the answer to all our problems. Little did we know it was more like the beginning of a nightmare . . .

9

LOVE FALLS APART

....

I sat holding baby David in the front room of my new home and looked around. There was no carpet on the floor, there were cracks in the walls, a gaping hole where the fireplace should have been, a musty smell of damp in the air and a sharp breeze whizzing through the rooms.

This was not the dream family home that I'd had in mind.

Dave was out at work all day so it could be me and the baby on our own from first thing in the morning until teatime. Sometimes it felt like a very long day. Soon after we arrived at our new home Mum and Dad moved into a house quite nearby so at least I could pop round to see them when I was feeling lonely. But it was tough.

I was desperately trying to play the role of housewife and mother, looking after the baby, cleaning up the house, doing the washing and cooking the food. But I had only just turned nineteen and had never lived away from home before. I could barely look after myself, let alone do all this other stuff as well. Not to mention the fact that it was impossible to keep that house clean because of all the building work. No sooner had I'd swept up, then another load of dust would blow in from outside. Talk about depressing.

Mum and Dad popped round whenever they could.

'Oh, you'll soon get this place sorted out, love,' Mum would say brightly.

It was only years later that she told me that she used to cry to my dad when they drove away.

Dave was doing his best to fill the holes, plaster the walls, lay the floorboards down and generally fix it up. And he really was trying his hardest. But there was just so much work that needed doing. I hated being stuck in the house all day on my own. I adored being with David but I had no friends and I felt pretty down. It was just so lonely. My baby was gorgeous but our conversations were all one-way!

For months the highlight of my day was walking down to the shops to buy something for our dinner. I felt very isolated, so as soon as Dave went out the front door, I just wanted to get out as quickly as I could. I'd bundle David into the buggy and go into town, or I'd take him out for walks just to kill the hours. Sometimes we'd pop round to my mum's and have our lunch there.

Dave and I started rowing a lot. He was mad at me because he felt I wasn't doing enough around the house and I was feeling increasingly low and isolated being stuck in the house on my own all day.

I think lots of couples go through these problems when they first move in together, particularly if they have children right off the bat. And in the end I guess we were a couple of kids who'd suddenly found ourselves playing at being grown-ups. And we didn't much like the rules!

Dave and I had only been together for a year and were at the stage in our relationship when we should have been going out for romantic dinners and having fun. Instead we were rowing about whose turn it was to put the bins out and who was going to heat up a pizza for our tea.

We were clashing more and more. Bringing up a baby is hard work, especially when you're living in a half-finished house which you can't keep clean and you're feeling isolated and lonely and you're nineteen and you haven't got a clue what you're doing.

We weren't making each other laugh any more – that was the main thing. When that happened it felt like the romance had gone.

However, we had baby David now, so we battled on and I hoped that things would start getting easier.

But, if anything, they just got worse.

Dave would work all week, and then he'd want to go out with his mates on the weekend and then on a Sunday morning he liked to play football. The only time I left the house without the baby was on the rare occasion that I managed to arrange a babysitter.

Dave was a lovely, lovely bloke and he was a great dad and a real hard worker, but we just had very different outlooks, and that became more and more clear as the months rolled by.

*

As the months passed we rowed more and more and more. It was obvious things weren't right.

By then I knew in my heart that we shouldn't be together. We were just making each other unhappy. But at the same time I still loved Dave. It was all so confusing. My mum and dad had been together for so long and they never rowed like this. I desperately wanted my relationship to be like theirs and I couldn't quite work out why it wasn't.

When I'd got pregnant I'd thought me and Dave would be together for the long haul; that was what I expected from a relationship. I was prepared to fight tooth and nail to keep us together, especially for David's sake. But nothing we did seemed to make things any better.

One of my mates said to me once: 'You've just got to get on with it. Living with a bloke isn't a fairy tale you know.'

But I didn't agree. 'Yes it is,' I said. 'Well, it can be. My mum and dad are still living their happy-ever-after thirty years down the line. And I want that too.

But no matter how much I wanted the happy ending, I could feel it slipping out of my hands.

Looking back, me and Dave were probably just too different for it to have worked. In the early days, when it had all been exciting and fun, we'd had a great time. But in all honesty I think that if we hadn't had David then we would have split up much earlier on. We grated on each other. We could really wind each other up and things would just explode. In the end we were rowing about everything.

My dreams of a singing career were on the back burner. Fairly soon after I'd had David I'd been asked to do backing vocals for a guy called Matt Darey who was quite big on the dance scene in London which was great fun. And I did the occasional gig, but that was pretty rare now. Instead I was throwing all my effort into being a good mother and girlfriend, but didn't really feel I was succeeding at any of it.

The reality was I was never going to be the kind of woman who's happy to stay at home scrubbing the kitchen floor and knitting. It just wasn't me.

'What's the matter, love?' Mum asked me one day when I was round at their house. I'd tried not to worry them about me and Dave, but they knew me well enough to know I wasn't happy.

'It's just all going wrong,' I admitted. 'We're rowing all the time and I don't know if we should be together any more.'

'Well think about it, love,' Mum said. 'You know your dad and me will be here for you. You've just got to think about what will make you happy.'

It dragged on like that for a while until I really couldn't bear it any longer. Dave and I could barely speak to each other without arguing. And neither of us wanted to split up for David's sake but nor did we want to expose David to the arguments. By then he was one year old, and becoming far more aware of what was going on around him.

We decided that maybe it would be best if we took a break from each other for a while.

I rang Mum. 'I'm coming home,' I said.

'Don't worry, love,' Mum said. 'We'll come round now and pick you up.'

Mum and Dad were there within the hour. We loaded up

my bags, David's nappies, toys and buggy and drove back to theirs.

I had desperately wanted the whole perfect family thing, so it was a sad day for me. But truthfully, I was relieved to be away from all the screaming and shouting. And while Mum and Dad never encouraged me to walk out I think they felt Dave and I might be better off apart, and they were pleased to have me home.

Me and David moved our stuff into my parents' spare room. David had grown out of his cot by then so he shared the bed with me.

I loved staying at Mum and Dad's. Mum looked after me and was a massive help with David. And I didn't feel I was spending my entire life cooking and cleaning either.

Dave and I carried on talking to each other on the phone every day and he came round whenever he could to see David. And of course, away from all the problems of that falling-down house and cooking and cleaning and sharing childcare, we started laughing together again. Even though I knew that we weren't really right together, there was still a spark between us.

And so, almost immediately, we got back together again, even though we weren't living together any more.

It actually worked really well like that. Not living together meant we didn't have anything to row about. It was like when we'd first started dating and we were able to enjoy spending time together without having to compete about who was working the hardest.

David enjoyed having his dad popping in all the time and I was chuffed we were all getting on better.

I did think we might be able to get things back on track between us, although I was still aware that there were issues we hadn't worked out. But at the time there didn't seem much need to worry about the future. We were just having a laugh again.

Then, almost six months after I'd left Dave, my period was late again.

Suddenly me and Dave were going to have to think about the future very seriously indeed.

10
SCRAPING BY

....

By the time I took the pregnancy test I knew I was expecting. I recognised the nausea and the crazy hunger from when I'd had David.

But this time I had a different feeling. This time I felt sick with nerves too. I knew now what having a baby really meant and the thought of going through another birth and bringing up a baby on my own was very scary. After all, me and Dave weren't even officially together any more.

The first person I told was Mum.

'Oh Kym,' she said. She didn't have to say anything more. I knew exactly what she was thinking, because I was thinking it too. Dave and I loved each other and got on great, but that wasn't enough. We just couldn't live together. How on earth were we going to cope with another baby to look after too?

Mum told Dad and we all sat down together and discussed it.

'Look, Kym,' said Dad. 'With or without Dave we'll be here for you.'

Again Mum and Dad were brilliant.

Next I told Dave.

We both knew the situation was far from ideal, but we were getting on well enough to talk about how we could make the best of things. Although it was a massive surprise, to say the least, and I was worried about how it would all work out, I still felt excited about having another baby. And I thought it would be great for David to have a little brother or sister.

Again there was never any question that I wouldn't go through with the pregnancy. It wasn't even discussed.

'Right, if we're having this baby we have really got to make things work between us now,' I said to Dave one day. 'Because it's not just about us any more. It's going to be about two children too.'

'I agree,' said Dave. 'We'll make it work this time. We have to.'

I stayed living at Mum and Dad's with David for a couple of months while Dave tried to finish off the house, ready for me to move back in again. We still saw each other all the time and we were getting on well.

When I moved back in, the house still wasn't totally finished but it was in a lot better state than it had been before. I was really hopeful that this time things would be better between us. I was twenty-one by then and more mature than when I'd first turned up with baby David. He had started at a nursery nearby which helped too, because it meant I had a reason to get up and out every morning. I even made a few new friends among the other mums. I didn't feel quite as isolated as I had when I first brought David home and even the household chores weren't so hard. Maybe I'd just learnt more of what was expected of me.

Mum and Dad were still living just around the corner and I saw a lot of my sister Tracey too. She'd just had her fourth child, a little girl she called Kimberley, after me.

Generally things were far smoother living back home with Dave this time round. And we were all so excited about the new baby that I really did think we were going to be able to make things work this time.

I couldn't help but worry though that the baby might be premature, like David was, and the doctors said there was a risk of that. To try to avoid labour starting early, they gave me steroid injections at thirty-three weeks.

In the end I went into labour on the evening of 26 November 1997, just a day before my due date. I'd popped into the loo at home when my waters broke suddenly and what felt like gallons of fluid poured out of me. My contractions started immediately and were really strong.

'Dave,' I yelled out the toilet. 'My waters have broke. I'm going into labour.'

'But Kym, I'm staining the front door,' he said. 'I'll have to finish it or it won't look right.'

That house and the bloody DIY was the bane of my life!

'Dave,' I shouted a bit louder this time. 'I don't care about the front door. Ring my mum and get her round here. I'm in agony.'

Dave immediately rang Mum and Dad, who came to pick

us up and take us both to the hospital. One of Dave's relatives kindly agreed to look after little David so off we went.

There wasn't much time to spare though. As soon as I got there the midwife sent me to a delivery suite and two and a half hours later Emily was born.

Mum, Dad, Tracey and Dave were all there with me in the delivery room.

'I want my dad in here,' I said to the midwife. 'It's not rude.'

At one point the midwives were worried because the umbilical cord had got wrapped around the baby's neck and I had to stop pushing. But they managed to unhook it and a couple of minutes later Emily popped out. It was certainly a very different labour to David's.

I hadn't known what sex the baby was going to be but when I saw she was a beautiful little girl I felt so lucky. She was perfect.

It was almost midnight when Emily was born, at 11.23 pm, and I was allowed home the following morning.

But no sooner had we got back to our house than David started throwing up. He'd come down with a terrible stomach bug. So there I was, the day after having given birth, looking after a newborn and a vomiting toddler. Oh God. It was horrendous.

It was over the next few months that the rows returned. A lot of them were about the same old things all over again. I felt knackered looking after a baby and a toddler as well as keeping the house tidy, washing and cooking. But I thought Dave felt I should be doing more to look after him too.

I felt sad that after all my hopes and best intentions, nothing had really changed between us.

I still loved him, I always had done, and sometimes we still laughed together but again we were getting bogged down in working, cooking and cleaning. We had no time for each other.

I think we both felt trapped in a relationship that wasn't making either of us happy any more. But we struggled on because we did want things to be OK, both for us and the kids. Dave was a great dad but it was becoming increasingly obvious we just weren't compatible.

The rows were getting so frequent and so bad that I knew they were making us fall out of love with each other too. This time, we were even losing that.

I knew we couldn't carry on like this. We'd given it our best shot, twice now, but it wasn't working. My parents would help support me and the kids if I left. It had reached the point where we knew what had to be done.

It was hard for David though, because he was three by then and old enough to sort of understand what was going on. Sometimes he would say to me: 'Where's my daddy?' Or, 'Are we going home yet, Mummy?' It would break my heart but I knew as long as me and Dave managed to stay on reasonable terms and showed him how much we both still loved him, then eventually he'd be OK.

Dave carried on being a brilliant dad and had the kids regularly. Neither David or Emily were ever left in any doubt about how much their mum and dad both loved them.

At first I was back in Mum and Dad's spare room again – but this time with two kids either side of my bed. We knew it wouldn't be for long though, and after a couple of months I found us a two-bed terraced house to move into.

Dave put a deposit down for us and my rent was paid by the Social. By then I was dependent on benefits and I was permanently skint. All my furniture was stuff that I'd been given by friends and family.

But the house was grim. It was next door to a pub and every night at chucking-out time there'd be pissed-up blokes clattering about outside the window. I was constantly worried they'd wake up the kids. Then first thing in the morning we'd be woken up by the clanking of the bloody beer barrels being delivered.

We'd only been in the house a few days when I noticed something that smelt like gas. As the days went by the smell just kept getting stronger and soon there was no mistaking it – the boiler was leaking.

Thank God I'd had windows open almost all the time, because I dread to think what might have happened to the children otherwise.

Dad was absolutely raging and rang up the landlord for me. 'I want her deposit back.'

'Well, I don't know about that,' the landlord replied.

'Really? Well I do,' Dad said. 'That place is dirty and shabby, but most of all it's dangerous. You can't rent out a place like that.'

So the next day I packed up all the clothes, toys and furniture and the three of us moved again.

We went back to Mum and Dad's for a short while and then found another house on Old Road in Ashton-in-

Makerfield. It was a three-bed terrace, like something straight out of *Coronation Street*. It was fine, but pretty basic, with that super hard-wearing office-style carpet on the floor.

My rent was paid by Social Security again and after that I never had much for us to live on. Dave gave me as much as he could afford for each child each week too.

Dave had the kids regularly and made a real effort to make sure they had everything they needed, and if I was really desperate he would try to help me out. But the rest of the time, everything else was down to me. Money was a constant worry. It makes me mad when people talk now about single mothers on benefits as if they're living the life of Riley. I know exactly how hard it is bringing up kids on the Social.

From the paltry money I had each week I had to buy food, the kids' clothes, nappies and bus fares to take David to nursery as well as my gas and electricity.

There was never quite enough money to get through the week.

I fell further and further behind on my electricity bills until they insisted that I go onto a pre-pay card meter. I'd have to top it up at the local shop and then when it ran out of the money, that was it.

There were plenty of times when the money on the card ran out and we were all left sitting in the dark. David was still just three years old and watching the cartoons on telly one afternoon when everything suddenly cut out.

'Mum, leccy's gone off again,' I heard him shout from the other room.

I hated the fact that he was so little and things like this

were becoming normal for him. It wasn't what I'd wanted at all.

Each time the leccy went off I'd have to get the kids' coats on, put Emily in the buggy then walk down the shops to top up the card. But sometimes, when I was totally skint, I'd have to ring Dad and ask to borrow a tenner. Mum and Dad did everything they could to help but they didn't have money to spare either.

Winter was the worst time because no matter how cold it was I just couldn't afford to keep the heating on. Each night I'd put David and Emily to bed wearing their dressing gowns on top of their pyjamas.

Most of the time I was totally skint, which meant shopping for food was a nightmare. I got most of our food in Aldi or a freezer shop in town called Heron, because it was so much cheaper there than anywhere else.

Me and Tracey would go halves on a bag of nappies because buying a whole bag would make a massive dent in my weekly budget. Tracey was still with her husband Malc, but he wasn't working so they were struggling for cash too.

Each time I went shopping I'd work out exactly what we needed for the week and that was all I'd buy. It was all pretty basic stuff. I bought Turkey Twizzlers and fish fingers because they were cheap and, since they were frozen, there was no danger of them going off and getting wasted. I'd also make spaghetti Bolognese because that was cheap and filling too.

It was a constant struggle trying to keep our heads above water.

David was really into Thomas the Tank Engine at the time.

Every day on our way to his nursery school we'd pass a toy shop with a big display of trains in the window.

'Mummy, have you got enough pennies today for a Thomas?' David would ask every morning.

'Not today, baby,' I'd say. And it would break my heart every single time.

I'd have loved more than anything to buy him that train but if I'd done that there wouldn't have been enough money for the rest of the week.

The worst thing about living like that was not being able to treat my kids to anything. I'd have to start saving months in advance just to get them a few bits and bobs for Christmas.

But I had to budget otherwise I'd get in all sorts of trouble. At one point I did get into debt with a catalogue company. I only bought a few clothes for the kids and myself but soon there were bills arriving and I had no way of paying them. I didn't ask Dave for money often as I knew I had to stand on my own two feet.

Mum and Dad helped me out in the end because it's extremely scary getting into debt when you've no way out of it. I never bought anything from a catalogue again after that. And I never had credit cards – although they probably wouldn't have given me one!

If the washing machine went wrong or the telly broke then I had to ask around for stuff that other people were thinking of chucking out.

I felt like some kind of scrounger, but what else could I do? The whole thing was demeaning and I hated it, but it was our life so I just had to get on with it. I did try looking for work but with no qualifications the only things I could find were really low paid. By the time I'd forked out for childcare I would have been out of pocket. Sometimes I felt completely trapped.

I don't think I really thought about the future much at that point. I was too busy getting through each day.

Because at this point, every day was a battle. We'd get up in the mornings and I'd get David and Emily dressed and give them breakfast. Then I'd put Emily into the buggy and we'd walk down the road to the bus stop to take David to nursery. Then me and Emily would go home, only to have to return a couple of hours later to pick David up again. On the way back I'd get whatever shopping I could carry, hanging all the bags of nappies or potatoes on the back of the buggy.

Sometimes Tracey or Dad gave me a lift but there was no way I could afford a car so we took the bus or walked everywhere.

In the evenings I'd cook the children's tea, read them a story and put them to bed. I'd wrap myself up in a thick jumper so I didn't need much heating on then watch hours and hours of telly. Sometimes some mates would come round and I did still have a laugh, so it wasn't totally grim. My best mates then were still Tracey Shaw, Clare (who later married my brother Jon), Faye Preston (who is now engaged to my brother David), her sister Kim and a guy called Braddy. I also used to hang around a lot with my brothers Jon and Dave and my sister.

Occasionally I would go out when Dave had the kids, but buying drinks in pubs was so expensive that I'd knock back a bottle of Lambrusco before I went out – it was a cheap way of getting in the party spirit!

One afternoon in the summertime I'd invited a couple of friends round and we were sitting chatting when I looked up and saw something black covering the bottom of the window.

'What's that?' I asked, getting up to look more closely.

As I got to the window I could see thousands and thousands of flying ants all over the pane of glass. Within a couple of minutes I couldn't see out of the window at all because it was entirely covered in the bloody things.

David walked into the room and started screaming. I don't blame him – it was like a horror movie! I wasn't sure what to do about the ants so I got the hoover and tried to start sucking them up, but then they began flying all over the room. Then everyone in the house was screaming.

It turned out there was an ants' nest under the window and they had been coming through the cavity wall. My dad came round and sealed the hole for me, which got rid of them – thank God. But I still felt bad having to bring up my kids there.

I tried auditioning for a couple of singing jobs but as soon as I told anyone that I had children, the work seemed to mysteriously disappear. I felt that it wasn't what people in the music industry wanted to hear.

So apart from the occasional wedding gig my career had pretty much ground to a halt.

It was sad, but I was having to come to terms with the idea that the life I was living might be it for me. With fewer and fewer opportunities coming up it became hard to see any way out of it.

We lived in that house for about two years, and we scraped by. But as David got older I found it harder to explain to him why I couldn't get him so many of the things that his little mates had.

Dave helped out as much as he could but money was tight.

One Christmas David was absolutely desperate for a Sega Mega Drive because his friend had one and he'd been playing on it round at his house. But they were a small fortune and I just couldn't afford it, what with getting presents for Emily too. In the end I managed to buy a second-hand one off my brother. David was chuffed, but I hated having to give my kids hand-me-down Christmas presents. I felt like I was somehow letting them down.

This wasn't the life I'd wanted for my kids and I found that very frustrating. When I first fell pregnant with David I'd been determined that I'd carry on with my career so that I could support them and give them everything they needed, but five years on, it just hadn't worked out like that. Every parent wants to give their child the best in life, and when you can't do that it rips your heart out. But there was no point in sitting around feeling sorry for myself; I just had to make the best of it for us.

And although it was a tough time, in many ways it was brilliant. I've got so many memories of those years that I'll treasure for ever.

The three of us were a very tight unit and we did everything together.

Little David had adored Emily from the moment she was born and I made sure he never felt left out after the new baby came along. I got him to help me change her nappies and get her dressed in the morning. It was so cute to see him helping to take care of his little sister.

When she got older they played really well together – although they had their cat-and-dog moments like any brother and sister! But really, I was so lucky. They were great kids.

I decorated their bedroom in our house using free tester pots because I couldn't afford big tins of paint. I created this under-the-sea picture with fishes and sharks and it didn't look too bad at all. The kids loved it.

The three of us played together all the time and they were such great company – however bad things were, one of them would always say or do something that could make me laugh.

One morning we were walking round to my mum's and David was holding on to the buggy and shuffling along in a really weird way.

'Oh for goodness' sake, David,' I said. 'Stop messing about.'

'I can't help it,' he said, and carried on walking in this really strange way all the way there. I was convinced he was just being silly and was starting to get annoyed.

It was only when we got to Mum's and I took him for a wee that I realised he'd put both legs through the same hole of his underpants when he got dressed. He'd been like that all morning! I cracked up when I realised. Poor David.

Dave and I were really big on making sure the kids were brought up with good manners. When it came to the kids we always had a united front. We always discussed how they should be brought up and that really helped. Maybe it was because we were quite hot on discipline that my kids were never really that naughty.

And in many ways I loved being a single mum because except when they went to their dad's house, it was just them and me. We were a brilliant team.

In the morning we would all cuddle up in bed together and at teatime we would sit round the table and talk about what they'd been up to at school or nursery.

And of course there was always music on and we'd be singing together around the house, like the von Trapp family!

I had a couple of dates after splitting with Dave, but nothing serious. But then, about a year after we split up, I started going out with a guy called Martin Murphy.

In fact, I actually went out with a friend of Martin's for a short while beforehand. He was a lovely guy but quite young in many ways, and just wasn't quite ready to be going out with a woman with two kids. While we were going out I couldn't help but notice his mate Martin and there was clearly a spark between us.

Martin was more mature and he seemed really nice. We could have a right giggle together and one evening we admitted that we both fancied each other. For a week or so there was a bit of an overlap and I was seeing both guys but I felt horribly guilty about it the entire time. In truth, the relationship with Martin's friend was hardly a relationship at all – I barely saw him. I stopped seeing the first guy and started going out with Martin properly. We hit it off from the beginning and I thought he was lovely. Maybe deep down

I knew he wasn't 'The One' but I really liked him and the relationship quite quickly became serious.

In the spring of 2000, in the run-up to my twenty-fourth birthday, I decided I had to start changing things in my life. I was still permanently skint and my career had hit the skids.

I was determined to try to offer my kids more. I'd always thought my escape route would be through singing but I just wasn't so sure any more.

'I've had enough of this,' I told Mum one day. 'I don't want to bring my kids up on benefits for the rest of their lives and I can't wait around for ever hoping that my singing career is going to take off.'

'OK,' said Mum. 'Well, what will you do?'

'If nothing has happened for me as a singer by my birthday then I'm going to enrol myself on a course in beauty therapy and find work as a beautician. I've got to get myself out of this situation. I've got to get us all out of this situation.'

It was hard to think about waving goodbye to my lifelong dreams, but the kids had to be my priority, and I decided I would do whatever it took to give them a better life – even if that meant giving up all hopes of ever being a singer.

11
AUDITIONS

....

I stood at the ironing board in my front room slowly working my way through the washing basket of crumpled clothes. David and Emily were sitting on the sofa watching *Paddington Bear*. That was one of their favourites.

It was late July 2000 and my twenty-fourth birthday had come and gone and there was still no sign of any more singing work coming in. I'd made my decision and I was sticking to it – in September I was signed up to start a beauty therapy course.

I'd loved playing with my Girl's World styling head when I was little, brushing her hair and doing her make-up, and I was pretty good at it on real people too! How could I go wrong?

Of course I would still far rather have become a professional singer; that had been my dream for as long as I could remember. But I had to face facts: it just didn't look like it was ever going to happen. There had been less and less work around for me and virtually the only singing I'd done in months was at home with the kids. David would sing, 'You are my

Sunshine', and me and Emily would belt out the *Teletubbies* theme tune over and over again. Hardly *Top of the Pops*!

No, I couldn't carry on hoping against hope that things were just going to get better. I had to get a job that would support my kids and get us off benefits. I certainly didn't want to be scrimping and saving for the rest of my life.

I was feeling pretty low generally. I was still with Martin, but I felt something was missing in the relationship. He had asked me to marry him and I'd accepted because he was a nice guy, but deep down I knew we weren't really right for each other.

I'd also been really upset to find out that David had been bullied after starting school. It had brought back all those terrible memories from my own schooldays.

'Is something the matter, love?' I asked him, after picking him up from school one afternoon.

'No,' he mumbled. But I could tell he was upset about something. We talked for a long time and gradually he admitted he was being bullied.

As the story came out bit by bit, I felt physically sick. I just couldn't bear the thought of him going through all those feelings I'd experienced.

'Don't worry, love,' I told him. 'Mummy won't let this happen again.'

The next morning I went straight in to the school and made an appointment with the head teacher. I was called in and told her the whole story.

'Yes,' she said, nodding slowly. 'I understand. You see, Mrs Cunliffe, David's biggest problem is that he's not very threatening and that's probably why this has been happening.'

'Hold on a moment,' I said. I was furious now. 'David's problem is that he's not threatening? What do you want me to do? Send him to karate lessons? Or maybe you'd like me to send him to school with a flick knife?'

'No, no, of course not, Mrs Cunliffe!' She started back-tracking like mad and said she'd speak to the parents of the bullies. But my back was really up by that point – and every time she called me Mrs Cunliffe it just made things worse. She obviously hadn't even bothered to find out that me and David's dad weren't married and my name was not Mrs Cunliffe.

That whole meeting only reaffirmed what I'd always thought about bullying: that people still think that the victims are somehow to blame because they're not standing up for them-selves. In reality, when you're being bullied you can't stand up for yourself. The bullies take that ability away from you.

So, all in all, as I stood there that evening with my pile of ironing, things were a bit rubbish.

Then the phone rang. It was my mum.

'Hiya, Kym,' she said. 'What are you doing tomorrow?'

'Taking David to school, doing a bit of shopping with Emily, tidying up toys, picking up David, making tea, doing more ironing. Pretty much the same as usual, Mum,' I said, being a bit sarky.

'No you're not,' she said. 'You're going to an audition.'

'What are you talking about?'

'There was an item on the local news – they're holding auditions tomorrow in Manchester to find people to be in a new pop band. You've got to go.'

'Oh Mum, if it has been on the telly there'll be hundreds

of thousands of people turning up,' I pointed out. 'It'll be a total waste of time.'

My confidence had been worn down over the past couple of years and I'd pretty much accepted my hopes of a singing career were over.

'Look, Kym, you're going,' said Mum firmly. 'Your dad will mind the kids and I'll come with you. It'll be great.'

I still wasn't convinced. 'Have you got any idea how many people will turn up there?'

'It doesn't matter,' Mum said. 'It might be a waste of time but unless you go along then you'll never know.'

I knew she wasn't going to take no for an answer.

'All right,' I said finally. 'I'll see you in the morning.'

Seven o'clock the next morning me and Mum were about third or fourth in the queue standing outside Granada Televison Studios. We thought we'd be the first. Goodness only knows what time the people in front of us must have got there!

Over the next couple of hours hundreds of people started turning up and by 9 a.m. the place was mobbed. There must have been more than three thousand people waiting.

'I told you,' I grumbled to Mum, looking back at the queue that stretched all the way down Water Street to the city centre.

'Well, we're here now,' Mum said. 'Just show them what you can do.'

The people in charge began letting us into the building in big groups of about fifty. First of all we were taken into one of the big studios and each handed forms to fill in. As we looked at the forms TV cameras kept moving up and down.

'What do you think they're filming for?' I asked Mum.

'Who knows?' she said. No one really had a clue what was going on. The whole thing seemed very odd.

Now viewers have seen thousands of people audition on television for shows like *Popstars*, *Pop Idol*, *Fame Academy*, *The X Factor* and *Britain's Got Talent*. But back then there had never been a reality show like this before and the whole thing was just weird.

I took out a pen and filled in all the available spaces on the form: Name, Address, Date of Birth, Marital Status. Nowhere did it ask about children.

'Do you think I should write down about David and Emily?' I asked Mum, staring at the form.

'Well, it doesn't ask,' she said. 'Just leave it and see what happens.'

We both knew that, ridiculously, having kids had counted against me when I'd been trying to get into the industry over the past few years. As soon as people knew I had children they'd worry I wouldn't be able to make recording times or be able to travel around the country. And however much I tried to tell them that they could count on me, I knew they didn't quite believe it.

After we had handed in our forms we were each given a number and told to wait until ours was called out.

Then a guy in his fifties with wavy hair went up to the front and started talking.

'Hi, my name is Nigel Lythgoe,' he said. 'In case you're wondering what this is all about, we're making a TV show which is going to be called *Popstars*. We're travelling all over the country carrying out auditions and seeing thousands of young hopefuls like yourselves. If you get through today, you will be invited back for more auditions in Birmingham. And if you make it through those, you'll be in the finals in London.

'And,' he said, pausing slightly, 'if you're one of the lucky five we select as winners you'll move to London to be part of the amazing band that we're going to launch.'

All round the room people were gobsmacked.

I just turned to Mum and said, 'We might as well go now then.'

'What?'

'Well even if I won, which I won't, I couldn't move to London,' I pointed out. 'I couldn't take David and Emily to London.'

Mum huffed a bit. 'Just give it a go, Kym,' she said. 'You're worrying about something that might never happen.'

I could hardly just get up and walk out after queueing for hours, so I sat there and waited for my number to be called out by a member of the TV production crew. Numbers were called out in batches of five and then you had to get up with your little group, walk into another room, then sing individually in front of the judges.

I only found out later who the judges were and how high up they were in the music and television industry. Nigel Lythgoe had been head of entertainment at LWT and in charge of shows like *Blind Date* and *Gladiators*. Next to him was Nicky Chapman, who had worked in music PR for years and represented the Spice Girls, Take That and David Bowie, as well as loads of other bands. The third judge was Paul Adam who was director of A&R at Polydor Records, which was to have rights to the finished group.

We'd been given a list of songs to choose between and I'd already selected 'My Heart Will Go On' by Celine Dion from the film *Titanic*. I'd done it in pubs and clubs so many times that I could have sung it in my sleep.

Some of the people who got up to sing had incredible voices. But some were pretty grim too! It was such a mixed bag.

When my number was called out I stood in front of the judges and gave it my best shot. I wasn't particularly nervous at first, but when I saw the TV camera right in my face and all the lights shining on me it was quite scary.

'Hi,' said Nigel. 'And what's your name?'

'I'm Kym,' I said giggling slightly. I'd automatically gone into my professional mode, acting all bubbly and confident even though I was feeling far from it inside.

Then I launched into 'My Heart Will Go On'. I knew it so well that I got through my thirty seconds without hitting any duff notes and I thought I'd done OK.

When I finished the judges stared at me for a bit and then Nigel Lythgoe said, 'Thank you. That was very good.'

Thing is, he'd said that to most of the people that day – even the rubbish ones – so I still didn't really have much indication what the judges thought of me.

So then I just had to sit down again and wait.

After all of the fifty people in my group had sung their song, a long list of numbers was called out. Mine was among them.

'All those people whose numbers have been called out are through to the afternoon auditions,' the TV guy announced.

That was me – I was through to the second round! I was so excited . . . that is, until I looked round at the hundreds of people who had been called back to the studio that afternoon for round two. With a sinking heart, I told myself there was no way I'd be getting through to the Birmingham auditions.

It was during our lunch break that I spotted Jon Hargreaves. Jon and I had known each other a while and it was great to see a friendly face. Then in the afternoon they called out our numbers randomly and put us in pairs to perform a duet – and by a stroke of luck I was paired up with Jon. It was brilliant because we already knew each other and we'd sung together before dozens of times.

We all had to sing 'Don't Go Breaking My Heart'.

We had about half an hour to practise the song and make up a dance routine, which was a bit tight, but we managed it.

Then we sat down with all the others again and waited for our number to be called.

When our turn came we got onstage and had a really good time. It was easier for us in some ways because we'd sung together before and we got on really well.

We were just getting into it when Nigel Lythgoe called out, 'Thank you, that's enough,' and we had to sit down again.

For a second time I had no idea what the judges had really thought. We had to wait until right at the end of the day when another list of numbers was called out.

Again mine and Jon's were on the list. 'If I've just called your number out,' said Nigel, 'congratulations. You're through to the next round in Birmingham.'

I was stunned.

It was really exciting just having got through the auditions and that evening I was once again back behind my ironing board.

Over the next few days the more I thought about the next stage of auditions in Birmingham, the more pointless the whole thing seemed.

I rang Mum to talk it through with her.

'I'm going to have to pack it in,' I said.

'Why? What's happened, love?'

'It's just silly me going to Birmingham,' I sighed. 'If whoever wins has to move to London, that rules me out completely. There's no point in me continuing any further.'

I felt gutted, but pulling out seemed like the only option for me.

'Look, love,' Mum said. 'Don't pack it in quite yet. Just keep on going and see what happens. Go and sing your best in Birmingham and we'll worry about everything else when we get to it.'

'OK,' I said reluctantly. 'I'll do it.'

I got the train down to Birmingham a couple of weeks later for the next round. This time there were going to be two full days of auditions, so all the contestants were staying overnight in a hotel. Mum and Dad had offered to look after David and Emily. They knew 'Mummy was going singing' and they loved staying with their grandma and granddad, so at least I knew they were happy and being well looked after so I didn't have to worry about them.

I was still so skint that I hadn't even been able to go out

and buy any decent new clothes to take with me. When the auditions were televised a few months later you can see that I'm wearing exactly the same black vest top from Morgan and trackie bottoms in nearly every single shot.

Well, we were doing a lot of dancing so I thought it was best to be casual.

At the hotel I was paired up with a girl who introduced herself as Jessica Taylor. She was lovely and we hit it off instantly, which was great because we made it right down to the final ten together.

That weekend I also met Suzanne Shaw for the first time. As it turned out, she would make it all the way to the band with me too – although neither of us dared hope for that at this stage in the game.

On the night we stayed over a few of us stayed up chatting in the evening. For me it was really strange being away from the kids for even a night but it was incredibly exciting. Jon, my pal from Blackpool, was also there and we all had a great time. I stayed up really late but I was careful not to overdo the booze because the following day was going to be so important. In fact, the only alcoholic drink I had all night was a single bottle of beer. The camera crews were filming us night and day so I didn't want to make an idiot of myself on telly.

However, the next morning my throat was really sore. I thought I'd better tell the television crew and they passed a message on to Nigel Lythgoe. But months later when the show was screened the scenes of me having a laugh that night in Birmingham made me look quite drunk. They are so cringey to watch now. And somehow they also managed to imply that I'd lost my voice the next morning by drinking and partying too much the night before. It wasn't true at all, but by the time the show went out I was learning quite fast how hundreds of hours of footage could be edited to make people appear in very different ways.

That day I struggled on with my sore throat as my group sang 'Monday, Monday' and 'Never Ever' by All Saints.

At the end of the two days we were all put into two different rooms. It was obvious that one roomful of people were through to the next round and the other roomful were going home, but as I looked around me I really couldn't work out which was which.

There were some people in my room that I thought were brilliant. But there were some really amazing people in the other room too. Whatever it was that these judges were looking for, it certainly wasn't obvious.

We waited for what felt like a lifetime and then Nigel Lythgoe stood in front of us. My heart was in my mouth, and everyone quietened down to listen. He smiled, and said, very slowly: 'Now, I'm afraid I'm going to have to tell you . . .' and then there was one of those agonising pauses that they do on all reality shows nowadays, '. . . that I want you all to come to London for the next round of auditions.'

Everyone was screaming and hugging. It was incredible.

I went home on a total high. After I got through each stage of the competition I could feel myself wanting to win more and more. I'd started out feeling totally negative about the whole thing. But as the weeks went by and the judges seemed to like my voice gradually my confidence had returned.

Maybe I could do this after all, I thought to myself. And the more I thought that, the more I wanted to win. This really could be the thing that changed my family's life for ever.

My only disappointment was that my friend Jon didn't make it through. He was so talented and I was desperate for him to get through to the finals. He was a real star, though, and wished me all the best for the next stage of the competition.

After a few days back home, doing the school run and loading up with frozen peas in Aldi, my excitement turned to worry again. There were so many incredibly talented people going through to the London auditions that I told myself it was ridiculous to get my hopes up. And say I did get through, what would I do about the children?

David and Emily were only tiny; I couldn't drag them to London. And besides, who'd look after them when I was working?

'Stop mithering about it, Kym,' Mum would say every time I brought the subject up. 'We'll cross that bridge when we come to it.'

But I couldn't help thinking about it.

'I can't move to London,' I said to Mum one day for the thousandth time. 'How could I move into a shared house with the children? That's just not how it works.'

'But me and your dad could help with them,' Mum insisted.

I sighed. 'I know you would, Mum, but the kids need me around. They can't just stay up here without me.'

'Listen, love,' Mum said. 'Sometimes you have to make sacrifices in life. You've got to think about what's best for everyone in the long run.'

I had to admit Mum knew what she was talking about

there. She and Dad had been making sacrifices all their lives for their children. They had scrimped and saved for years after Dad lost his business but they always made sure us kids had everything we needed. Even so, I couldn't bear the thought of being away from my children.

I even hated leaving them for two days to go down to London for the finals. I gave them both hugs and kisses in the hall at Mum's, then said goodbye to my parents.

'Sock it to 'em, kid,' Dad said, giving me a hug.

'Go on, love, you can do this,' Mum added.

I wasn't so sure. By this point I knew I wanted it, I knew I really wanted to win. *Popstars* could be the thing that changed all our lives for ever. But there was still a long way to go and I knew I was up against a lot of people who seemed far more talented than me. I didn't really think I had much chance of making it through to the final ten.

I went down to London on the train. There were other people I recognised from the auditions in the same carriage. Some of us chatted about how nervous we were feeling. It was nice knowing that other people were bricking it, same as me.

The London auditions were held in rehearsal rooms in Brixton. There were so many of us there, but still just a fraction of the thousands who had come along to auditions across the country. Still, it seemed like a massive number of people to be whittled down to the final five band members.

Over two days we had to do lots of different tasks to see how we would cope with being in a band. It wasn't just about singing any more, they told us. It was about the entire package.

We had to do trust exercises, where one of us would lead

another blindfolded across a room and another where we had to fall backwards and rely on someone else to catch us – me and Suzanne were fab! I guess that was all about whether we could be team players.

Then we had to sing in different group set-ups. After that we had to answer questions at a mock press conference. There were people pretending to be journalists asking questions which they thought might trip us up.

One of the questions was, 'Have you ever smoked marijuana?' and one of the girls, Jessica, went, 'Yeah, yeah, I have.' The rest of us were all thinking: *Oh my God, they'll get rid of her now!*

She actually made it through to the final ten, but it did make us all think very carefully about our answers.

One of the pretend journalists asked me: 'If one of your fans wanted to get a tattoo like yours, what would you say?' Back then I had one Chinese symbol at the top of my arm that I'd had one afternoon with my mate Tracey Shaw – she had been throwing up in the gutter outside the tattoo parlour because she was so queasy! And I also had a panther etched on my bum although it actually looks more like the Slazenger logo!

I really had to think on my feet. 'If they were an adult then I'd say it's their choice, but if they were under eighteen then it's illegal.'

The judges were watching our every move all day but we had absolutely no idea what they were thinking. Nigel, Nicky and Paul were always nice to me, but I still didn't know whether that meant they liked me enough to keep me in the competition.

At the end of the first day we were all put into a room then one by one we had to walk what we called 'the Green Mile' into the judges' room where we were told if we would be staying or going home.

People walked back and some were crying and others were smiling all over their faces. But with each person that came back from their meeting with the judges I was more and more confused. It seemed that some of the best people were being eliminated. I was convinced that if they were out, I would be too.

When it was my turn to walk the Green Mile to the judges' room I was certain I'd be going home. But Nicky and Nigel were smiling at me. I was staying for another day. I felt like the breath had been knocked out of me.

Throughout the whole audition process it was really disappointing when anyone was sent home because we'd built up a real team spirit. But with just a day left to go, I finally felt like I had a chance of winning. For the first time in years, my lifelong ambition of being a professional singer was maybe, just maybe, within my grasp.

The next morning there were just twenty of us left. There was more singing and group work and then we were told more people were going to be eliminated. That was incredibly scary because we knew all that hard work and hoping would mean absolutely nothing if we went out then.

I'd dreamt of being a singer all my life and now I was so close. If I could just make it into the band it would change my kids' lives for good. It was the first-ever reality music show and so I had no idea then how big a deal it would turn out to be, but I knew it was going to be a huge step forward for us.

That's why I had to win. I had to get into that band and give my children the lives they deserved.

At the end of the second day we were separated into two rooms – ten people in mine and five in the other. I looked around at the people left in my room. There was Jessica, who I'd become friends with in Birmingham, and Suzanne Shaw, who I'd met there too. The others in the room I didn't know so well, as they'd come up through auditions elsewhere in the country.

Then Nigel Lythgoe stood in front of us and after a pause that seemed to last a million years he said, 'Congratulations. You are in the final ten.'

We all started screaming, 'Yes! Yes!' and were jumping up and down like mad things.

But then we remembered that in the other room our friends were being told they were going home, so we felt awful for them.

And it still wasn't over. We still had to find out whether we'd actually made it into the final five who would form the band.

We were told that we would be visited at home by one of the judges in the next week and they would break the news to us in person. Eek!

The next few days were horrific, waiting to find out whether I was in the band or not. I was on eggshells the whole time, daydreaming about what might happen if I made it into the band, and then telling myself not to get my hopes up.

The production crew arranged for my judge's visit to happen at Mum and Dad's house one morning towards the end of

October 2000. I didn't want them coming to my house as it was still a bit grotty – I didn't want those flying ants on national TV!

David and Emily weren't there that day. I still hadn't told the production crew about the children and I was worried sick about how I would do it. Obviously I would have to tell them sometime but I just wasn't quite sure how I'd do it. But I knew it could only be a good thing for the children if I succeeded. This was going to be what changed all our lives for ever. As Mum kept saying, 'Worry about breaking the news to the TV crew if and when you need to do so.'

I knew that maybe I should have told someone but I also knew for a fact that I wouldn't have been down to the final ten if I'd burst out one day and said, 'By the way, I've got two little children called David and Emily and they're gorgeous.' No way. I'd have been straight out of there!

Obviously they would never have said it was because of the kids, but I'm certain they would have found an excuse for binning me. Single motherhood just didn't fit with the young, glam image they were going for.

The way I saw it, I was so close to making it now and I could see how *Popstars* could really change everything for me and the kids. It was a massive gamble but I had to take it.

On the morning the camera crew were due to arrive at Mum and Dad's house we sat waiting for them, nervously drinking cup after cup of tea. We were all on pins. The camera crew came round first just to check the lighting and sound, but they weren't giving anything away. It was all I could do to stop myself grabbing hold of them and yelling, 'Am I in? Tell me! Tell me!'

Then, finally, at around one o'clock, Paul Adam arrived. I was delighted to see Paul because he was my favourite judge. He was very warm and I knew that even if it was bad news, he'd break it to me gently.

Paul came and sat with me in the front room. The camera was trained on my face and it was taking all my effort not to shake with nerves. At the same time another cameraman was filming Mum and Dad in the kitchen, listening in.

'So,' said Paul, and then he paused for ages and ages and ages and ages. I think I aged a good few years in that pause! 'I'm afraid . . .' then he paused again. At that point I thought it was over. I thought I was out but Paul, being a nice guy, was struggling to tell me. I felt devastated but I really didn't want to burst into tears on camera. But then I heard Paul finishing his sentence, '. . . I'm going to have to ask you to come to London.'

I was so shocked that I slapped him straight across the leg for putting me through such misery.

'Oh my God,' I screamed. Then I was hugging Paul and jumping up and down.

Mum and Dad were in the kitchen being filmed saying: 'Is it a yes?'

'It is, it is. It's a yes!'

I ran into the kitchen and me, Mum and Dad all hugged each other and then I started crying. Mum was crying, Dad was crying. Everyone was bawling away. It was just an amazing moment.

'Oh Kym, I'm so proud of you,' Mum said. And then we were all sobbing like idiots. What a carry-on!

Mum and Dad were both as proud as Punch. I've never

seen them so made up before. But really, if it hadn't been for them, I would never have been there.

I was desperate to find out who else had made it through to the band. On our last day in London we'd come up with a secret code that we would use to text each other our news. If it was a 'yes' we were to write 'rice' and if it was a 'no' the code was 'beans'. It was all meant to be so top secret that we weren't even supposed to tell each other if we were in the band or not.

There were frantic text messages going up and down the country until we all found out who had made it into the band. It was me, Suzanne Shaw, Myleene Klass, Danny Foster and Noel Sullivan. The five who hadn't made it were Jessica Taylor, Kelli Young, Michelle Heaton, Tony Lundon and Kevin Simm.

I felt really sorry for Jessica and the other four who hadn't got through, because I knew just how much we'd all wanted it.

That evening we were all just floating on air. I still couldn't quite believe what was happening. Paul Adam and the TV crew told me I had a fortnight before I was expected in London, where the band would all be living together in one house. Then we'd have three months to work together and record tracks before releasing our first single. Almost every moment of our days would be filmed for the TV show, which would begin airing in January 2001.

In the meantime I wasn't supposed to tell anyone what had happened to avoid news of the final five leaking out to newspapers before people had seen the show on television.

So the only people I told were my closest family.

Dave and I decided it would be better for the children to

spend most of their time with my parents but still see him at weekends, as before.

I hated the thought of spending even a night away from the children. And even though I knew I'd be travelling back whenever I could and Mum and Dad would bring the kids down to see me, I still didn't want to be away from them.

'They'll be safe and happy here,' Mum would reassure me. 'You've got to take this opportunity – for them, and for yourself too.'

But it was still agony telling the kids I was going away for a while. When I'd had the auditions I'd told them I was going off singing so little David sort of understood a bit about what was happening. Emily was still too young though.

'Mummy is going away singing again,' I told them the night before I was due to travel down to London. 'But I'll be back all the time and you can come down to visit me too.'

'OK, Mum,' said David. He was never one to make a big fuss. Emily was as good as gold too. I'm not sure she really understood what I meant.

Leaving them the following morning was heartbreaking. I knew I would be travelling back up to see them as often as possible but they were my babies and I hated being away from them. But I knew I had to take this chance and it wouldn't be forever.

Popstars sent a car to my house to pick me up and take me to London, which was the height of luxury. And as I stepped inside it, I truly felt like I was stepping into a new life. It was so totally different to anything that had happened to me before. But even though I was so excited I felt desperately sad too. Saying goodbye to my kids was heartbreaking. We'd been a team, just the three of us, for so long and now I was on my own. I cried all the way to London and cuddled their teddy bears, which I'd taken with me.

But I knew I had to do it. This was our big chance. Our chance to change everything.

12
REALITY BITES

·········

It was the most amazing house I'd ever seen in my life: four huge bedrooms, two living rooms, a garden room, three bathrooms and a music room with mirrors on the walls so we could practise our dance moves.

It was the kind of mansion that I'd only ever seen on telly before. But for the next three months it was to be our home.

Only that morning I'd woken up in my cramped little terraced house with the flying ants. Everything seemed to be changing so fast, it made me dizzy.

I lay down on my bed in the room I was sharing with Myleene Klass and tried to think it all through. I'd been selected from thousands of people to be here as part of Britain's first-ever reality TV pop band and record a single with Polydor, one of the country's biggest record companies. It felt like all my dreams were coming true.

I should have been happy as Larry. But inside the only thing I could think was, *I miss David and Emily*. The next three months away from them stretched ahead of me like a lifetime.

Since I'd been selected for *Popstars*, my entire life had become surrounded in mystery.

The show's producers were terrified that the tabloids were going to track us down and print the identities of the final five before they had been revealed on the show. So there we were in this house in God-knows-where in London and with a new mobile phone number that I was only supposed to give to a very select few people in case the press tracked me down. Plus I wasn't allowed to tell anyone – even my parents – exactly where we were or what we were doing.

I can sort of understand why they were being so paranoid, because it would have ruined the early part of the show if the viewers found out who won. But so much secrecy did make our lives pretty difficult.

I went home to visit the children whenever I could but when I was in London it was like I'd fallen down the rabbit hole, into a completely different sort of life.

The five of us bandmates moved into the house in Mill Hill, North London, in early November 2000. Me and Myleene shared a bedroom, which put me in the position that a million blokes in the country would like to be in – I've seen Myleene naked and yes, she is gorgeous!

The second part of the *Popstars* series was to be filmed more like a documentary, following our time in the house as we got to know each other, began singing together and then went on to start recording.

The first day at the house was very strange. The car that had collected me from home had then gone on to pick up Suzanne Shaw from her house in Bury, Lancashire, so the two of us turned up together. When we arrived Myleene, Danny and Noel were already there. Myleene was originally from Norfolk, but had been living in London for a while. Danny was from East London. Then Noel arrived from his home in Cardiff.

When we were all finally there we were so excited that we just ran around the house screaming and laughing. Coming from my tiny little home, the house looked like the most beautiful place I'd ever seen in my life before. None of us could believe it.

The next few days we spent gradually getting to know each other. We were all from very different backgrounds and in normal circumstances we'd probably never have met. But we'd been thrown together and at that time I think we all believed we were going to be the best of friends.

Noel liked to be the clown of the group and he was always having a joke and a laugh. He'd been working in Ibiza as a holiday rep and was Mr Party Party Party. Myleene was quite settled in London and had her family and boyfriend nearby. We came from totally different backgrounds – she'd studied classical music for one thing! – but actually we had a fair bit in common, in that we were both pretty outspoken and capable of standing up for ourselves. Danny was a very warm, genuine guy who wore his heart on his sleeve. He was very close to his family, as was I. He was still quite young and out to have a good time. And so was Suzanne. She was still only nineteen and seemed much younger than me.

I was the only one with children and responsibilities and

so right from the start that made me feel very different to the others.

At first, though, we all got on well together. In those early days none of us really knew what to expect or what the future held. But everything that was happening to us was so exciting that we just went with it and had a laugh together. After all, we were all having the adventure of a lifetime. We'd been in London a couple of weeks when we sat down with our management team to decide on a name for the band. There were lots of suggestions being thrown around but in the end we settled on Hear'Say. It sounded cool and unusual. I liked it.

Around that time the runners-up formed a group called Liberty, which then became Liberty X because of a court battle with another band with the same name. We were all dead happy that they'd got the chance to be in a band too. I kept in touch with Jessica for quite a while and I was pleased it had worked out well for her too.

Each morning the five of us in Hear'Say would wake up in our big house and go off to rehearse together, work out dance routines, record tracks, take part in photo shoots or have meetings with the record company.

I felt like I was learning more and more about the record industry with every day that passed.

What I wasn't quite so keen on was being filmed every moment for the TV show. That said, after a while you did just sort of forget the cameras were there. After a bit I could act quite normally even when there was a lens stuck in my face.

I've always worn my heart on my sleeve and after a while I was saying exactly what I thought about things without a second thought. I've never been the type to mind my Ps and Qs. That did mean, though, that they had to do a lot of bleeping when the series was screened the following January. Oops!

My auntie Dilys said to Mum one day, 'Kym is doing so well, but does she really have to swear quite so much?'

She's dead funny, auntie Dilys. She comes across as very well-to-do but she is actually wonderfully down to earth and absolutely lovely. She has always been so supportive of my career, even lending me money to record tracks before I entered *Popstars*.

What I hated about the constant reality-show filming was having to do things a second time if they had missed something. Something that was said or done spontaneously the first time just felt kinda corny when doing it a second or third time, just so they could get it in shot. It was a bit like being a human video player. Stop, rewind, replay. Fast-forward to the next good bit!

I was living in an amazing house, with great people, working hard at a job I loved. All in all, I'd have been having a great time if it wasn't for being apart from David and Emily and not being able to tell everyone I was working with about them. I never once lied or pretended not to have children. It was just never asked. I had missed out on jobs in the past because I was a single parent, and I really needed that job. I had to get David and Emily out of that house. It was killing me not being able to share with everyone the truth about my beautiful children. But it had been so long by that time and there never seemed to be the right moment to tell them.

I pinned up pictures of my kids next to my bed, but kissing

a photo goodnight didn't come close to stroking David's hair or touching Emily's chubby little cheek.

Apart from the auditions I had barely been apart from either of them since the day they were born. Aside from school, nursery, and their visits to their Dad, the three of us had been together every minute of every day for their entire lives. Now we were living at opposite ends of the country. I'd worked out with Mum and Dad that if I couldn't get back home to see them each week then they would drive them down and we'd all stay together at a nearby Holiday Inn. So I always saw them at least twice a week – but still the thought of actually being away from them for most of the time for three months was killing me.

I missed the kids like mad and felt really low. What made it worse was that I couldn't talk to anyone else in the house about it. Like all parents, I was desperate to boast about my lovely children, but I couldn't. But I wasn't deliberately keeping them a secret, I just could never quite find the right time to break the news. The whole thing seemed to be snowballing out of my control and although I knew I would tell someone about Emily and David at some point, I just wasn't quite sure how and when to do it.

Looking back, maybe it was obvious to some people. At times I was quite withdrawn, and there were pictures of two little children all over my bedroom.

I wanted to shout it from the rooftops that I was proud of my children so I was feeling very guilty about keeping quiet about being a mum, but I thought that if they found out I'd be kicked straight out of the band. I was so close, I couldn't bear to throw it all away.

Night after night I'd worry about whether I was hurting my kids by being away from them. The thought of them missing their mum tore me apart. But at the same time I also knew this was, without a doubt, the best opportunity I was ever likely to get to give us all a better life. I had to stick it out, for all our sakes.

But after a couple of weeks down in London I decided I just couldn't take it any more. I had to come clean about David and Emily. If I couldn't be with them, I needed to at least be able to talk about them and I hadn't even been able to do that.

The first person I confided in was a guy called James Sully who was our lawyer who'd been brought in to help us with our contracts when we first signed up for the group. I really trusted James and found him easy to talk to. He's still my lawyer now.

I rang him at his office one day and said I had something to tell him.

'It's like this,' I said. 'I've got two children.'

'Right,' said James, very calmly.

'I just want to get it all out in the open now,' I said. 'The only reason I didn't say anything sooner was it never seemed the right moment. And I've never been asked if I had kids – I'd been dismissed out of turn just for being a mum before. But I'm proud of my kids and I want to be able to talk about them. So if I get kicked out now, I get kicked out. That's the way it'll have to be.'

'OK, I see your point,' James said. 'Leave it with me and I'll speak to Nigel.'

My next step was to tell the rest of the band. Later that

day when we were all in the house I took a deep breath then laid down some pictures of David and Emily on the table.

'Er,' I said, 'I just thought I should tell you that these are my kids.'

'Oh my God,' said Noel.

'Oh my God,' repeated Suzanne.

'I have to admit I guessed when I saw all the pictures, but I didn't like to say anything,' said Myleene.

'Why didn't you tell us?' Danny wanted to know.

'Well, you never asked,' I said quietly, still not quite sure how they were taking the news. 'And I had to do it. There's so much discrimination against single mothers and I'm pretty sure I wouldn't have been chosen for the band and be sitting here with you now if they'd known.'

'So what are you going to do now?' someone asked.

'Well, I've told James and he's telling Nigel so I'll just have to see.'

I spent the next few days wondering if Nigel was going to haul me in and have a go at me, but he didn't say a word. I saw him at rehearsals and he visited us at the house, and he just acted perfectly normally towards me. After all that worry it was a bit weird!

For two weeks nothing was mentioned about it at all. Then one day we were at the LWT studios when I got a message saying Nigel wanted to see me in his office.

I walked upstairs to his office but before I even got there I saw a *Popstars* camera crew outside his door. My stomach turned over.

It didn't take a genius to work out what this was all about.

By this point I'd already realised that *Popstars* wasn't just about making a band but also about making good TV, so any dramatic moment was bound to be captured on film. This confrontation was too good to miss.

I walked in to Nigel's office and sat there with the camera trained on my face as he started talking. He got straight to his point.

'I'm very disappointed that you thought the fact that you have two children would mean you wouldn't get into the band,' he said.

Then he went on and on at me about how I should have just told them about David and Emily right from the start.

It sounded like he was reading from a script – he obviously thought it was Oscar-winning stuff. The whole meeting felt like it had been set up for the benefit of the camera crew and my role was to look like a lemon on national television.

At first I tried hard to stay strong, but then I could feel myself starting to cry and then there was nothing I could do to stop it. I felt humiliated and as if I had lied. But I had never, ever lied. To me, lying is saying you haven't done something when you have. No one had ever asked me if I had children. If they had done I would have told them the truth. After such a long time not knowing whether it would be a big deal or not, I hadn't offered the information because I was terrified it would have meant the end of a fantastic opportunity.

But that day in Nigel Lythgoe's office, I was made to feel like a sneaky, lying, selfish cow when all I'd ever done was try to get a better life for me and my kids.

The meeting with Nigel wouldn't be aired for another couple of months, but I already knew that I'd be shown crying as if

I had been caught cheating. Who cared if that was totally humiliating for me?

At the time I felt I'd been used, and because of that I was hurt and angry. Those feelings stayed with me from then on, really. I felt they were simply chasing TV ratings. It really seemed to me like that was far more important than the band, and certainly more important than the individual performers.

When that meeting was shown on television it just made everything worse. I felt it came across as though I had deliberately lied about having children and was just being utterly selfish. But I had never, ever lied about my children. All I'd tried to do was the best thing for all of us.

The only good thing to come out of it all was that from then on I could talk openly about David and Emily. I felt like a huge weight had been lifted off my shoulders and that made things a little easier for me.

I still missed the kids terribly, though, and was constantly dashing home when I could get a couple of days off. And Mum and Dad were brilliant at bringing them down to see me in the car. When I couldn't see the children for a few days they would send me envelopes full of pictures they had drawn for me. David wrote me a card saying 'Good Luck' in his best handwriting. I kept everything they sent me and I still have them all, which are now in a frame at home.

Christmas 2000 was an amazing time. I'd only been in the band a few weeks but compared to what I was used to, it felt like I was earning a fortune. It was brilliant being able to save up a bit of money to treat the kids to some really nice presents.

I went back to my mum and dad's and we were all there together for a few days, relaxing, playing and, like a lot of people in the country, eating and drinking a bit too much!

When I got back to London the following week I had probably put on a couple of pounds – all those mince pies! Then it was back to our routine of living on takeaways because we weren't allowed out to the shops in case we were spotted by photographers. Going to the gym was a no-no too.

So maybe I was a little bigger than I had been when I arrived at the house, but I was still only a size 10. Hardly a heifer!

Whatever size I was, I certainly don't think I deserved the next public humiliation that I received from Nigel Lythgoe. Imagine being told on camera, in scenes that would be watched by millions of people, that you're fat. That'll make you feel great about yourself – especially after having an eating disorder!

Nigel had come to the house one day when we were all just hanging around. I was wearing a Man United football shirt, so I admit I wasn't really looking my best. But still!

After calling us over, Nigel started giving us this lecture about how as popstars we were going to be on display all the time, and had a duty to look good.

Then, looking at me, he said, 'Christmas is over and the goose has gotten fat.' For a moment I wasn't quite sure what he was on about.

And then it clicked.

'Do you think I'm fat?' I said, absolutely fuming mad then.

'Well,' he said. 'I think you needed to lose weight before Christmas and I think you need to lose weight now.'

Ouch! I was furious, but really hurt too.

'You are bang out of f***ing order,' I said. The camera stopped filming at that point, but the row carried on going.

We walked into the kitchen then and I tore strips off him. Yeah, he was some high-powered telly executive and I was a single mum from Lancashire, but I wasn't scared of him. I didn't care who he was – the way he was treating us was wrong.

It wasn't so much what he'd actually said – although that was pretty bad. It was the fact that he was now going to show it on television because, it seemed to me, he knew publicly humiliating someone would be good for ratings.

I felt like I was being bullied all over again. It was like being back in the school playground and hearing some kid telling me that I was fat and ugly and having that horrible sick feeling inside. That was the kind of bullying that had made me throw up my meals for a year. And here was Nigel, slagging me off about my weight on national television.

But I wasn't a frightened little kid any more. I was a grown woman with children and this time I wasn't going to take any abuse.

'Look, I'm trying to make a TV show,' he said again, holding his palms up.

'I don't give a f*** about your TV show,' I replied. 'I'll walk out of it now.' And I was so angry that I meant it.

Suddenly it was horribly clear. I felt like me and the others were just puppets or characters in a soap opera. We were presented as caricatures of ourselves and we were being used to make viewers laugh or gasp with shock. And that was a horrible feeling. I, for one, was sick of having my strings pulled. Nigel seemed to have forgotten that I was actually a real person with real feelings.

He carried on ranting about his show but I'd heard enough and stormed out of the kitchen. Myleene tried to calm me down but then I just started screaming and swearing at her too. I can see now that I was a bit of a loose cannon at that time and very confrontational. Looking back I must have been quite hard for the others to live with.

At that moment I was ready to quit the group. I had signed up to be in a pop band, not to be made a fool out of in front of millions of people. If this was the price of being in his show, I'd rather not pay it. I was away from my babies and now I was being treated like a character in a TV show!

I spent the next day thinking about what I should do. Then that evening Nigel turned up at the house again and came in to see me.

'I'm sorry about what I said yesterday, Kym,' he said. 'Let's just put it behind us, shall we?'

I didn't really know what to say. Of course there was no camera crew there when he came to apologise. No, when the series went out on television all the viewers at home saw was him calling me fat. It became a national talking point and probably helped Nigel win his TV nickname 'Nasty Nigel'.

People might think, *Well if you go on a reality show you should know what to expect* but none of us had a clue what we were getting ourselves into because this was the first-ever programme of its kind. Maybe now people go into those shows knowing they risk losing their privacy and being publicly humiliated, but back then we had no idea. We really did think it was all about the band!

Years later I was reading an interview with Nigel Lythgoe in the *Mirror*, and he was asked if he had any regrets.

He replied: 'Yes. The way I spoke to Kym Marsh about her weight.'

I think it was nice of him to say that so long after the event and I like to think that maybe later he realised that the band members weren't just puppets he could treat however he liked, we were real people.

What was amazing to me was the amount of letters of support I received after the row was screened. After all, I was a normal-sized girl. I wasn't stick thin, but why, everyone was asking, should I be?

I also got letters from girls with eating disorders writing about their own experiences of being told they were overweight or feeling that they were fat.

There are so many women who have issues about their weight that people really do need to think carefully about the kinds of messages they're giving out to viewers – especially young, impressionable ones.

It was January 2001 when all five of us in the house sat down together to watch the first episode of *Popstars* as it went out on ITV. The first half of the series was going to show the audition process and then the second half would be about us living in the house together.

None of us knew what the viewers would make of it because, like I said, there hadn't been anything else like it on television before.

'Do you think anyone else is watching this?' Myleene asked me.

'Who knows?' I laughed.

But when the viewing figures came in for the first week it was clear the show was a massive hit. Suddenly we were all thinking, *Whoa, hang on a minute, this is going to be really, really big.*

Within days it felt like the whole country was going *Popstars* crazy. There were stories about the contestants in all the newspapers and magazines and it was getting talked about on radio and telly shows all the time.

The first time I was recognised in the street was really weird. 'Oh, Kym, is it you from *Popstars*?' this woman asked me. 'Er, yes,' I mumbled.

'Good luck then,' she said. I don't think most people realised that the auditions had been finished months before and that I had made it through to the band. It was just as well though, because we were still sworn to secrecy about everything.

Life in the house was totally full on, and any spare time I had I wanted to spend with the children. That's why I ended up deciding to call things a day with Martin. Even though I'd really liked him, it was just incredibly difficult keeping the relationship together when we were so far apart. Before I'd started auditioning for *Popstars*, Martin's mum was diagnosed with cancer. I'd done everything I could then to support him and the family and I was very sad because she was a lovely lady. When she seemed to be getting better we were all incredibly relieved. But by this point I had already realised that our relationship wasn't working and I just didn't feel the same way about Martin anymore. It was getting more and more difficult to keep it going. But then very sadly we found out his Mum's cancer had returned. It was an awful situation because I didn't feel we could stay together because his mum was poorly even though I was really upset for them both. There was never going to be a good time to end it and eventually the break-up was inevitable.

I think Martin was really hurt by the relationship ending and a while later he told his story to a tabloid newspaper. The report made it sound like I'd dumped him after his mum was diagnosed with cancer again but that was never the case. I still feel very sorry if Martin was hurt because that was never, ever what I wanted. His mum was an amazing person and it was an incredibly sad situation.

So there I was, single again, missing my kids like crazy and working like a mad thing in London to make my dreams a reality.

One evening all five of us in the band were invited to a TV recording of *An Audience with Ricky Martin* and for the first time I walked up a red carpet. We'd had our hair and make-up done professionally and been given new outfits to wear, which was fantastic.

It was a bit weird though because the show hadn't finished yet and no one had a clue who we were. Someone from the record company asked Emma Bunton to have her picture taken with us. She was lovely about it but she must have been thinking: *Who the hell are this lot?*

Halfway through the show I went to the toilets and met Tina O'Brien, who played Sarah-Louise in *Coronation Street*. She was incredibly down to earth, just smoking a cigarette and chatting to me, but all I could think was: *That's her off Corrie!*

My life was changing so much, so quickly. It was hard to keep up.

*

As *Popstars* got more and more popular the papers were desperate to find out which five of us had made it through the audition process and into the band.

Sure enough, after a couple of weeks some of our names were leaked to the press, which was a real shame for the viewers because it ruined the surprise. And it was very odd for us too, suddenly seeing old school pictures of ourselves in the tabloids.

Even though our names were leaked, the producers were desperate that we shouldn't be photographed coming out of the house, because that would confirm the stories.

Later that same day all hell broke loose – the papers had found out where we were living and there were photographers outside the house in Mill Hill.

For a while, we stayed barricaded inside with the curtains drawn, wondering what the hell we were supposed to do. But we couldn't stay locked inside all day. In the end we each had to wear one of those weird face masks from the film *Scream* and run down the front steps to a car that was waiting outside.

We were driven to a meeting with the record company but when we arrived there we had to put our *Scream* masks back on again to get from the car to the offices. Then a reporter got hold of my phone number, so I had to immediately hand over my mobile to the production team. It was a couple of days before I got a replacement, which was horrible because it made it really hard to ring David and Emily.

That day was crazy because by midafternoon we were called in to LWT and told we wouldn't be allowed to return to the house in Mill Hill now we'd been found. Instead we were being sent to a place in Highgate. By the time we arrived there it was quite late and I was exhausted.

I was sharing a room with Myleene again but when I walked into the room I hated it. I had none of my photos of the children or their drawings around me and I hadn't spoken to them all day because I hadn't got a phone. All our belongings were still in the other house and we didn't even have any clothes for the next day.

On top of that I knew reporters had been sniffing around my mum and dad's house and I was worried for them.

All in all, I'd had a really bad day. I was pretty stressed out by it all and I was feeling like I'd just had enough. I had to wear glasses to shield my identity, like we were in a spy operation or something.

I'm sick of this, I thought, and I flipped a bit.

So when the scenes of us arriving at the house were shown on TV all you could see was me walking around the house still wearing my shades saying, 'Well, I'm not staying here!'

Suddenly, the diva was born! Watching those scenes now I cringe and I can see how volatile and difficult I was back then. But people watching that at home weren't given any idea of why I was in such a bad mood that evening. They must have just thought I was a spoilt little cow.

Unfortunately, I felt that I was portrayed like that from then on in the show. I am not the only person who's taken part in a reality show and felt that what the public see, after hundreds and hundreds of hours have been filmed and edited, is not the true you.

With me, I think *Popstars* created this persona of a stroppy diva because it made good television. In reality, I'm not like that at all, but I bet that's how a lot of people still think of me. Yes, I'm feisty and speak my mind, but can't we all be?

At the time, there was nothing we could do about it. We had no control over the way we were being portrayed on-screen. In fact, the first time we saw the edited footage was when we sat down to watch the show at the same time as the rest of the country.

We even missed quite a lot of the shows because we'd be out rehearsing. I hated seeing myself on television. I found it really, really cringey. Plus I'd find it really upsetting to think that David and Emily were hundreds of miles away watching me on TV instead of seeing me in the flesh.

The members of the band were revealed officially on the show halfway through the series. We were away recording at the time but when we got back there was an unveiling for the press and a massive party for all our friends and family at the house. It was a great night. And after that it became so much easier for all of us because there was no longer any need for all the cloak-and-dagger stuff.

We were even allowed out of the house! Amazing!

Around that time we started recording our first album from which one of the tracks would be selected to be the debut single. The single was chosen by the time we were unveiled. Most of the album was recorded at a studio in Trondheim in Norway, so we flew first to Oslo and then had to get in a tiny little plane for the second leg of the journey. I have a fear of flying and I was so scared that Myleene had to sit with her arm around me for the entire trip.

Recording the album was fabulous. I'd never experienced anything like it before. We all had to sing different parts of the song and then the producers decided later whose voice would be used on which lines.

'Pure and Simple', which was selected from all the tracks on the album, was actually recorded in London. It had been written by Tim Hawes, Pete Kirtley and Alison Clarkson. We put all our energies into getting that song right. Because it was all very well being recognised from a TV show, but what really mattered was whether our music was successful.

I guess the five us of were quite different people too. And although at first things were pretty much fine between us, gradually our differences did become clearer. Looking back I can see maybe I wasn't an easy person to live with then. If something was winding me up, I made it quite clear to everyone. And if I was stressed or feeling down about being away from David and Emily I'd let that show too. And because I had the children I wanted to spend all my spare time with them. So maybe the others did think I wasn't joining in with them as much as I could, but my situation was just so different to theirs.

In March 2001 'Pure and Simple' was released. The *Popstars* series was set to climax with a live show in which we would discover where the single had reached in the charts.

All our families were there for the final, and it was incredibly exciting. Emily, who was still only three, and David, who was nearly six, were even interviewed on the stairs by Davina McCall.

'So Emily, who do you think is going to be number one?' Davina asked.

'Erm, erm, erm,' she replied. Then finally: 'The *Popstars*!'

Then Emily sang a few lines of the song. She was so sweet. A few minutes later it was time for the official countdown. The five of us in the band stood around the radio with the telly cameras trained on our faces.

Westlife had been number one the week before with their version of 'Uptown Girl'. Westlife were massive and no one was sure whether we would be able to knock them off the top spot.

It was going to be between them and us, and so hearing who'd got number two was crucial. None of us had been allowed to read newspapers or watch television all week so we knew nothing about the midweek sales figures or who the media thought would be number one.

Finally the DJ said, 'And at number two it is . . .' It was so quiet you could have heard a pin drop. And then I heard the first notes of 'Uptown Girl'.

We all started screaming. It was fantastic. Our families were all hugging each other and going mad too. The noise was insane.

I just couldn't believe it. *Number One*. Eight months earlier I'd have been at home listening to the charts on the radio in my tiny kitchen. Now we were at the top of the charts! People talk about dreams coming true, but this was really it! It just didn't seem real.

The five of us were sped off across London on motorbikes to do a live web chat. It was so cool. And on the way back the TV producers sent us a white stretch limo. But it all felt a bit too glitzy for us; we'd rather have been on the bikes again.

We got the limousine chauffeur to stop off at a McDonald's drive-thru and treated ourselves to Big Macs all round. It was hilarious – goodness knows what all the other people eating their Chicken McNuggets must have thought!

That evening we had another massive party at our house. David and Emily were there and it was a fabulous night – one I'll never forget. 'Pure and Simple' was a massive hit – it sold 500,000 copies in the first week, putting us in the *Guinness Book of Records* as the fastest-selling debut single of all time.

Being number one was a dream come true for all of us. For me, it meant my life and my children's lives would be changed for ever.

13

THE WAY TO YOUR LOVE

·········

Hear'Say was big, big news. We were number one and it felt like everyone was talking about us.

As the first reality-TV pop band, we were a new phenomenon and everyone had an opinion about us. That said, if you read the papers, a lot of the opinions were pretty nasty.

But half a million people had gone out and bought our single in the first week alone – so we can't have been that bad!

About a week after hitting the number one spot we made a show called *Meet the Popstars*, which was like *This is Your Life* for all of us. Our families all came on-set and so did loads of people who'd known us when we were growing up. Kevin Kinsella and Carol from the Starlight Roadshow all sent messages and it was really emotional.

I was disappointed though, because I'd been told Emily and David couldn't be there and what with all the craziness I hadn't seen them for a few days. Then, when I was sitting on a sofa on the stage with Davina McCall she suddenly introduced them and two little people came running over to me – it was them! They gave me big cuddles and I couldn't stop grinning and crying. It was the best surprise I could have had.

Everywhere we went it was Hear'Say fever. We were invited on to *This Morning* and we did *Top of the Pops*, which was brilliant. Not only that, but we were on all the kids' TV shows and did dozens of photo shoots for magazine covers. Me, Myleene and Suzanne even made it onto the cover of *GQ*. How glam is that?

We were suddenly living a real popstar lifestyle. We were given Vespa scooters to ride around on – which we never learned to ride – and loaned swish cars for the year.

More importantly, we had some amazing performances lined up for us. Later that year we played Party in the Park and even the Royal Variety Performance where we met the Queen. Elton John, who'd recently just called us 'the ugliest band in pop' (ouch!), was playing the Royal Variety Performance too that year. He obviously felt a bit guilty when he saw we were on the bill, so he sent us a message asking if we'd like to go up to his dressing room.

'He can come down here if he wants to see us,' Myleene said. She was great like that. And he did! He came down to our dressing room and apologised for being immature and unkind. That was definitely one of the most surreal moments of all time!

In May we released our second single and then there was another whirlwind of interviews, photo shoots, TV shows and promotional work. It was an absolutely manic time.

I should have been loving every minute of it. But behind the scenes I was struggling. For legal reasons I can't go into the details of what happened but at the time I had to be in London for the band and my children had to stay in Wigan with my Mum and Dad. As I said I'm not allowed to explain why that had to be the case, but I can say that it was a very difficult time and I was very anxious about possibly being separated from my kids.

I travelled up North as often as I could to see the kids, but it was getting more and more difficult because of the band's massive workload. There was also a tour lined up for the summer and I was terrified I might not see them for weeks on end. Mum and Dad were brilliant at driving them down South to see me but I still missed them terribly.

I was also feeling quite lonely in London. We were all still living together in the big house in Mill Hill, but I felt tensions were building between us. Increasingly I had a sense that I was the odd one out in the group. It was a horrible feeling.

Apart from the other band members, I knew virtually no one in London. I'd been used to having family and friends around the corner but now I felt totally isolated. It was bizarre: in my career I had everything I'd ever dreamt of, but in my personal life I was really unhappy.

I think that the rest of the band picked up on my mood, and maybe that added to the strained atmosphere between us. We were all under a huge amount of pressure. After 'Pure and Simple' went to number one, our album went straight to the top of the charts too. We had masses of exposure. We were on everything, in everything, and I couldn't help but think people might soon be sick of the sight of us. And that wasn't just me being paranoid. At the same time as our success was growing, I got the definite impression that some people just wanted us to fall flat on our arses. That only added to the pressure.

So, all in all, by the time our second single, 'The Way to Your Love', was released, I was feeling lonely, stressed and, actually, pretty sad.

We were booked to perform the new single on *Top of the Pops*, and all five of us turned up at Elstree Studios one evening in May to record our slot. Before going onstage, we all went for a drink in the studio bar. We'd met up with Mark Lamarr, the host of *Never Mind the Buzzcocks*, which a couple of us had appeared on a few weeks before. He was a really nice guy and we had quite a laugh together.

We'd been there for about twenty minutes when I noticed a familiar blond guy on the other side of the room.

'Look, there's Jamie Mitchell off *EastEnders*,' I whispered to Myleene. We might have had a number one single and album but I was still pretty star-struck!

He was with Natalie Cassidy, who played his on-screen girl-friend Sonia, and a few of the others from the cast.

'He's quite cute,' I said. 'Except he looks about twelve!'

I didn't think any more about him after that – I was too nervous thinking about our *Top of the Pops* performance!

But when we got up to leave I had to walk past Jamie Mitchell, as I thought of him, because he was stood leaning against the cigarette machine.

'Hi, I'm Jack,' he said as I walked past him. 'Nice to meet you.'

'Oh, hi,' I said. 'I'm Kym. Nice to meet you too.'

I stopped for a minute and we had a quick chat.

'You're the one with the kids aren't you?' he said, smiling.

'Yes,' I laughed. That was what everyone said to me every-where I went – that moment when Nigel had confronted me about having children had obviously stuck in people's minds.

I explained I was there to film *Top of the Pops*.

'So, er, are you going to be in the bar afterwards?' he asked.

'Yeah, I probably will be,' I replied. I could tell he was flirting with me and, to be honest, I kinda liked him too. He was being really sweet to me and he had a very open, honest face. Close up he looked older than he did on television.

'I'll see you later then,' he said.

He leant forward to give me a kiss so I quickly pecked him on the cheek and darted out of the bar.

As I walked away I couldn't help but grin. I could sense there was something between us but I thought maybe I was imag-ining it. Surely he wouldn't be interested in me, would he? At the time his face was plastered all over the teen magazines.

In the end I didn't go back to the bar after we finished filming. I was knackered, so I just got a cab home and had an early night while the others went back for another drink. The more I thought about it, the more I convinced myself there was no way 'soap heart-throb Jack Ryder' was seriously going to be interested in someone like me. I figured that I must have imagined the whole thing.

But the next morning, Myleene and the others were desperate to tell me what had happened in the bar after I'd gone home.

'You'll never guess who was asking about you last night,' she said.

'Who?'

'Jack Ryder.'

I laughed. 'No. Shut up!'

'Seriously, he was,' Myleene said. 'I think he likes you.'

It was really flattering, but I didn't for one moment think anything more would come of it.

A week or so later, all five of us went out for dinner. I was planning to go straight back to the house afterwards but Suzanne was desperate to go to a nightclub called Red Cube.

'Oh, come on, Kym, come with me,' she kept saying.

'But we've got to be up really early in the morning,' I said. 'I just don't want to.'

'Pleeeeeeasssse,' begged Suzanne. 'You'll enjoy it when we get there.'

In the end I caved in. 'OK,' I sighed. 'I'll come with you.'

We went into town and were immediately ushered into the VIP area of the club. Being swept to the front of the line always made me feel really embarrassed. After years of queuing in the rain outside bars and clubs back home, I just couldn't get used to it.

Me and Suzanne were just standing having a drink when I turned around and there was Jack Ryder, right in front of me.

'Oh, hi, how are you?' I stammered.

Straight out, he asked me, 'Why didn't you go to the bar the other night?'

'Er, I was a bit tired.'

Jack seemed to have forgiven me for flaking out though because soon we were chatting and having a laugh together.

He was charming and funny and we got on really well

together. There was a fair bit of flirting going on too. Jack explained that nightclubs weren't really 'his thing' but he'd been dragged along by a couple of mates.

The first time I'd met Jack all I could see was Jamie from *EastEnders*, but after spending a short time with him it was easy to see he was actually very different to his character. He was nineteen, but was actually very mature for his age with a sharp sense of humour. I was twenty-four, but it certainly didn't feel like there was much of an age gap between us.

Jack was so easy to talk to that the hours just flew by. It gave me a bit of shock when I finally checked the time on my phone and saw how late it was. I knew I had to get back to the house – we had an early start in the morning.

'Right, I'm off now,' I said, picking up my handbag.

'Well, give me your phone number then,' Jack said cheekily.

We exchanged numbers and I kissed him goodbye – just a peck on the cheek, mind!

'We'll stay in touch,' he said.

But I didn't realise how quickly! I'd only just got in the cab on the way home when he started texting me.

'I really like you and would love to see you again soon,' he texted.

'I really like you too,' I wrote back. And I did. He seemed so genuine and normal and I was crying out for friends like that in London. And yeah, I fancied him too.

But the whole thing was a bit surreal. Only a few months earlier I'd been a single mum who spent her evenings in front of a pile of ironing. Now I was being texted by the hottest soapstar in the country.

We texted backwards and forwards all night – just about

silly stuff really. A few days later he sent me another message saying he was going on holiday the following week and would be in touch when he got back.

'Yeah, fine,' I wrote back. 'We're actually away too, shooting a video.'

'Where?' he texted.

'Marbella.'

'No way,' he replied. 'Me too.'

It turned out that we were both going to be in the same resort at the same time. It felt like fate was throwing us together.

We texted each other all the time we were in Marbella and then one evening we arranged to meet. The others in the band were going for a drink for Danny's birthday, which in hindsight I really should have gone to, but I wanted to see Jack. I told them I was nipping round to see Jack. He was staying nearby with his brother and a mate.

I turned up at their apartment with a couple of beers in a carrier bag.

'No, thanks,' said Jack. 'I don't drink.'

'Oh, I do,' I giggled. 'I hope you don't mind if I have one then.'

I hadn't noticed before that Jack didn't drink. He explained that he'd got drunk once and it had made him do stupid things and feel really sick so he'd simply decided never to do it again.

That evening we sat up chatting for hours. It felt like we could talk about anything. By the time I said I ought to be getting back to my hotel it was really late.

'Why don't you stay over?' Jack said. So I did. But it was all very innocent. We lay next to each other on the bed for ages not even touching. I think we were both too scared to make the first move. Finally we kissed and then we cuddled all night long.

That was when I realised that I really liked Jack. He wasn't just another guy trying to get me into bed; he was a really sweet, genuine, funny person.

When we both got home from Marbella we met up again and from then on we were a couple.

There was five and a half years between us but the age gap didn't bother me in the slightest. I actually didn't really notice it much. It was only other people who commented on it. For some reason it seems to be totally acceptable for a man to go out with someone younger, but not for a woman.

From the very beginning, Jack and I spent virtually every moment of our spare time together.

While all this was happening, I moved out of the *Popstars* house and into my own flat just off Camden High Street while the kids shared their time between me, Dave and my parents. I didn't know anyone nearby and I hated being there on my own, so most of the time Jack stayed over or I'd go round to the flat he shared with his brother in Shooter's Hill, South London.

We were mad about each other and that was a great feeling. If I ever said, 'I'm off home now,' he'd beg me to stay at his. We were together constantly.

He was very much pursuing me and that made me feel confident. I was happy and felt really good about myself for the first time in ages. I'd struggled with my self-confidence so much, but being with Jack gave me a massive boost – especially since he was always dead keen to be with me.

The only times it would be a bit tense between us was if

his friends came round. That was the only time I was conscious of the age gap because when they were together Jack and his mates could be a bit immature. Their humour was very much about taking the piss out of people and I did find it slightly childish.

But when it was just the two of us it was absolutely fantastic. The relationship was incredibly intense right from the beginning. We were so close.

Jack was very open with his emotions. It took my breath away the first time he told me that he loved me. I told him that I loved him too, because I did.

The only time I'd ever felt that strongly about someone was with Dave, the father of my children.

Within a few months I knew this relationship was serious, so I really wanted Jack to meet David and Emily – I didn't want to introduce the children to him any sooner than that. It meant the world to me that the kids and my family got to know him too. One weekend my friend Michaela had a barbecue and all my family were going. It seemed the perfect opportunity to take Jack up North and introduce him to everyone.

It must have been so strange for my family – suddenly there was someone from *EastEnders* with them in the garden! My family weren't used to being around actors or celebrities, but they soon realised that Jack was pretty down to earth and everyone ended up getting on like a house on fire.

Best of all, the kids immediately took a shine to Jack. When I introduced him to Emily, I said to her: 'Do you know who this is?'

She looked at him for a long time and then said, 'It's that man off *Emmerdale*!'

'Almost!' Jack said. Emily was so adorable at that age. Just thinking about it makes me smile.

We were on the way back from Wigan to London on the train when we realised there were reporters on the train watching us. When we pulled in to Euston, Jack and I got off at opposite ends of the train so the photographers couldn't get a snap of us together. We didn't want to parade our relationship to the world because it was still early days. But the papers had got wind that something was going on between us and for a while it felt like we were being followed everywhere we went.

I found it quite daunting because I'd never known anything like that before and as far as I was concerned it was just me going out with a new fella. In every interview I did I was asked about our relationship. I found it so weird – I honestly couldn't understand why anyone would be interested in that.

We'd only been together a short time when Jack asked me to move in with him. And we'd only been going out a couple of months when I actually did in the August of that year. By then I knew I'd fallen for him – hard. One day I suddenly thought to myself, 'This is it. This really is it.'

Jack sometimes came with me if I went home to visit the kids and they loved it when they came to stay with us. Jack was great with them and he'd come to the park with us or play with them and their toys. I'd been dead nervous to start with about how they would all get on, but it worked out brilliantly.

Everything would have been perfect if David and Emily had been with me, but for legal reasons I unfortunately can't go into they had to stay at my parents' house.

We saw each other almost every weekend but the time we were apart was still very upsetting for all of us. One weekend Mum and Dad brought the kids down to London but when it was time for them to go home again David went and hid under my bed and refused to come out. I tried talking to him, coaxing him, even pleading with him to come out, because it was getting late and my poor dad still had to drive all the way back to Wigan. But David just wouldn't budge.

I just wanted to cry.

Emily was still only three and she would cry, 'Mummy, Mummy!' as they all drove away. Her voice would just tear into me. It was heartbreaking every single time it happened.

Nothing is worse than seeing your children in that kind of pain. What made it even harder to take was the fact that I felt completely to blame for what they were going through. I was working so hard to build a better future for the three of us, but if I hadn't been on *Popstars* in the first place we'd never have been apart. But I had gone onto the show in the first place to try and build a better life for my kids. It killed me that they were not able to come with me. At this time it was a no-win situation.

Having Jack around was the only thing that kept me sane at that time – particularly as my band's workload was getting totally mad. Hear'Say were riding high – and we were running around like headless chickens, trying to keep it that way.

Looking back, even in the early days there were a few things about my relationship with Jack that signalled that we were very different people. In all the time we were together the only thing I ever saw him drink was one Smirnoff Ice, while

I had always enjoyed getting together with friends and having a couple of drinks and maybe going out dancing.

As we spent more time together it became clear that not only did Jack not like drinking, but he gave the impression that he didn't like other people drinking either. I'd never been a massive boozer but I did enjoy a few glasses of wine or Bacardi and Coke. After we got together, though, I felt I should just cut all that out. There wasn't much opportunity to drink anyway because we pretty much just stayed in together. After that first night, we virtually never went out as a couple.

It wasn't long before I figured out that he hated things like premieres and awards ceremonies. He seemed to hate nightclubs too, and being around people who were drinking and getting drunk. I guess when you're sober but are surrounded by drunken people, it can be annoying, so I can see where he was coming from. Occasionally just the two of us would go out for dinner, but that was rare. Jack was also very sensitive if people were staring at us and asking for autographs. I think deep down he was just quite shy. Problem was, we were both very well known at that point and it really couldn't be avoided. I'd be dead chuffed that people liked the music we made, but he just seemed a bit uncomfortable with it all.

So instead of parties and premieres and romantic dinners, Jack and I stayed in most evenings and watched films. Jack was really, really into movies. To be honest, staying in was fine by me at that point because I just wanted to be with Jack. Also, my days were so busy recording and working with the band that I kind of liked staying in and watching telly.

There were times when I'd think, *Here I am, in London*

in my mid-twenties, and I could go to any club that I want but I'm sitting here watching Star Wars *again.* But Jack never seemed keen on going out, so I never pushed it. Instead we'd just cook our tea then cuddle up on the sofa to watch telly.

At that time I thought it was brilliant that Jack was so different to guys I'd met before. Most blokes are only interested in beer, sex and football (not always in that order!) but Jack wasn't like that at all. He was a proper actor who'd been working in the business since he was sixteen. He seemed very sorted and I guess I figured I should try to be more like him myself. So that's what I did.

After I moved into Jack's flat we had a few conversations about our future. Although he didn't ask me to marry him at this point, there was no doubt in either of our minds that we were in it for the long haul.

Jack was so open about his feelings and that was like a breath of fresh air for me. I never had to worry about whether he liked me or not, which meant a lot to me.

Although things with Jack were going great, I was still living apart from my children and it was agony.

The legal situation that was keeping us apart looked like it was going to be resolved, one way or the other, soon and the prospect of having my kids living with me again was the only thing that kept me going. I was very anxious about the outcome, but determined to remain positive so I set about looking for a suitable family home for all of us. I couldn't expect the kids to live in the centre of London; it would have been too much of a culture shock for them.

I also needed somewhere that had easy access to the motorway so I could easily get them to Wigan at weekends. That was when I settled on the idea of St Albans. It was a nice town with good schools, it was handy for the M1 and I could be in the centre of London in forty minutes.

I found a lovely four-bedroom detached house – the kind of place I could only have dreamt about living in a year earlier. I set about buying the house. Jack was very supportive during the awful time when I was apart from my kids and he'd try to keep my spirits up.

In December 2001, just seven months after we'd met, and only a year since I landed my place in Hear'Say, Jack proposed.

I was on my way home from work and had called him to say I'd be in soon. But he was really offhand with me on the phone, as if I'd done something to upset him.

When I got back to the flat he wasn't there but there was a note on the table saying: 'Turn on the video recorder'. It was all a bit weird but I did as instructed.

After a few seconds Jack's face flashed up on our TV screen.

He was speaking straight to me, saying: 'There's a torch in the bedroom. I want you to go and get it, then go outside, turn left and keep walking.'

That was all he said. This was starting to feel really weird. But again I followed his order, got the torch and went outside.

I remember it was freezing cold, but luckily I was still wearing my coat. I was thinking, *What the hell is all this about, then?*

I didn't have to wait long to find out.

When I got to the end of the path I saw the light of Jack's cigarette. He was standing in the darkness. As I walked up to him, he didn't say a word at first but then he went down on one knee and said, 'Kym, will you marry me?'

At first I couldn't quite believe what was happening. It was all a bit too surreal. Yes, we'd talked about spending the rest of our lives together, but now he was actually proposing I was stunned.

For a second we were both just standing there, looking at each other.

'Yes,' I said. There was nothing else to say.

We hugged and both started crying. It was totally incredible.

Here was this guy who I figured could have any girl he wanted, but he wanted to marry me, a single mum who had been called fat on national TV. Take that, Nigel!

It was hugely flattering. But that wasn't the reason I said yes. I loved him. In fact, I loved him very much. Jack gave me a real sense of security and the feeling that I had one ally in this strange new world. He made London feel like home. Maybe there were some things about us that were pretty different but I was determined to change, to be more like him. That way, I reckoned, everything would be fine.

We went back upstairs to the flat and rang our families and friends. We were both totally made up.

That Christmas was totally amazing. I had a gorgeous new fiancé and for the first time in my life I had enough money to really treat the kids to everything they wanted. No hand-me-downs this time around! I don't generally believe in spoiling children, but that year I thought they deserved it.

It was the biggest Christmas any of us could have imagined. When David and Emily came downstairs on Christmas morning and saw the piles of presents they both just said: 'Wow!' They didn't know where to start!

It made my day to see them that happy. I'd got a huge tree for the corner of the room and underneath it was a pink Barbie car for Emily. David had everything he'd written on his neat little list for Father Christmas. After years of barely scraping by neither of them could believe it.

After we'd opened our presents, I took everyone out for Christmas dinner at a fancy restaurant. There was no way Mum was doing the washing-up that year!

But for me the best present came a little later, when at last David and Emily came back to live with me in March 2002. I'm really sorry I can't go into what kept us apart for legal reasons, but the day they came through the door of our lovely new home to live with me at last was one of the happiest days of my life. I was over the moon to have them back with me and couldn't stop grinning.

Finally my home life was everything I had ever wanted. Which was just as well, because professionally things were about to get a whole lot more complicated.

14
HEAR'SAY FALLS APART

·········

Meeting Jack had given me something to smile about in my personal life for the first time in ages. But that late summer and autumn of 2001, while we were busy falling in love, was a miserable time for me in the band.

Like I said, for a while I'd had a vague sense that I was an outsider. As time went on that feeling hardened into an absolute certainty.

I'm sure the others probably felt I was choosing to keep myself apart from them at that time. To start with, when the others went out clubbing I was often back up North to see the kids. And then when I started going out with Jack, all my spare time was spent with him and he hated going out.

And when some of the others went on holiday together, I didn't join them. To be honest, I wanted to go on holiday with my children. I hadn't seen Emily and David properly for months and so when I had a week off I took them to Disneyland Paris and we had the time of our lives.

So I guess I was slightly apart from the others. Some of that was my choice, but a lot of it was just down to being in a totally different situation – what with the kids and Jack and everything. It wasn't that I didn't want to be part of the group, because I really did. It was the only reason that I had been living at the opposite end of the country to my children. I knew the band was the best way to build a better future for the kids and I loved performing.

But more and more I got the feeling that the others didn't think I was a team player. At first it wasn't a big issue between us, but I could sense little niggles.

Then I began to get the feeling that the others were talking about me behind my back. It seemed like everything I did was being scrutinised. There would be raised eyebrows when I said something or meaningful glances exchanged when I walked in the room. It all made me feel pretty isolated and lonely.

No one ever told me what their problem was with me, so I could only guess. I suspected there was some unhappiness in the way the vocals had been shared out on the album but there was nothing I could have done about that – they were decisions made by the producers. And I think maybe there was some unhappiness about the attention I was getting in the papers because of Jack and my family situation. I think they thought I enjoyed it, but I really didn't want that attention at all.

There were obviously bad feelings though, and by this point we were bickering over lots of silly things.

I'm very aware I can be hot-headed and often I'll speak first and think later. And I'm sure I was incredibly irritating at times so I have no doubt that I was equally to blame for the tensions that were mounting between us. I just feel sad that no one was able to sit us down together and work through those issues before they exploded.

Because when they did explode – backstage at Jerry Springer's chat show – it was horrific. Things had started to go wrong before we even got to the television studios that evening where we were due to perform a song and have a quick chat with Jerry. We'd gone for an early evening meal at a pub next door to the studios. There was the five of us there and our tour manager, Jamal. I finished eating my dinner and was just waiting for the rest of them to finish theirs when a lady came over holding a baby.

'Hi, there,' she said, really politely. 'I just wondered if you would all mind having your picture taken with my baby – she was born on the day you went to number one.'

'Of course,' one of the others said. 'But we're just eating at the moment. Would you mind coming back when we've finished?'

'Oh, sorry, I can't,' the lady said. 'I've got to dash off now and I can't wait.'

She looked really disappointed and as I'd finished eating, I went, 'Don't worry, I'll have my picture taken if you've got to go.'

The woman seemed really pleased, so me and the baby had a quick snap taken of us together and I sat down again. There was a horrible silence at the table and I could immediately tell something was wrong. No one was speaking to me.

At the time I was pretty confused because I thought I was just being nice. But thinking about it, I bet the others were furious because they reckoned that I was pushing myself forward again.

Without saying a word to me they finished their meals, got up and walked out the pub.

I looked at Jamal, who just shook his head.

'I'm sick of this,' I said, fighting to keep my voice steady. 'I'm sick of every little thing that I do being made into a massive deal.'

It just seemed so unfair. It wasn't like I'd gone off and done a cover shoot on my own for *Vanity Fair*. I'd had a snap taken in a pub with a baby!

But by then I think the others were becoming hypersensitive about everything I did. Thing was, I could only speculate as to why I was annoying them so much because no one had actually told me what the problem was.

As I walked round to join them at the television studios I could feel myself getting really angry. I'd had about enough of being treated like this. I stormed into the dressing room of the show and the most almighty slanging match broke out.

Finally all the stuff that had been brewing for months was blasted out into the open.

'The problem with you,' Noel said, 'is that you're selfish in the studio.'

I was fuming.

'Selfish?' I said. 'Selfish?' *Sitting here with you lot making my life a misery when I could be at home with my kids?* 'I'm not selfish. I'm here because I want this band to work.'

To me it was obvious from what some were saying that they'd been talking about me like this for months.

Suzanne interjected occasionally and Danny sat very quietly as the rest of us carried on shouting at each other.

After a while Myleene stormed out of the dressing room, but I followed her out into the corridor. I was ranting and raging by then and I'm well aware that I was responsible for refusing to let the situation drop.

We had a massive shouting match outside but someone eventually split us up because we were due out onstage at any minute.

It all boiled down to this idea that I was somehow 'pushing myself forward' – it drove me crazy. I felt like I couldn't do anything right. I don't think Danny ever felt like that, but I got the impression the rest of them did.

Maybe I did get attention in the newspapers, but that wasn't deliberate. In fact, I'd have been more than happy if most of the stories about me had never been written. But when we went along to do interviews, journalists often wanted to know about the kids and what it had been like bringing them up as a single mum, as well as my new relationship. I did speak a lot about Jack and the kids because I was so happy at that time and maybe I went on a bit too much about them rather than the band or the music. But I was very new to the situation and still wet behind the ears. And because Myleene and I were quite outspoken, perhaps we did get more attention than the rest of the group but it was frequently negative. The papers often speculated about the relationship between Myleene and I and would cover pages with stories about rows that sometimes had never happened.

We might have rowed more than the others, but we were both very passionate people who cared deeply about what we were doing and each other, and perhaps we were more similar than either of us realised.

That said, I never intentionally went out to hog the limelight.

As for being selfish? My priorities were certainly different. There were things that I didn't want to do and places I didn't want to go because I'd rather be with David and Emily. On the days I wasn't with the kids I could get very down, so maybe they thought I was just being moody. But the move to London and the total change in lifestyle had been much more extreme for me than for any of the others and I don't think they ever really got that. But I guess I shouldn't blame them for that. Until you have kids of your own, it is virtually impossible to understand how much they influence every single decision you make.

But if I was selfish, it was for David and Emily's sake. I've definitely got my faults – I can be fiery and very outspoken – but I honestly don't think I'm selfish. I never once asked for special treatment or for extra lines to sing or for more money because I was doing more solos. My conscience was clear on that front.

But whatever I said, they seemed to have convinced themselves I was trying to push myself forward by singing lead vocals on the singles, by going out with someone from *EastEnders* and by getting my name in the papers.

Going out onstage on *Jerry Springer* after the row was just awful. We had to perform the single and at one point me and Myleene had to put our arms around each other. It felt so fake. I hated every minute of it.

To make matters worse, our row had been overheard by staff at the TV studios and the next day the story of our slanging match was all over the newspapers. That was all we needed! Again, it was all about me and Myleene.

Fortunately after a few days we were able to put the row behind us and move on. But although we were able to get on with each other on the surface, a lot of the niggles remained. Looking back I wish I had thought more about the feelings of the others in the group. And I wish I'd been able to explain honestly how I was feeling too. But we didn't do that and unfortunately the problems between us just festered.

In the midsummer of 2001, Hear'Say went off on tour. By then we'd had two number one singles and a number one album. But I could already feel the tide was turning against us.

Things weren't helped by the fact that we took a mobile recording studio with us on tour. That meant we were doing gigs in the evenings then trying to make a new album during the day. Our critics thought we were being greedy by rushing out a second album just months after our first. It also seemed a bit desperate, as if they knew they had to make as much money out of us as they could before the Hear'Say bubble burst.

That tour was a tough time for me. We were literally working night and day. I've never had a problem with hard work but I missed the kids and Jack terribly.

I loved performing live and seeing all the fans was incredible but looking back I feel sad that we were starting to fall apart as a group.

*

After the tour, the tensions in the group started becoming more obvious. Communication between us was completely breaking down and there didn't seem to be anyone around to help us rebuild it.

Our third single, 'Everybody', was released in November 2001 and went to number four in the charts. Of course that was still a really good chart position, but after two consecutive number ones our critics took it to mean that our star was falling.

Everything seemed to be turning sour. One day I was called in for a meeting with our manager, Chris Herbert. He told me I was being moody and bolshie. Of course, that just made me even more pissed off. I was a twenty-five-year-old woman with two children and I was being treated like a naughty schoolgirl. To be honest I could be moody and bolshie and bad-tempered. But I wasn't the only one like that. We could all be pretty grumpy at times.

By the end of the year my life in the band was really difficult. We weren't getting on at all.

Then, at the beginning of 2002, we were invited to play to British troops stationed in Oman. There was a big meeting to discuss it with our management from the record company.

Geography was never my strong point and I had to ask exactly where Oman was! I knew it was in the Middle East, but like most people I'd have struggled to put my finger on it on a map.

'Oh, that's a bit scary!' I said, as we talked about where it was in relation to the wars going on in Iraq and Afghanistan.

Then we talked for a while about what we'd have to do

on the trip, security issues and how long we would be away for.

At that point I knew I really didn't want to go. Obviously I wanted to support our troops, and again for legal reasons I can't go into details about what was going on at that point, but I can say that I needed to be in the country for my children. The whole reason I'd gone into the band in the first place was to give the kids a better life. They will always come first.

I mulled it over for a bit, then told Chris Herbert that I really didn't want to go. He and the others all accepted it and everyone seemed fine about it.

Or so I thought.

Shortly afterwards, at the beginning of February, I got a call from a PR guy that we knew saying the *Sun* was planning to run a story which said I'd refused to entertain the troops in Oman because I was scared I'd get blown up.

I felt sick. From what the PR guy was saying it seemed that story could only have come from someone who was in the room that day – someone in the band or our management team. And although I'd said I was scared about the idea of travelling to Oman – who wouldn't be nervous about going to a war zone! – it certainly wasn't the reason I didn't want to go and I definitely never *said* I was scared of being blown up. Maybe I did have some questions about what security would be like over there. But frankly there were much bigger things going on for me behind closed doors that meant I just couldn't leave the country at that time.

I was so hurt that someone I trusted had given a story like that to the papers with the obvious intention of making me look selfish and callous.

'Where did they get that story from?' I asked.

The PR paused for a while. And then he named one of the other band members.

I was gutted. Despite all the frictions that we'd had between us, I'd loved every member of the band so much and I'd never thought any of them would do something like that. I felt utterly betrayed. Apparently they had written evidence too.

'So, have you got any comment then?' the PR asked.

I didn't even pause. 'I quit,' I said. 'That's my comment.'

I put the phone down and burst into tears. Jack was with me and he put his arms round me and hugged me but nothing really helped. I was so angry, so hurt and felt so totally betrayed. But my decision was made – I was out of the band.

And so that was how I left. Looking back, I'm really sad about the way it all ended. The worst thing about it is that I eventually discovered that it wasn't even the person he said it was who really leaked the story. I don't really want to name names now about who I thought it was at the time and who it actually turned out to be. It's in the past now and I don't feel there is anything to be gained from picking over old wounds.

But I'm sorry that I quit through a newspaper rather than sitting down with the rest of the band face to face and telling them I'd had enough. I very much regret the way I left the group because all I ever wanted was for us to talk about things straight. Maybe if I'd confronted them, the confusion about who had leaked the story to the newspaper could have been sorted out and we could have tried to deal with our differences. But by that point I just felt totally isolated. To be honest, I think I would have left anyway but not under those circumstances. I was desperately missing my kids and just wanted to be with them. Being in the band wasn't the dream come true I thought it was going to be.

I do wish though that we'd managed to have a conversation to clear the air before I quit. Maybe then it wouldn't have been so bitter between us all afterwards.

After dropping my bombshell to the PR guy, I rang Chris Herbert and told him that I was going and the reasons why. I was still very angry and upset – not in a good place at all.

Chris tried to talk me round but I wasn't budging.

'You don't think you might change your mind?' he asked.

'Nope.' I felt so betrayed; I didn't even have to think about it.

I felt our management was partly to blame, too. When all the bitching had started someone should have taken us aside before it had a chance to escalate. Then again, maybe we should all have done more to stop the situation getting out of hand.

Months of feeling isolated and excluded had taken their toll on my self-confidence. I thought if I carried on in that situation it would destroy me. But I had to accept a lot of the problems in the band had been of my making too.

There had been plenty of times where I hadn't considered the feelings of the others and maybe, because I had a life outside of the group, I wasn't as involved in some things as they would have like me to be. But I'd loved Hear'Say and all the people in it and I was truly sad when my time with it was over.

It hadn't been an easy journey for me, being the fat girl from Hear'Say who'd snatched the kid from *EastEnders*. But

Popstars and Hear'Say had changed my life. And for that I'll be forever grateful.

The worst thing was that I knew I had to break the news to my parents. As ever, they were incredibly supportive. They knew how unhappy I'd been, and although they were worried that I was walking out on what was, at this point, one of the biggest bands in the country, they were pleased I would be away from the situation that had been getting me down.

The next few weeks felt very strange to me. I was relieved to be away from all the hassle, but I felt quite lonely too. I'd spent night and day with the other four for more than a year and, despite what had gone on at the end, I had loved every single one of them. Also, after months and months of working non-stop, I had nothing to do. Added to that, I had taken on a big mortgage on our new house in St Albans, just as I'd become unemployed. Thankfully Jack was still working, which meant we would be OK financially for a little while, but it wasn't that long since I had been totally skint and I never wanted to be in that situation again.

But once I got the news I'd been waiting for and I knew the kids were finally coming down South to live with me, I was just delighted that I'd be around all the time to help them settle into their new home and school.

When Emily and David arrived at the beginning of April 2002 it was just amazing. I'd decorated David's bedroom in Manchester United colours and created a little princess room for Emily. The house felt like a proper family home. Not a flying ant in sight!

I'd worried about how the kids would cope having to

leave their old friends behind, but in the end they were absolutely great. They adapted really quickly and saw their Dad regularly.

Mum and Dad also offered to move down at the same time as David and Emily so they could look after the kids if I was working. That was a massive help for me, because although I was no longer in the band, I soon found work doing photo shoots or promotional jobs and personal appearances. After having spent all that time living apart and having worked so hard to get into Hear'Say I didn't just want to give everything up – and we needed the money too!

It was a big step for Mum and Dad moving down South, where they didn't know anyone apart from me and Jack, but as ever they were 100 per cent behind me. I have the most amazing parents in the world and I'll always be grateful for their unfailing support through everything, it really means the world to me.

They'd been renting their house back home so it helped them out a bit financially too, as Dad wasn't working either. He hadn't really been able to work since his heart attack, which was tough for him. The long-term plan was to get them their own place nearby, but in the short term they would be staying in the spare room.

Soon after I quit the band, Hear'Say ran a massive open audition for my replacement. It was kind of weird knowing they were doing that, but I managed to put the whole thing out of my mind.

I do wonder, though, if the way the replacement was found ultimately led to their downfall. Thousands of people auditioned to become the new fifth member of the band but out of all of those they chose a guy called Johnny Shentall, who was then the fiancé of Lisa Scott-Lee who'd been in Steps.

Hear'Say's team kept saying, 'No, he was chosen fair and square and the band had never met him before.' But then one of the newspapers printed a picture of us performing at the *Top of the Pops* Awards and there was Johnny dancing behind us. It made them look like liars and I think it really annoyed the public.

People seemed to turn against Hear'Say after that and by then other reality music shows were coming thick and fast too. There was *Popstars: The Rivals, Pop Idol* and *Fame Academy* and each one brought with it another new band or solo artist fighting for the top spots in the charts.

The whole thing must have been a nightmare for them. They were badly advised and it wasn't their fault. I think maybe some of the band blamed me for their sudden collapse in popularity. What I'd hear from mutual friends was that they reckoned that if they'd stuck with the original line-up, the fans would have remained loyal. I don't know whether that would have been the case or not, but there had been so much over-exposure in the first place. I felt that maybe Hear'Say's shelf life was already coming to an end, and the bad feeling over the new line-up just made things worse. In fact, Hear'Say could have turned me leaving to their own advantage. After all, I was the one who got all the bad press for walking out, while the band got loads of attention auditioning for my replacement. But whatever the reason, the damage had been done.

Their next single reached number six and a couple of months later, in October 2002, the band split. It had lasted just over eighteen months.

The *Popstars* dream was over.

15
MARRIED LIFE

....

Our wedding was booked for 10 August 2002, at St Albans Cathedral, to be followed by a reception in a marquee in the grounds of Cheneys Manor, a gorgeous stately home nearby.

Jack and I were both incredibly excited. The four months since David, Emily, Mum and Dad had moved in with us into our new home had been hectic, but things seemed to be settling down.

I loved our house because it felt like a proper home. It was a modern four-bedroom detached house on the outskirts of St Albans, with a little garden where David could play football and Emily could run in and out of her red plastic playhouse.

After the council house that I'd lived in as a kid and some of the rented places I'd had when I was on my own with the children, this place seemed a palace. It was a different life for David and Emily and something I would never, ever have been able to give them before. It was just wonderful.

I was so happy to have the kids with me again and Jack was great with them too. Their school was just around the corner and they quickly made new friends. Every other weekend Dad or I would take them back up North to see their dad. It was a long journey for the children – going all the way up there on a Friday night only to return again on Sunday evening – but we managed to make it work.

I'd also signed a solo recording deal. My manager Chris Herbert called me one day to say that Paul Adam, who had been our A&R man at Polydor, was moving to Universal Island. And he wanted to sign me there.

I was delighted. The thought of performing as a solo artist was just brilliant. We set to work, thinking about tracks and putting together an album.

All in all, things were good.

The only thing that used to frustrate me sometimes was the amount of time Jack and I would spend cooped up in the house together when we weren't working . But Jack never ever wanted to go out and so we rarely did.

We spent our evenings slobbing out in front of the television, watching movies. That was what Jack liked to do, so I went along with it. If Jack had to do things he didn't want to do he couldn't hide it and would get moody. Few things seemed worth the hassle of upsetting him.

Very, very occasionally I'd wonder if we really were right together, but when that thought crept into my mind I'd push it right out again. I loved Jack and I was convinced that was more important than any differences in our personalities.

Around the time that David and Emily moved in with us, Jack announced he wanted to quit *EastEnders*.

He'd been in it for four years and had been thinking about

leaving for a while. He was incredibly popular with the viewers and both he and his agent were convinced the job offers would come pouring in once he left. Jack took his acting very seriously and he wanted to have a go at all sorts of different things, not be typecast as Jamie Mitchell.

I wanted him to be happy, so I backed him all the way.

The week before our wedding I arranged for Mum and Dad to take David, who was then seven, and Emily, who was four, on holiday to Ibiza for a week. Up until then me, the kids, my parents and Jack had always gone away together, but as I was working again then I wasn't allowed any more time off in addition to my honeymoon. But it didn't seem fair that the children and Mum and Dad should miss out on a summer holiday so they went without me.

The day before they were due to return home, Mum rang me.

'Oh Kym,' she said. 'Emily's come out in chickenpox.'

'Oh no,' I said. I hated the thought that she was poorly and I wasn't there for her but Mum assured me she was in good spirits.

'What I'm really worried about though is that they won't let us on the plane home,' Mum went on.

'What?' I gasped.

'Well, they don't let people fly when they're contagious,' Mum said.

I could feel myself going into a full-scale panic. The wedding was just days away but I couldn't possibly go through with it without my kids or Mum and Dad there.

I was worried sick but, thank goodness, Emily was checked out by a doctor who said she was no longer contagious and could fly home. I was so relieved.

They all got home safely and we started packing up our things for the wedding. The night before we were all staying at the Edgwarebury Hotel. But no sooner had we all sat down to enjoy a drink at the lovely reception we'd organised when I looked at David and saw spots forming all over him too.

'Oh no,' I squealed, and rushed around checking his temperature and getting him to lie down on the hotel bed. But there was nothing we could do. He was also coming down with chickenpox.

Within a couple of hours he was covered in them. But David was incredibly brave about it and was still adamant that the next day he wanted to go ahead with his job as ring-bearer in the ceremony. After all, he'd been looking forward to it for months.

'Wouldn't you rather just sit with Grandma tomorrow if you feel poorly,' I said stroking his head.

'No,' he said. 'I want to do my job.'

When he and Emily had gone off to sleep, I left them with Mum and went back downstairs. Afterwards Jack's mum came back to my room. The pair of us had a few more glasses of wine and a real giggle. I hadn't really drunk in months because I felt Jack didn't like it but that evening reminded me how much fun it could be. I didn't do anything outrageous at all – I was just doing what most people do every weekend. But since I'd been with Jack I'd rarely been out at all.

Maybe by then it was glaringly obvious to close friends and family that Jack and I were very different people. The newspapers kept going on and on about the age gap between us as if I was some kind of cradle-snatcher. I thought that was a bit ridiculous. After all, I was only five and a half years older. Dave had been seven years older than me, but because he was a bloke no one ever batted an eyelid.

No, in all honesty the age gap was the least of our problems. It was our personalities that were most at odds. But we were very much in love and so no one ever said anything about that to me. Basically, I was prepared to do anything to make Jack happy. I was happy to change myself and be whoever he wanted me to be, so long as we were together.

The morning of my wedding I woke up feeling a bit rough from all the wine I'd drunk. But that was nothing to how poorly David was feeling. He had spots all over his body.

'I still want to be the ring-bearer, Mummy,' he said, getting dressed up in his little suit. He was so determined that I could hardly stop him.

He looked brilliant as he stood in the cathedral, carrying a little cushion with the rings lying on top of it.

Emily was a flower girl, along with my niece Kimberley. They looked so sweet, but Emily had a right face on her all day because she wasn't allowed to get handfuls of petals and just chuck them everywhere she wanted.

Then my bridesmaids were my sister Tracey and a friend I had met through her called Michaela. Then there was my old mate Tracey Shaw, Jack's sister Violet, Jack's brother's girlfriend Celia and his *EastEnders* girlfriend Natalie Cassidy. They wore beautiful cornflower blue dresses which were all the fashion at the time.

As for me? I wore an ivory corset-style bodice covered in

tiny crystals with a floor-length skirt and a really long train. To finish off the look I had a full-length veil and I carried a posy of yellow and cream roses.

The skirt and bodice had had to be taken in twice because I'd lost so much weight since quitting Hear'Say. I was eating more healthily than I had before because I had more time to cook proper food. And I'd also asked a guy called Paul Younane who was the physio on the Hear'Say tour to become my personal trainer for a while. So all that, plus a large dose of pre-wedding nerves, got me down to a size 8 for my wedding day.

I felt better than I had in years when Mum and Tracey helped me into that incredible bridal outfit on the morning of the wedding. I had no doubt that this was going to be the one and only time I ever got married and I so wanted it to be perfect.

Dad was giving me away and went with me in the car to the service. After all those evenings he'd spent driving me here, there and God-knows-where to do gigs, now he was sat next to me in the black Range Rover on our way to my wedding in a cathedral.

'I'm so proud of you, Kym,' he said squeezing my hand. He was chuffed to bits.

'Thanks, Dad,' I said. 'Thanks for everything.' And I really meant it.

Inside the cathedral Dad walked me down that long aisle to a string quartet playing music from the movie *Meet Joe Black* which Jack and I had watched over and over again together. It was our piece of music. Everywhere I looked I could see my friends and family all looking so happy for us.

My uncles, aunties, nephews and nieces were all there, as well as Jack's friends from *EastEnders,* my mates from Liberty X, and people I'd met in the music industry. None of my band-mates from Hear'Say were there though. It was all still too raw and we hadn't spoken to each other since the split. It was a shame they weren't there. I felt by then that I'd handled the split badly and I missed them.

In the cathedral I felt like I really was playing the role of the princess in a fairy tale. This was my happy ending. It was just over two years since Mum had dragged me to that first audition for *Popstars* in Manchester. It was unbelievable how much my life had changed.

When I got to the front of the church Jack was standing there sobbing. He seemed so upset I thought maybe he'd changed his mind about the whole thing.

'Are you OK?' I whispered.

'Yes,' he said. 'It's just you look so beautiful.'

OK! magazine was covering the wedding and with the fee they paid us we were able to have a fantastic reception, with the most amazing food and wine. It was brilliant to really treat our families, who'd supported us through everything.

Looking at the pictures of the wedding that day, it really does seem perfect.

But do you know what? I hate to admit this, but deep down I don't think I really enjoyed it.

When we got to the reception all my family and friends were there and ready to party. I really fancied a drink to cele-brate with them – and to help my headache from the night before – but I didn't think Jack would be happy if I did.

So on my wedding day I stuck to Coca-Cola all day because

I was frightened of upsetting my husband. And we hardly got any family photographs because Jack said he'd had enough of having his picture taken after a short while.

Jack and I ate our meal, chatted to our friends and danced a bit but then as the evening rolled on I thought he was getting a bit tired and fed up. Some of the guests were getting a bit merry – not that I blamed them, it was a wedding after all! But Jack seemed to find it irritating.

So at about half eleven he turned to me and said, 'Come on, Kym, people are getting drunk. I've had enough, let's go.'

I looked around at all the people I loved, enjoying themselves. Then I turned back to my new husband. 'Oh, OK,' I said. 'If that's what you want.'

I was disappointed but I didn't want Jack to be in a bad mood on our wedding night, so we quickly said our good-byes and left. It wasn't even midnight and the party was still roaring on when we got back to our hotel room.

Even though my wedding day might not have been every-thing I would have wanted, I was still very happy to go to bed that night as Mrs Kym Ryder. Because despite my niggling worries about our relationship, I did love Jack very, very much.

The next morning we were due to fly to Corfu on honey-moon. David was still poorly with the chickenpox and I hated the thought of leaving him.

'I'm not going to go to Corfu,' I said to Mum. 'I'll cancel it.'

'Don't be ridiculous, Kym,' she said. 'He'll be better in a couple of days and look, the spots are already beginning to dry up. He'll be here with me and he couldn't be in better hands. This is your honeymoon. Enjoy it.'

I still wasn't convinced but after a whole load more persuasion I agreed to go. But the whole trip was a catalogue of disasters.

For the entire flight all I could think about was David's chickenpox and when we arrived I was constantly on the phone home. Jack had been insistent that we should go somewhere 'off the beaten track', but in reality that meant us being stuck in a villa halfway up a mountain in the middle of nowhere. There was nothing around for miles: no restaurants, no shops, no bars, nothing. We spent the week living off beans on toast.

The fun didn't stop there. No sooner had we got to the villa than I got stung on the bum by a wasp! Then we got locked out of our apartment and were chased up the road by a rabid dog. And then photographers turned up and some pictures of us ended up in the paper. So much for getting away from it all!

While we were out there I also got a phone call from Tracey saying that Tony Anderton, my friend, the guy I'd gone out with for a few weeks when I was at Cansfield High School, had died. He was the lad who'd once run up and down the street in little Trevor's bonnet. Even though it had only been a playground romance we'd stayed friends for years afterwards, only losing contact as we got older. I was stunned.

Tony must have been going through a really bad time because he'd taken his own life. He'd done it the previous Saturday, the day Jack and I got married.

Tony had been one of those guys who lit up a room and I couldn't imagine how he'd got so low. He was the last person you would expect to commit suicide – he was the life and soul of any party and always seemed happy. I felt so sorry for him and his family.

With that awful news and everything else that was going wrong on our honeymoon, Jack and I felt we'd had enough.

'Shall we go home?' I asked Jack one evening after another meal of beans on toast.

He sighed. 'Maybe we should.'

I was missing the kids and we were both always happier at home, so we booked ourselves some flights. It's probably not a good sign to go home from your honeymoon a week early, but we just weren't having a good time.

Jack and I were just walking out of the arrivals gate at Heathrow Airport when I saw a couple of photographers looming towards us. *What now?* I thought.

'Hi, Kym,' one of the journalists said. 'We just wanted to know how you feel about Tony Anderton killing himself?'

'Er, I, I don't want to talk about it,' I stammered. I hadn't expected this at all. How did they even know about it?

'Do you think he did it because he was still in love with you and couldn't cope with you marrying Jack?'

What? It was a completely ridiculous idea. I hadn't seen Tony for years and he probably hadn't even known I was getting married that day.

'No, no I don't,' I said. I was totally thrown by all their questions and didn't know what more to say.

The next day the story about poor Tony's death was in the newspapers. He was described as my 'ex-boyfriend', which was totally misleading. We'd gone out for maybe two weeks when we were kids, and since then he'd had his own family and his own life. It was just wrong that now he was being dragged into the papers because of me. I felt overwhelmed with guilt.

His funeral had been arranged and I desperately wanted to go, but there was no way I could do it now because the press would be watching out for me all day and that would be awful for his family.

So I sent a message of condolence with Tracey and kept away from the service. But even so, press photographers still took photographs of the poor guy's coffin being carried into the church and a picture of the flowers that I'd sent. They even doorstepped his sister, trying to get her to sell a story.

I felt awful that I'd caused all this extra upset for Tony's family when they were already going through so much. Times like that, I hated the attention that my job brought, especially since so much of it was entirely out of my control.

Back home we got back into a routine. Jack was still at *EastEnders*, and I was working on recording a new album. David and Emily were settling in well at school.

But that autumn Jack's behaviour began to grate on me more and more.

'Shall we take the kids to Thorpe Park?' I suggested one weekend.

'Nah, don't think so,' said Jack.

'Why not? They'd love going on the rides and stuff.'

'There'll be loads of people there and they'll all be staring at us,' he said. 'It'll be awful.'

'But that's hardly fair on them,' I pointed out. 'Why should the kids be stuck at home just because we're in the public eye?'

'Look, I just don't want to go,' he said.

So that was it. We didn't go. I knew how moody he could get and it didn't seem worth pushing the point any further. Yeah, I wanted an easy life but I also really didn't want to upset him. Jack was my husband and I loved him.

But it irritated me more and more that the kids were missing out like that. I'd take them on days out on my own, or with my parents. Still, I wanted Jack to be there with us too and it upset me that he wasn't.

With Mum and Dad living in the same house they could see all too clearly what was going on between us.

Maybe they'd had doubts about how well suited we were from the beginning but if so they didn't say anything for ages. Gradually, though, I could tell they were getting concerned about the way things were going.

'I worry about you sometimes, Kym,' Mum said to me one morning.

'Why? What do you mean?' I said, trying to sound upbeat.

'You've changed since you've been with Jack. You don't go out any more and you've lost some of your sparkle. And I don't think it is good for the kids seeing you like that.'

'You reckon?'

'Yes,' Mum said. 'I worry that you're changing for Jack. And I don't think you should change. You were lovely the way you were before.'

'Thanks, Mum,' I said, trying to smile. 'But you know what Jack's like. He doesn't mean any harm, but he just likes me staying here at home with him. It's all that he wants.'

'Hmm, maybe he does,' said Mum. She didn't say any more. I could tell by the way she looked sometimes when Jack was talking that she thought we weren't right for each other.

If an invitation to a party or a premiere came in the post, more often than not Jack would look at it and say, 'Well, we don't want to go to that.' I felt he sometimes looked down on the celebrity side of the business and that he thought of himself purely as an actor and took that side of things very seriously. Me, sometimes I just wanted to go out and have a bit of a laugh. After the years I'd had as a single mum with not enough money to keep the leccy on, I couldn't see what was wrong with having some fun.

And that's what upset Mum and Dad a bit. They'd seen me struggle for years and years and then, just when I should have been having the time of my life, I barely left the house.

I know I've got a fiery temper and I am not an easy person to live with at all. But when we finally split up there seemed to be a general view that it was all my fault. But unless you're actually in a relationship it is impossible to know what is really going on. I took so much flak at that time that I just want to take this chance to tell my side of the story.

Maybe it was because I was five years older than Jack with kids and was known to be quite feisty that everyone assumed I was the one controlling the relationship. Because he looked young they thought he was under my thumb. But things are sometimes not quite what they appear.

Jack could withdraw and sometimes he'd go for days without speaking to me. It created a terrible atmosphere in the house, so I'd do anything to avoid that. I don't know if it was deliberate but the effect was that it felt to me quite controlling. He was never nasty or violent or anything like that, but it definitely felt to me like he was calling the shots in our marriage.

But he could be incredibly thoughtful too. He was always hugging me and kissing me and was totally open with his emotions. He helped out around the house and did all the cooking. He loved cooking so I never had to do a thing in the kitchen. No more fish fingers and Turkey Twizzlers for us! In many ways, he was a top bloke to live with. He was neat and tidy and organised. And he was great with the kids, playing games with them and chatting with them when they got in from school. And his family were lovely.

So for all the negative things there were also a huge amount of positives. And because of that I kept on trying to push aside all my worries about our marriage.

Looking back, I think I was in denial about our differences for a long time.

Then in November 2002, three months after we married, Jack decided to leave *EastEnders*.

I think he had hoped they would leave the door open for him to return but in the end they killed off Jack's character, Jamie, and he was gutted. I think he'd hoped that he might be able go back there one day after he'd had a chance to try some other acting work.

But the writers made sure there was no chance of that when Jamie was hit by a car driven by Martin Fowler, played by James Alexandrou. The episode was shown on Christmas Day 2002 and was watched by 16 million people.

After he'd left Jack had done an interview in the *News of the World* in which he criticised the show and some of his co-stars. It went down really, really badly at the BBC.

It was the end of Jack's career at *EastEnders* and quietly I worried it might be the end for him with the BBC too. Jamie had been such a popular character and loads of his fans were devastated about him going but again I seemed to take the blame. It was entirely Jack's decision to leave and to do the *News of the World* interview but again I was perceived as this older, domineering woman forcing Jack to give up his job. How people thought I would gain from that, I don't know!

We remained confident he'd get loads of offers of work because Jack had been so popular in the show. He was a young, talented actor. I was sure it was only a matter of time before he was snapped up.

I certainly hoped our confidence would prove correct because, apart from anything else, we needed the money. I'd got an advance for my album but by then I knew the way the music industry worked. The advances might sound like eye-watering amounts of money but unless you have massive hits you actually see very little of it: a million-pound deal is not how much money you receive, it's how much money is spent overall on however many albums.

All I could do was hope that the New Year would bring a new beginning for us all.

16
GOING SOLO

·········

I'd had almost a year out of the spotlight and loved being around for the kids so much, sorting out the wedding and getting our new family home just so.

I was also recording my debut album and by the beginning of 2003, I was ready to really throw myself back into my career.

My debut solo single was called 'Cry' and was due to be released in the April of that year. It was written by Espen Lind who had worked with Beyoncé, Lionel Ritchie and Jessica Simpson. I flew over to Norway again to record some of the album on which it would feature which was called *Standing Tall*.

Being a solo artist was great because I was able to choose the style of music I wanted to record. Plus it was a lot quicker in the studio, which meant less time away from the kids.

Back in Britain I was hurled into the bedlam of photo shoots, interviews and appearances to publicise the release. That was the part of the music industry that I'd never really loved. For six weeks before a single is released you have to do absolutely everything your record company asks you to do to promote the song.

And as much as I was enjoying working again, I quickly became quite cynical about the music industry. It was pretty clear to me now that it didn't matter all that much how good the song was or my talents as a singer. It seemed more about getting the public to buy into me as a person and I began to feel a bit like a product.

I felt like a product that shoppers would either like or hate, no different to a new type of breakfast cereal. And I just felt really uncomfortable with it all

So I found a lot of the promotion work really annoying, but it had to be done. And doing it as a solo artist was pretty scary too. Everywhere I went and every interview I did, I was on my own. And if the single succeeded or failed it was down to me too. I knew there were a lot of people willing me to fail because they were unhappy I'd ever left Hear'Say, so that made it all pretty stressful.

When 'Cry' went straight in at number two in the charts I was absolutely delighted. I'd done it – on my own this time. I could hardly believe it.

Suzanne Shaw called me to say 'Congratulations' and I was really pleased. I invited her round for lunch and we got on really well. She apologised for what had gone on at the end in Hear'Say and I apologised for the things I'd said and done too. It was great to put all that behind us and feel we could be mates again.

But while my career seemed to be getting back on track, things with Jack weren't so good.

He still didn't want to go out – but now he started to take issue with me going out on my own too. Fairly soon after I'd joined Universal they'd thrown a big party, which Jack and I were invited to. I thought it was really important that I should be there because Universal were pretty much keeping a roof over our heads – and I wanted to go anyway since it looked like it would be a good night. But Jack couldn't see that.

But on the evening of the party, just as I was about to start getting ready, Jack began complaining of a migraine.

'I feel terrible,' he said. 'I'm really not well.'

I didn't even bother putting my dress on; I knew we wouldn't be going to the party. I suppose I could still have gone on my own but I didn't want to take the risk that Jack would withdraw and there would have been a terrible silence for days.

It was often the same when I had a promotional event I had to attend. At one point my tour manager was so worried it might damage my career that he rang Dad and asked him for advice. We'd often have a big row on the phone before I had a public appearance to do and then I'd be crying and really upset minutes before meeting hundreds of people.

Then when I got home he'd be moody, then I'd get angry and it would all end in another row. Looking back, maybe I should have sat down and explained to Jack how much I loved him, but that I was finding his moods really hard to cope with. And maybe he could have been honest about what he was feeling too. Maybe he was feeling he wasn't getting enough of my time and attention but I didn't see that at the time. And sadly we didn't talk things through. Instead, I just kept trying to avoid situations that I thought might annoy him. It worked for a while, but at the same time I was getting more and more frustrated.

One evening my mum said to me: 'What is all this "yes Jack, no Jack, three bags full Jack" business? Why don't you do something you want to do for a change? When was the last time he even took you out for something to eat?'

I couldn't answer that. We never went anywhere, except on birthdays, when we might go somewhere with the kids for a burger. Even then we'd be straight back home and Jack would be watching TV again or playing computer games.

We did make friends with other local parents, but we still very rarely went out.

It was really getting me down.

In July 2003, my second single, 'Come On Over', was released around the same time as the album, *Standing Tall*.

Again it was another round of public appearances and crossing my fingers that the British public still liked me enough to go out and buy my records. And again, I felt pretty disillusioned with the publicity machine. All my life I'd loved music and I'd loved singing, but somehow I felt it was all about image and what people thought about you. It was destroying all the enjoyment of the job for me.

The single reached number ten in the charts and so did the album, which wasn't bad at all. But in the press it was written about as if it was a total disaster. Of course it was going to be hard to do better than the debut single, but lots of critics seemed in a hurry to write me off.

I was away for weeks doing promotional work and Jack

and I were only speaking on the telephone, which was really tough.

At the same time there were loads of stories in the papers saying that our marriage was in trouble. The speculation just added to the pressure on us and we were rowing all the time.

We decided we needed a break from each other to get our heads straight and to work out what we really wanted. I was adamant that I still wanted my marriage to work. I just hoped that after some time apart we could start again.

Jack went to stay with his dad but we carried on talking. Neither of us had been married before. Marriage had been a lot harder than we'd thought it would be and we were both equally to blame for the breakdown in communication between us.

But we still loved each other and having that trial separation reinforced that in our minds. After about four weeks apart we arranged to meet one evening on Primrose Hill in north London. We talked for hours.

'I love you,' I said. 'And I really want to make this work. I want us to start again.'

I was worried that Jack was thinking of walking away but gradually that evening we talked things through and decided to try again. I just wanted to make him happy and I was determined to do it.

Maybe deep down I still knew things weren't quite right but I thought with enough hard work we could make them right in the future. That was what I hoped, anyway.

It was a really hard time in the music business. It was just at the point that illegal downloading was taking off and everything was changing. The record companies were losing money hand over fist and dropping artists like no one's business.

I knew if my third release didn't do well then I would be dropped by Universal.

But with hardly any budget set aside to promote me this time, that was a hell of a lot to ask for. This time my prayers weren't answered. My next single, 'Sentimental', scraped into the top forty at number thirty-five. And that was the end of my solo career.

It was January 2004 when I was called to a meeting with my manager Chris Herbert to be told the news. I was pretty much braced for it, by that point.

'I'm sorry, Kym,' Chris said. 'But I've heard from Universal and I'm afraid they're not going to renew your contract.'

I'm not sure what reaction he was expecting but I was actually pretty relieved.

'That's fine,' I said. 'I thought it was coming. I had a great time while it lasted.'

I had enjoyed recording again but everything else about the music industry had started to get a bit old; the endless promotional interviews, the road shows and the parties where you had to kiss arse just to get publicity for your song.

To be honest, there was no way I was going to consider signing another record deal – and not much chance of being offered one anyway.

Of course there were people who were delighted that I'd been dropped by my label. It was like they still saw me as the diva I'd been portrayed as on *Popstars* and they were loving that my career had hit the rocks. There were articles in magazines saying my fifteen minutes of fame was up and one newspaper had a picture of my head going down a toilet.

That made me really mad.

I thought to myself, *Do you know what? My time is over when I say it's over, and not when you decide. I've worked too hard for it to be any other way.*

I still wanted a decent career, but not necessarily in the music industry. What's more, I had to find some kind of work for the kids' sake. I'd created this new life for them and I couldn't suddenly just yank it all away again.

In fact, I had to do some pretty quick thinking. Our money was starting to run out. I'd signed a big deal when I joined Universal, but what people forget when they read about these multi-million-pound deals is that all the costs of recording the singles and albums have to be deducted from that sum. The artist can be left with virtually nothing and I really didn't make much money at all during my entire solo career.

And by then Jack hadn't been working for more than a year, apart from a few weeks in panto. When he first left *EastEnders* he'd been offered a few roles but he'd turned them down, confident something better was going to come along. But it didn't and eventually even the offers of smaller parts dried up too. Jack's agent had told him there would be jobs in America and people queuing up to meet him in the British film and TV industry, but sadly it all came to nothing.

I was starting to panic about money. Jack had been working since he was sixteen and had never known what it was like to be skint himself. I could remember all too well and was determined it was never going to happen again. With the money I'd made from Hear'Say I'd been able to put down a deposit on our house in St Albans, but there was still a hefty mortgage to be paid every month.

But despite the situation getting increasingly desperate, Jack did not want to do anything other than straight acting. Loads of times I said to him: 'Have you considered doing voiceovers?' or 'What about applying for some presenting work?'

He would just reply: 'No, I'm an actor.'

I felt it was really important that we both kept ourselves in the public eye because once you disappear from view in showbiz you might never work again. But Jack just wasn't interested in being seen in the right places or doing things he didn't want to do, just to maintain his profile.

Ultimately, it was all down to me. I picked up absolutely anything I could get. While I was looking for another job, I did photo shoots for magazines, personal appearances and promotional work. I'd have been at the opening of the envelope if someone hired me to do it. So long as it paid, I was up for it. After all, I wasn't going to let a bit of pride get in the way of giving my kids a decent life.

What really wound me up was that while I was going out and pimping myself out to any magazine that would have me, Jack was holding out for his dream acting job. It wasn't like I was desperate to appear in magazines week after week; I did it purely to pay the bills. But Jack didn't seem to worry about that.

Looking back I realise that we'd had such different experiences with money in the past, that we just had very different attitudes to it. But we were charging through my savings and

I began to feel more and more anxious about how we were going to keep our lovely new roof over the kids heads.

One night we had a massive row about whether he should do a reality show that he had been offered. He was dead set against the idea.

'Well, you've been on a reality show, so it's OK for you to do those things,' he said, 'but I'm not going to.'

I was furious.

'I know you might not want to do it,' I said. 'But you've got responsibilities and anyone in that situation has to go where the money is. You can't always only do things that you want to do. We're a team'

But he wouldn't budge.

I guess the difference was that I knew what it was like to have nothing. I'd lived on my arse; I'd licked envelopes and delivered Betterware catalogues to make ends meet. Now that I had a public profile I could earn money by doing relatively little work – easy stuff, in the grand scheme of things. And so could he. Which was why it made me so livid that he refused to do it.

It upset me too that there was no sense of us being in this predicament together. It would have been great if he'd taken some of the pressure off my shoulders. After all, he wanted to keep the nice lifestyle he was accustomed to. But no, I knew that if we were going to keep the house, it was going to be all down to me.

One day I visited my accountant to work out exactly how much money we had left. It wasn't looking good at all. We were only months away from having absolutely no way of paying the mortgage. What would we do then? There was no way I could go back to the life I'd had before *Popstars*, when I couldn't even afford to put a decent meal on the table. I didn't want to have gone on this whole journey for nothing. It would have been too bloody awful.

That night I sat with my head in my hands. 'What are we going to do, Jack?' I asked.

He didn't have an answer.

There was more worry at that time when Dad was told he needed a heart bypass operation. He'd gone for a check-up with his GP and tests showed something wasn't right with his heart. After the heart attack he'd had no one wanted to take any risks and he was booked in for an angiogram. Dad wanted to wait to have the test on the NHS but the waiting list was so long and I wanted him to have it immediately. I didn't want to take any chances with Dad's health so I offered to pay for him to be seen privately. He didn't like the idea at first but eventually he caved in.

And I'm so glad he did. The angiogram showed that one artery was completely blocked, another was 90 per cent blocked and the remaining two were 70 per cent blocked. He was a time bomb just waiting to have another heart attack.

The doctor said he needed a quadruple bypass. Again I couldn't bear the thought of him waiting on an NHS list for months on end so I paid for him to be treated privately and within a fortnight he'd had the operation.

Mum, me and my brother Jon went to the hospital on the day of the op with Dad. I could tell he was scared that day. I could see it in his eyes and I'd never ever seen that before. But as the hospital porters wheeled him down towards the operating theatre he put his fist up and shook it as if to say: 'I'm fighting this.' It was an emotional moment as he disappeared round that corner. We were all terrified it would be the last time we saw him alive. My dad is not usually an emotional person and he never got upset in front of us, but we could see he was in a bit of a state as they wheeled him in. The three of us then sat in a waiting room for nine or ten hours waiting for news and drinking endless cups of coffee but we didn't hear anything. We finally got a call to say the operation had been successful, but he wasn't yet out of the woods. The surgeon later came down to speak to us and said it had all gone well. We were all so relieved. I was a bit worried my Mum was going to kiss him. He'd literally just saved my dad's life, yet for him it was all in a day's work.

The first time I saw Dad afterwards was truly shocking. He was out cold in intensive care, covered in a foil blanket and connected by dozens of wires coming out of him to a bank of machines. Mum sat next to his bed and cried. Me and Jon were in shock.

But my dad has incredible spirit and two days later he was up and waiting for us at the lift when we went in to visit him. And within a couple of weeks he was out in my back garden messing about with Emily's skipping rope. The nurses said he was a star patient and that his positive attitude meant he healed unusually quickly. A lot of people naturally feel very frightened after going through that kind of procedure, but my dad's positivity really speeded up his recovery. The doctors had done an incredible job and without them I'm sure he wouldn't be here today.

*

Soon afterwards I got a call from Chris saying he was thinking of putting me forward for an audition for the part of Annette in *Saturday Night Fever* in the West End stage production of the movie.

'Would you fancy it, Kym?' Chris asked.

'Yeeeees,' I screamed.

I was really quite nervous in the audition because I'd never done anything like that before. I had to talk with a real Brooklyn 'New Yoik' accent, but I'd always loved doing different voices. When I used to help out Mum delivering the Betterware catalogues, I'd put on a different accent at every house we went to. It was so funny.

When I landed the role in *Saturday Night Fever* it was a massive relief. At last we had a bit of security. We certainly weren't going to be rolling in money, as there was just my wage coming into the house, but it was enough for us to relax a little.

Before the show started I was sent for singing lessons to teach me how to breathe properly and how to place my voice and make it sound more dramatic. In musical theatre you are telling a story with the lyrics, so you have to deliver them totally differently to the way you would in a pop song.

I was also sent for lessons with a speech coach for the Brooklyn accent, but after three classes the teacher said I didn't need to go back again. That gave me a real confidence boost.

Saturday Night Fever was eight shows a week. It was really hard work but I loved it from the beginning. My character, Annette, was in love with the lead guy, Tony Manero, but he didn't want to have anything to do with her. Then my character gets raped at the end of the show. It was dramatic stuff, and the music was all the Bee Gees hits. Good job I loved them, because I could never get them out of my head after I started on the show!

My first night was 6 July 2004. It was terrifying but totally amazing. When we arrived at the Apollo Theatre there were massive posters of me and the rest of the cast all over the walls outside. It was unbelievable. For me, appearing on a West End stage really was a dream come true.

Jack, the children and Mum and Dad were all there that opening night, clapping and shouting like maniacs.

Emily adored the show and she came to see it over and over again. Fortunately she didn't understand the more shocking parts of it as they weren't literal and there wasn't any violence or scenes of a graphic nature, it was all just hinted at. But she knew every word to every song. At the end of each show we'd do a medley of all the songs and everyone in the audience would be on their feet dancing. At that point Emily would come running down to the front and start dancing with the cast. She knew the names of all the actors and would bring in pictures that she had coloured for them.

I met some fantastic people in *Saturday Night Fever*. On my first day I was introduced to a woman called Katie Roddy who was going to be my dresser. We got on brilliantly from the beginning. She was just so genuine and fun to be with that we had a fantastic laugh. In fact, she's now one of my best friends.

The rest of the cast were brilliant too. Sean Williamson, who'd played Barry in *EastEnders*, joined at the same time as me to play Monty the DJ, and Gerard McCarthy, who went on to play Kris in *Hollyoaks*, was in it then too. He's also still one of my best mates.

You know, it was hard work and I had to be extremely disciplined, but it taught me a heck of a lot about acting.

If there was a matinee performance I had to be at the theatre at midday and if it was just an evening show I had to be there at 5 p.m. The downside was that I didn't see much of the kids if they were at school. Thankfully Mum and Dad were there to help look after them.

We did have a fantastic laugh in that show but I had a terrible run of bad luck too.

First of all, Gerard McCarthy managed to break my nose backstage halfway through a performance. I loved Gerard and didn't want to get him into trouble, so at the time we told the show manager that we'd been rehearsing a dance routine and Gerard had accidentally knocked into me. But the truth was much sillier than that. Gerard had actually been messing about, swinging round a pole. I'd stepped out of my dressing room and was about to go back onstage when he came flying round, shouting 'catch me, Marshy!'. His elbow went crunch, right in my face. I could smell the blood and my nose immediately swelled up to twice its normal size.

The worst thing was my microphone was still on so the entire auditorium could hear me saying, 'I've broken my nose, I've broken my nose.'

Gerard was almost crying because he felt so awful. It was mayhem. They quickly sent on my understudy with a hand-held microphone while I was put in a cab and taken to hospital.

Once I got there, an X-ray showed my nose was definitely broken. I needed four days off work while it healed.

When I went back to work it was still horribly painful because every time you sing it resonates your nose and that was agony. Even worse, I had to go back into hospital and under anaesthetic have my nose manipulated back into the correct position. What a nightmare!

While I was having the treatment they put a cannula into my vein, but then that became infected and I got a blood clot in my hand. And no sooner had I got back to work than someone accidentally hit me right on the hand where the clot was. So then I had to be rushed back to hospital for the second time in the middle of a show.

When I got there a camera crew was filming one of those 'day in the life of a hospital' shows. 'Oh Kym,' they went. 'Can we film you?' I didn't have the heart to say no, but it was so embarrassing.

My hand got better but then at around Christmas time, I got laryngitis. I didn't feel I could take any more time off sick so I battled through. My throat was dead painful and I couldn't hit all the notes, but I carried on anyway. I'm sure anyone who came to see me in the show that Christmas time must have thought I was absolute rubbish.

My contract for the show was for six months, which took me just into 2005. By then the show wasn't doing quite so well and although they asked me to stay on, they wanted to cut my money.

I wasn't earning very much compared with a lot of people in the West End anyway, and I just couldn't afford to continue on less money so I decided to walk away. I was gutted it was over, really gutted. But doing the show had given me the acting bug and it had also given me the confidence to think I really could be an actress.

Back at school I'd enjoyed drama and always got high marks in it, but somehow I'd forgotten that over the years while I'd been putting all my energy into singing.

But now I knew it was what I wanted to do.

In my last couple of months in the show I'd realised that if I was serious about acting I needed to get an acting agent. I was still with the same music management company I'd been with for years, but they weren't going to be able to help me break into television and film.

So over a couple of nights I invited two agents to come and see me in *Saturday Night Fever*. They'd been recommended to me by other people and I just hoped one of them might agree to represent me.

As soon as I met Vivien Wilde I knew she was the woman for me. She turned up at the theatre with her dog, Princess, a little Chinese crested dog with just a few tufts of fur, so it looked kind of weird.

'Would you mind if I leave her in your dressing room?' Vivien asked.

'Er, no, that's fine,' I replied. 'So long as you can smuggle her in there.'

Normally agents leave at half-time if they come to see a show, but Vivien stayed for the entire performance. 'I had to stay because you were just wonderful,' she said afterwards. I was delighted.

It was only later that she admitted she had gone to check

on Princess at half-time only to discover she'd done a few poos all over my dressing room. Vivien actually spent most of the second half trying to clear up the damage!

The next day we spoke on the telephone and Vivien agreed to take me on.

Vivien is fabulously eccentric, and she has a great reputation in the business. Everyone enjoys working with her. She can be a Rottweiler too, and will really fight for me when she needs to. Fairly soon afterwards I was asked to attend an event with Tim Henman to encourage kids to play tennis. Some of the photographers were asking me to hitch up my tennis skirt at the back like the girl in the famous poster.

Vivien stomped over to the photographers and asked: 'And is Tim Henman having his butt pictured like that too?'

'Er no,' the snappers replied.

'Well there's your answer then,' Vivien snapped.

Once I'd signed with Vivien we sat down for a big conversation about where I saw my career going.

'So, what is it you would like to do?' she asked me.

'Well, I'd love to be on *Coronation Street*,' I said. Yeah, me and every other actress in the country!

I'd grown up with *Corrie* and to me it was still the biggest thing on British TV. I thought she'd laugh, but that's not Vivien's style.

'OK,' she said. 'Well, it might take a couple of years, but yes, I'm sure you can do that.'

I couldn't stop grinning. As far as I was concerned, I was on the road to Weatherfield.

17
NEW GIRL ON THE STREET

· · · · · · · · ·

'So, Kym, how do you feel about playing nude scenes?' the casting director asked me.

'Um,' I said with a sense of rising panic. 'Um, I'm not quite sure.'

What I actually felt about the idea was sheer terror, but I wasn't going to tell him that. It was my first audition for television, and I was trying out for the role of Anika Beevor in the *Footballers' Wives Extra Time* spin-off show. OK, so it wasn't Shakespeare, but it was an acting role.

Thankfully I didn't have to worry myself too much about the prospect of stripping off in front of the cameras because I didn't get the part. But just getting called for auditions gave my confidence a real boost. At least I was getting my foot in the door.

'Some people can be a bit snobby about actresses who've come from the music world,' Vivien explained. 'You're just going to have to be very patient.'

I tried my best, but I couldn't help but keep getting my hopes up.

Then the makers of *The Royal* said they wanted to see me too. That was the first time I met Steve Frost, now known as Steve November, who was producing the show, and later went on to produce *Coronation Street* and is now Executive Producer on *Emmerdale*.

I didn't land a role, but after the audition Vivien told me that the feedback had been really positive.

'Just be patient,' she kept telling me. 'We'll get there.'

Next I was called to audition for a BBC3 comedy called *Grown Ups* with Sheridan Smith and then I did another one for *Dalziel and Pascoe*. For that job it got down to just me and Jennifer James, who'd been in *Corrie*. In the end, Jenny got it, but I was pleased for her because I think she's fab.

With each audition I gained a little more confidence and had a better idea what I was doing. Sometimes I would be sent a script in advance but other times I'd just get it when I turned up on the day. Either way, I'd have to sit down at a desk in front of the producer or director and casting director. It was just like having a job interview, except there was a camera in your face all the time.

My next audition was for a role in an episode of the daytime soap, *Doctors*. And bloody hell, this time I got it!

When Vivien rang me with the news I jumped up and down with excitement. It was brilliant. It was my first step to where I wanted to be.

The storyline in my episode was that I'd been caught selling a watch which belonged to someone who'd been found dead so I was under suspicion for killing him. She was innocent, just a petty thief, but I had to wear a trilby and a trench coat so I certainly looked pretty dodgy! The show was aired in October

2005 and even I could see when I sat down to watch it that I still had a lot to learn. All my family and friends said I was great in the part, but looking back I think I was pretty rubbish.

I was still pretty green, but at least I was finally getting the opportunity to learn the ropes. The director on *Doctors* was really nice and made me feel very relaxed and gradually I got the hang of what I was doing.

He would say things like, 'I want you to pick up that glass there' and then, 'turn right there' so it wasn't too complicated. But how I delivered the line was down to me.

Soon afterwards I landed another part in an episode of *Holby City*, which was to be screened early in 2006. I played the girlfriend of someone who had been shot in the arse. In the storyline she didn't know he'd been shot in the bum because it had happened a long time ago but then he started vomiting and it turned out he had lead poisoning from the bullet.

They were a lovely, lovely bunch of people at *Holby* and because I felt a bit more confident by then I really enjoyed myself.

Back then Jack was quite enthusiastic that my acting career was taking off. And I, of course, was made up.

That said, while it was great getting encouraging noises from casting directors, that didn't pay the Tesco bill. At the end of 2005 I signed up to do panto in Stoke-on-Trent. I didn't have much choice, because by then I hadn't worked regularly since *Saturday Night Fever* at the start of the year. Jack had done a bit of theatre work and a short film called *Popcorn* but we were getting desperate for money.

My pot of Hear'Say savings was long since empty and we

had to cut right back on our spending. I knew it would only take one regular job to turn things around but I began to worry: *What if I never get that one job?*

Both Jack and I had credit-card bills and a couple of times we were in shops and our cards were refused because we hadn't paid them off. It was so humiliating – especially since we were pretty recognisable. I didn't want to go back to my old life where there wasn't enough money to pay the bills or buy the kids toys. I remained adamant that that wasn't going to happen.

When the bills were really racking up I'd do a magazine shoot or personal appearance, which might tide us over for a while, but pretty quickly we'd be back in the same situation again. I was desperate for a proper job.

That's why landing the panto was such a relief. It was Dave's turn to have the children that Christmas so I didn't even have to worry that they'd be missing out by having me working.

I was starring alongside Jonathan Wilkes in a production of *Mother Goose*, which had been written by Eric Potts – who, funnily enough, played Diggory Compton in *Coronation Street*.

I moved into a temporary flat in Stoke two weeks before the show opened while we rehearsed. I didn't know anyone living up there and I was quite lonely.

Since Jack wasn't working I asked him to come up and stay with me for a while, but he didn't want to. He didn't mind popping up for a night at the weekend though.

I was bored and lonely so when the cast or crew suggested going out for a drink after work I'd jump at the chance. But

Hear'Say, the first reality TV pop band (left to right): Noel Sullivan,
Suzanne Shaw, Myleene Klass, Danny Foster and me

'Pure and Simple' getting to Number One was a dream come true for all of us.
For me (far right), it meant my children's lives would be different for ever

Performing solo at Party in the Park, London, 2003

As Annette in *Saturday Night Fever*, with Stephane Anelli as Tony, 2004. Doing the show gave me the acting bug again

My first professional panto, *Mother Goose*, with Jonathan Wilkes, 2005

New to Weatherfield: with my on-screen family, the Connors, on *Coronation Street*, July 2006. (left to right) Sean Gallagher (who played my brother Paul), Rob James-Collier (my brother Liam) and Ben Thompson (my son Ryan)

My first ever appearance as Michelle on Corrie was opposite my favourite character, Liz, played by Beverley Callard. I was terrified!

David carrying the rings, and Emily as bridesmaid

Jack and I at our wedding in 2002 – it really was a lovely day

Accepting the award for Best Newcomer at the National TV Awards, 2007. An incredible feeling, and such a relief when the papers gave my dress the thumbs-up the next day!

Jamie and I visiting the Hard Rock Café, New York. I was pregnant with Archie at the time

At the British Soap Awards, May 2008, the night I met Jamie

With Jamie at the British Soap Awards, May 2009, putting on a brave face for the cameras. I had to keep shoving ice down my top because I'd just had my boobs done!

Performing 'Pie Jesu' in the semi-final of *Popstar to Operastar*, February 2010

Celebrating 50 Years of
Coronation Street with (left
to right) Julie Goodyear,
Betty Driver and Sue Jenkins,
December 2010

With Jamie's sister,
Charley. She and his
family are now some
of my closest friends

Emily and David in
2011 – it's scary
how quickly they
are growing up

Jamie and his son Billy,
trying to teach Polly the
offside rule already!

Gorgeous Polly –
our happy ending

then Jack started getting irritable when he rang my flat in the evening and I wasn't at home.

I felt he was checking up on me all the time and it felt like he was trying to control me. It really did seem like he was only happy if I was stuck indoors, even though I knew I'd be having a miserable time. The thought that I was going out and having a laugh with some colleagues seemed to be just too much for him.

A big party was being thrown after the first night of the pantomime and all my family had been invited. There were also local reporters and photographers there, so I had to go and talk to them – the whole point of the do was to publicise the pantomime.

But again I felt Jack had a problem with me mingling with other people because he felt uncomfortable with people he didn't know. I felt it had reached the point where if I wasn't by his side 24/7 then it was a really big deal. So again it turned into a massive row between us.

And that night was worse than others because Dad got involved too which made Jack furious. Mum and Dad felt I was changing to please him. And of course they didn't like that.

But Jack felt my parents were interfering in our marriage. It was horrible and some awful things were said.

I know it must have been hard for Jack living with his in-laws, but ages later Mum explained that she had been worried about the way Jack behaved towards me from the time I lost my record deal. Apparently she'd talked to him about it and he had said something like, 'I love it when Kym is down because she needs me then. I don't like it when she's strong; I like it when she needs me.'

Understandably, Mum thought there was something pretty wrong with that. What husband wants his wife to be miserable, just so she needs him more? She didn't say anything about it to me at the time, but she said Jack's words stuck in her mind for ages.

Jack was fuming after the row with my dad. He seemed to be angry that my parents took my side in everything – but then that was hardly surprising.

'I don't want them back in our house,' Jack said that night.

I just didn't know what to say. He was my husband, and I felt like he was forcing me to choose between him and my folks.

Mum and Dad went to stay with my auntie Pam for a couple of days over Christmas. But with Jack adamant that they had to move out, we had no idea how long they might be there for.

'I'm so sorry, Mum,' I said, on the phone.

'Don't worry, love, it's not your fault,' she said.

I felt totally stuck in the middle between my parents and my husband. I loved them all, and I just didn't know which way to turn.

That Christmas Day I quickly popped presents round to my parents who spent it with Tracey. For the rest of the day I was stuck in a pub in Stoke-on-Trent with Jack. The kids were still in Spain with their dad.

Even after Christmas Jack and my parents didn't make up. And by then there was no way they'd move back in anyway.

That Christmas only got worse when little David returned

from Spain with a really painful wrist, which he'd hurt when he fell over while playing football. I took him to hospital where they discovered it was broken.

Then on New Year's Eve, me, Jack, the children, Tracey and her kids and my big brother Dave and his girlfriend Faye were all invited to another party being held by the panto organisers. Jack didn't want to go, but I managed to persuade him by telling him it was important for me to keep in with the people I was working with. I knew he didn't really want to be there so it was the same old story. We were just very different people.

By the time it came to everyone singing 'Auld Lang Syne' he wouldn't even stand with me. By the time we left the party he was in a terrible mood and on the way home we had the most massive barney. It was awful because the kids were there and we had always tried to keep any arguments away from them. I really wish it hadn't happened but I was so sick of his behaviour that night.

Everything that had been going on over the last few months poured out. I was mad at him for falling out with my parents and he was angry at me because he thought I hadn't stuck up for him.

Then I said some really hurtful things to him. I'm not proud of that, but I was so angry. He'd hurt me and he'd hurt my parents and all the time I'd been trying to keep him happy. Now I'd had enough.

When I'm really angry like that I can say some terrible things in the heat of the moment. But the minute the argument is over I forget all that and try to clear the air. Jack didn't find it as easy to move on though.

It was such a bad row that Jack drove back home to St

Albans in the middle of the night. I got the kids to bed and then tried ringing him when he was halfway down the motorway.

'I'm really sorry about everything I said,' I told him. 'I shouldn't have said those nasty things. Please come back and we can try to sort things out.' I actually didn't really think I was entirely to blame for the row, but I just wanted to put things right and make Jack happy.

We talked on the phone a few more times and I kept on begging Jack to come back. In the end, he did drive back up North again on New Year's Day. When he got back I did my best to cheer him up and put him in a better mood.

It could be exhausting trying to keep him happy though. It was really wearing me down. Looking back, I have to take on some of the blame here and acknowledge that if I hadn't tried to change who I was in order to be with him, then maybe a lot of this wouldn't have happened. Because if somebody doesn't love you for who you are, it's never going to work. But when you fall in love with someone, and you really fall in love with them, it's too late by the time you realise there might be some cracks in the relationship, because you're already in love.

That night was a real turning point for me. I knew for certain my marriage was in serious trouble. But still I kept hoping things would get better. I wanted to keep my family together.

Sadly there was no improvement in relations between Jack and my parents and he refused to let them back in the house. In the end, I had to find them a house to rent back up North.

They packed up all their belongings and drove up there. I'd go to visit them and when I left them to drive back down the M1 again I was heartbroken. I missed having them around so much.

The kids really missed having their grandparents around too. They were so close. Throughout all the mayhem of the last years and all the personal problems we'd been through, my mum and dad had been a constant in their lives and the kids were beside themselves when they moved so far away.

The only good news around the start of 2006 was that my acting career was building up.

My next audition was for a part in a late night spin-off of *Hollyoaks*, called *Hollyoaks: In the City*, written and produced by Daran Little, who is now a good friend of mine. I went up for the part of a high-class escort who would be appearing in two episodes. To my surprise, I got it and I was chuffed to bits.

But just before I was about to start filming, Vivien called me.

'I've got you an audition for *Coronation Street*,' she said.

'Oh my God,' I replied. 'What is it?'

'Well, it's only for four episodes, but who knows what might happen?'

It probably sounds awful, but I was actually a bit disappointed. I was worried that if I got the part and appeared in four episodes then that would totally scupper my chances of getting a bigger role in the show in the future. And more than anything I wanted to land a long-term role in *Corrie*.

'You'll be perfect for the job,' Vivien said. 'It's to play a singer who comes in to audition to be in Liz McDonald's boyfriend's band.'

But I was terrified that if I landed the part this would be my first and last appearance in *Corrie*.

*

Things were pretty hectic around then because I'd also agreed to compete in the *Making Your Mind Up* contest to choose the British entry for the Eurovision Song Contest. I really was totally over the music industry but Chris Herbert, who was still managing the music side of my career, thought it could be good for me.

'But isn't Eurovision just totally cheesy?' I asked him. 'Will this really help my career?'

'It'll be fun,' Chris insisted.

So I went along with it. Chris arranged for me to sing a song called 'Whisper to Me' which had been written by the guy who wrote 'Pure and Simple'. Have to say, it was a really lovely tune. I sang live and it all went really well, although I didn't win. To be honest, I was pretty happy I didn't. By then I'd set my heart on acting. The contest was won in the end by Daz Sampson, who sang 'Teenage Life' surrounded by four dancers dressed up as schoolgirls. I thought it was all a bit sleazy, but obviously someone liked it!

I was down in London for the launch of *Making Your Mind Up* on the day they wanted me to audition for *Corrie*. There was no way I was going to be able to get up to Manchester in time so they agreed for someone to see me the following day at the ITV studios in London.

I'd already been told I had to learn how to sing 'Time After Time' by Cyndi Lauper, because that's what my character would be performing on-screen. I wasn't worried about the singing part of the audition, but the acting terrified me. I didn't really think I had a hope in hell of getting the part. I didn't think they'd really want some girl who was already known to the public for being in Hear'Say. *Coronation Street* just didn't tend to use people who were already recognisable like that. It wasn't their thing.

I did the audition as best as I could but then I went home and put it out of my mind. I honestly didn't think I would hear any more about it.

Then a couple of days later I got a phone call from Vivien. *Coronation Street* wanted me.

'Oh my God,' I started screaming. I couldn't quite believe it. It was still only four episodes but it was *Cor-o-na-tion Street*!! The country's biggest show.

Jack was with me when I got the news and he was delighted for me. And when I rang Mum she was chuffed to bits – she'd always been a massive *Corrie* fan. Now her daughter was going to be in her favourite show!

I arranged to go and stay with Mum and Dad for a few days while I was filming my episodes.

On my first morning at *Coronation Street*, Dad dropped me down at Granada Studios again, which brought back memories of when Mum had stood and queued with me almost six years earlier when I'd gone to the same place for my first *Popstars* audition.

And this time I was even more nervous than I had been way back then.

'Good luck, babe,' Dad called out as I got out the front seat of his car. 'Just give us a ring when you want to be picked up.'

'Thanks, Dad.' I was so scared but dead excited too.

I went inside the studio gates and one of the production team introduced me to the rest of the crew. Everyone was absolutely lovely to me, but I was still a bag of nerves.

The make-up department was being renovated at the time so I had to go to a caravan outside to have my face done. Then someone showed me to the visiting artists' dressing room, which was where all the temporary cast members got changed.

Then I had to go and sit in the green room and wait to be called. I was sat there feeling sick with nerves when the actor William Roache walked past me.

I was like, *Oh my God, it's Ken Barlow. It's Ken Barlow!!* I'd grown up watching him on the telly. I'd watched him setting off to work at the *Weatherfield Recorder*, I remembered his affair with Wendy Crozier and I'd sat through all those rows with Deirdre while Tracy was upstairs listening to her tapes!

Everywhere I looked there were more familiar faces, people that I'd seen in our front room for years and years. Now they were here in the flesh, right in front of me. My favourite character had always been Liz McDonald. I think she's hilarious – and her dress sense is really something else!

My very first scene was going to be with Liz, so that was quite scary. But when Beverley Callard, who plays Liz, came over to me that first day I discovered she was a real sweetheart.

'Now don't be nervous,' she said, putting her arm around me. She must have been able to see the sheer terror on my face. Beverley was so kind that day, trying to put me at ease. Since then she has become one of my best mates.

From the scripts I'd been sent I knew I was going to be playing a character called Michelle who was auditioning to be in Vernon Tomlin's band. Vernon was going out with Liz, who wanted to be the lead singer herself. So of course when Michelle turned up it was going to be a proper catfight.

I was also well aware that there would be plenty of people who wanted me to fail going into the country's most popular soap. As far as they were concerned, I was 'that girl from Hear'Say', and now I suddenly fancied myself as an actress. But the role of Michelle was a massive opportunity for me and no way was I going to screw it up. I gave it everything. I learnt my lines really carefully and went over them again and again until they were stuck in my head.

Even though Beverley and Ian Reddington, who played Vernon, were lovely, it was still very scary singing in front of them and the crew. It wasn't like recording a single, where you'd be in this quiet studio and you'd know you could do as many takes as you needed. The cameras were rolling and I had to get it right so we could shoot the rest of the episode.

My first scene took place in a pub (not the Rovers!) where the band was supposedly rehearsing. Liz was singing with the band and when she finished I was seen for the first time. The camera focused in on Michelle clapping. Then it was my big moment. I still remember those bloody lines!

Michelle was supposed to say, 'Follow that, as they say,' as if she was dead impressed, then: 'I'm Michelle. I'm not too late, am I?' She then proceeded to get up and sing 'Time After Time', much to Liz's fury.

When the scene was finished, I felt fantastic. I really loved doing it!

My second scene was in the Rovers, which is always tough for someone joining *Corrie*. It's a pretty intimidating set because it's so familiar. Also, you know that over the years all the greats of *Coronation Street* – Bet Lynch, Hilda Ogden.

Annie Walker, Albert Tatlock and Elsie Tanner — have all stood at that bar. It can be very scary to suddenly find yourself there too, walking in their footsteps. In that scene Michelle was shown chatting with Vernon about what kind of music he wanted to make. The camera panned up from my foot and revealed my fishnet tights and short black dress. Then there was a shot of Liz McDonald looking really annoyed. It was pretty funny playing the femme fatale for once!

The storyline went that Liz became more and more jealous of Michelle until the pair of them had a big bust-up. Michelle told Liz that she had never been interested in her fella and then she disappeared out of the show again.

As far as the plot was concerned, Michelle was still in Vernon's band, but she wasn't seen on-screen again. So after I wrapped up my four episodes, I said goodbye to the cast and crew and left the set – perhaps for good. That was when the waiting game began. I'd done my best, but was it enough? Would I be asked back?

The Granada press office had asked me to do interviews for magazines because it was a bit of a talking point that a former Hear'Say band member was going into the soap for a while. The press officers kept saying things like, 'Who knows? If things go well you could be around for ages.' I just kept my fingers crossed.

I desperately hoped I would be asked back but, realistically, I had to accept that four episodes was probably my lot.

When my first *Corrie* scenes were screened, me, Jack and the kids sat round and watched the episode together. When the credits rolled up, and my name was there under 'Michelle', I felt really proud.

Next I started rehearsing then filming my spell as Kay, the escort in the *Hollyoaks* spin-off. It was then that I had to do my first screen kiss – with another woman!

I was dead nervous about it but the actress I was kissing said: 'Don't worry, I've done it before. It'll be fine.'

But then when I leant in to kiss her, she clammed her lips tight shut.

Oh! I thought, a bit offended. Surely I wasn't that bad?

During the gig playing an escort, Vivien got a phone call saying I might get called back to *Corrie*, but I still felt it was too much to hope for. But *Hollyoaks: In the City* asked me if I could carry on there too. It was a fantastic opportunity, but Vivien felt we should hang on just a bit longer in case *Coronation Street* came back with an offer.

The waiting seemed to go on for weeks and *Hollyoaks: In the City* wanted to find out if I was going to be staying or not. Money was still tight and I was scared that I might hold on too long and lose that job too.

Finally, in June 2006, Vivien got a phone call from the *Coronation Street* casting director. They definitely wanted me back.

When Vivien called me with the news I was at home cooking the kids' tea. The minute she said they wanted me as a regular character I started screaming in the kitchen. I was over the moon.

It was just two years since I'd gone into *Saturday Night Fever* in the West End, my first real acting job, and since then I'd worked my way up to a part in the country's biggest soap. It was just amazing.

When I rang my parents and told them, they were so happy for me. They were absolutely delighted.

'Oh I wish your grandma was still here,' Mum said, getting all tearful. 'She was such a big *Coronation Street* fan, she'd have been thrilled.'

It's only when a character becomes a regular in *Corrie* that they get a surname. And so that was when Michelle became Michelle Connor.

Soon after I was called in for a meeting with *Coronation Street* producer Steve November, who I'd first met at the auditions for *The Royal*. He told me a bit more about Michelle's character. He said Michelle was going to be a barmaid who'd been recommended to Fred Elliott by Vernon and that she would become Steve McDonald's love interest.

Steve Frost then explained that soon after my arrival the viewers would also be introduced to my son and two brothers who would be taking over the factory.

There was certainly plenty of scope for drama.

My contract was initially for six months, with the option of it being extended for another six months and then another year after that. So potentially it could be two years. It was a dream come true.

There was no way I could commute from St Albans though and be away from the kids all week. We would have to move to Manchester all together. Jack and I had always agreed that we would move to be close to work for whichever of us got a steady job first.

I could tell Jack was understandably nervous about the thought of moving so far away from his family, but he agreed.

Work hadn't picked up much for him and I felt really bad for him because it must have been hard. Before we left St Albans he had landed a role in *Family Affairs*. But then he discovered the show was being canned and decided it wasn't worth taking the part. He did have some theatre work and when he was doing that he was just like his old self again. I just desperately hoped he'd get offered something permanent.

David was eleven and due to start secondary school that September, so we decided to wait until the summer holidays so as not to disrupt him too much.

I wasn't sure how the kids would react, and David was a bit nervous about it. He isn't as confident as Emily and it was a bigger deal for him. Emily was only in Year Three and although she was sad about leaving her friends I knew she'd soon settle into her new school. Being nearer to their dad would be great for them too.

We put our house on the market and quickly got an offer. Then we just had to find somewhere up North. We looked in a village called Appleton near Warrington, because it was only forty minutes for me to get in to work, there were good schools around there and it was close to my parents and Dave, the kids' dad.

Mum and Dad were going to look after the children again for me while I was working. Jack was still going to be at home all day, but he was still looking for work. He hadn't been thrilled about the move so I wanted to make things easier on him.

I split the money I got out of our house in St Albans into two and put down deposits on two places – a family home for me, Jack and the kids in Appleton, and a house for Mum and Dad in Runcorn. I'd put a big deposit down on the St Albans house from my Hear'Say earnings. But still, when I used that money to buy the house up North, I made sure it was in both our names. However rocky things had been between me and Jack, I never thought we'd break up. We were a family, and I wanted to keep it that way.

I was determined to make my marriage work. I still wanted what my mum and dad had got – to be with someone for the rest of my life. For a while I'd even thought that Jack and I might have a baby together one day, but he was never keen on the idea and I didn't push it.

Obviously things weren't great between us but I still loved Jack. The worry was that with all the rows and tensions between us it was getting harder and harder to keep that love alive.

18
WALKING AWAY

·········

Michelle Connor was hurled straight into the thick of it on *Coronation Street* with an ongoing will-they/won't-they relationship with Steve McDonald.

At the beginning Michelle was going out with a guy called Sonny who, it turned out, had been having a gay affair with her mate Sean Tully. It was totally brilliant being at the centre of such beefy storylines, and getting to do emotional scenes where I had to scream and shout and cry. I never found crying on-set difficult. I'd just go away and have a bit of quiet time to get myself feeling melancholy then go back and do the scene. Pretty soon I'd be crying like a baby.

Working behind the bar at the Rovers also meant I got to work with lots of different cast members straight away. I actually felt like I slotted in pretty quickly. The people I was working with most of the time, like Beverley Callard, Simon Gregson and Antony Cotton, were fabulous – brilliant actors and top people too.

Me and Beverley often found it hard to do scenes together

because we were laughing so much. I always seemed to have to give her bad news, and every time I did it we'd get the giggles. We just cracked each other up.

I'd been a bit worried about uprooting my family, but in the end the kids settled into their new schools well. Plus it meant being back up North and the kids being nearer to their Dad. It was a bit harder for David at first because he was starting secondary school and he got a bit of stick for having a mum in *Corrie*, but gradually he found his feet. Little Emily was fine from the beginning. She's more confident than her brother, and everyone always wanted to be her friend.

It was great living near the rest of my family again too.

The only bad thing was that we quickly realised we'd made a bit of a mistake with the house we bought. It was a nice enough place but it was quite small and we all felt a bit cooped up in there.

Jack joined a gym around the corner and we even made friends with some people in our road who had children at the same schools as David and Emily. I thought we were settling in well, but Jack wasn't happy up North. He missed his family and even though they came to visit he still wanted to be back down South, which I fully understood.

Jack landed another theatre tour, which was great. Then, finally, he got a break when he landed a role in a new daily ITV medical soap, *The Royal Today*. It was his first big television job since leaving *EastEnders* and we were both made up. But just a couple of weeks into filming they let him go, saying it wasn't his fault, but they'd made a mistake with the casting. They said he looked too young for the character they had in mind.

Jack was devastated. He'd had such a bad run of luck and now he was back to square one. By then it was three years since Jack had done any television work and he was feeling really down. It was so unfair because he was so talented, but even though I was trying to keep his spirits up I just felt that he resented me for having a job.

It reached the point where Jack didn't want *Coronation Street* being on in the house. I'd always watched all the soaps and I'd grown up watching *Corrie*, but now it just wasn't worth the hassle.

The whole situation was really awkward and again I felt like I was treading on eggshells around the house. I loved my job, but I didn't want to rub his nose in it.

Right from the start, the response I got from the public was incredible. You can never, ever overestimate how popular *Coronation Street* is in this country. It's like being in the Royal Family!

Even though I'd had people recognise me in the street when I was in *Popstars* and Hear'Say, that was nothing to the recognition I got once I joined *Corrie*. Everyone you meet has a view on your character and storyline, and it's fab to feel people care so much about what you're doing.

Michelle Connor and the entire Connor family became really popular with the viewers. I couldn't believe it. After all the bad press I had after I left Hear'Say it was nice to feel like people liked me! But I was still really shocked the following year when I was nominated for a string of awards. I was even more stunned when I actually won some of them.

My first nomination was for Best Newcomer at the TV

Now Awards in Dublin. Jack couldn't come so I invited Mum as my guest. It was lovely to have mum there as it was the first award I'd ever won.

Then soon afterwards I was nominated for Best Newcomer again at the British Soap Awards. This was a big one for me. Jack agreed to come with me for the ceremony down in London. I was crazy with nerves and excitement and when I heard the words: 'And the winner is . . . Kym Ryder,' I nearly collapsed. I leant over and kissed Jack and then went up to collect my award. I felt like my feet didn't touch the ground.

That year I also won Best Newcomer in the *TV Quick* Awards and at the Television and Radio Industries Club (TRIC) Awards. And I was also nominated for best actress and for best couple with Simon Gregson at the *Inside Soap* Awards.

It was absolutely amazing. But Jack never came to any more awards ceremonies with me after the Soap Awards.

He said he hated going to them and I didn't push the point. That hurt though. I loved my husband and I wanted him by my side.

To make matters worse, I got the impression that he didn't really like me going to those awards dos either. He didn't like it when my mum sometimes put my awards on the side in our front room either. You know what mums are like, she was just very proud. She's still got my certificate from when I came third in the egg and spoon race, and I've definitely kept everything David and Emily have ever won.

Secretly, I felt crushed that the awards seemed to annoy him so much. For years the thought of getting a part on television had seemed like a total impossibility. Now I'd snagged a great role, and was even winning awards for it, but I wasn't allowed to enjoy it.

I did feel bad for Jack because it was awful for him not working and very, very unfair. But no matter how much I tried to make him happy there was nothing I could do to fix his work situation. And I had to keep working, we needed the money. Plus I loved my job and the people I worked with.

Even at home things were changing. He'd always been great with the kids, but now he seemed different towards them and the kids really felt it.

Things were getting worse but I kept on trying, hoping that once he got a job things would get better. I felt like I was spending all my spare time trying to reassure him. I loved him but it was taking it out of me.

Then in October 2007 I was nominated for Best Newcomer to Television at the National TV Awards. The ceremony's held at the Royal Albert Hall and it's really prestigious.

I was down to the final four contenders for the award and I was really excited. But Jack decided not to come so I took Mum instead.

I had a full-length red Philip Armstrong dress, which was split to the thigh, made for me specially. I felt amazing and when the newspapers printed their verdicts on all the frocks the next day it got a thumbs up from everyone. That's always a massive relief!

That night Mum and I sat in our seats at the Albert Hall shaking with excitement.

I really didn't expect to win because I was up against some really good people: Jo Joyner from *EastEnders*, Joe Gilgun from *Emmerdale* and Gemma Merna from *Hollyoaks*.

The guys who played Max and Bradley in *EastEnders* were presenting the award and when they read out the names of the final four I could feel my heart beating really fast.

Then suddenly I heard the words 'winner' and 'Kym Ryder'. It was just mad. I could not believe it. Mum started crying and all the cast of *Corrie* were up on their feet as I made my way to the stage.

I'd written a speech just in case I won, but I really hadn't given it much thought because I was so convinced that I wouldn't. Then when I got up in front of all those people my mind just went blank. All I could think was 'Oh my God, I'm standing up in the Albert Hall'. I thanked everyone at *Coronation Street* and all my family for supporting me and the public for their support and for voting for me and then my legs were trembling so much I thought I'd better sit down.

I was ushered off the stage and into a press room at the side where each winner was interviewed and had their picture taken. I was still shaking with excitement when this woman reporter stood up and said, 'I know you thanked your family, Kym, but don't you think you should have thanked Jack personally?'

'Why?' I was a little confused because as far as I was concerned Jack *was* my family. Not only that, but her tone was a bit off, like she was trying to get a rise out of me or something.

'Well, I mean you wouldn't be able to do what you're doing if it wasn't for him, would you?' she said, smiling slyly.

What a bitch! She didn't know the first thing about what was going on in my life. There were so many people shouting out questions that I pretended I hadn't heard her, but her words kept ringing in my ears. That must be what people thought about me. But I *had* thanked Jack because he *was* my family. And really it was my parents who looked after the children most of the time when I was working. If I'd had to thank every one of the people who had helped my career, I'd have been on stage for hours!

I walked out of the press room and burst into floods of tears. My biggest moment had been ruined. I felt like someone had let all the air out of me.

I immediately rang Jack on my mobile phone and told him what the journalist had asked.

'Well,' he said. 'She had a point.'

And that was it for me. I was done.

I'd tried to support Jack and keep him happy for years and years, then, at the biggest point in my career, he didn't even congratulate me. It felt like he sided with the random journalist instead.

I felt totally let down. It seemed that whatever I did for Jack, it was never going to be enough.

I found my mum and told her what had happened and she gave me a hug. We went to the after-show party, but on what should have been one of the best nights of my life I had to work hard to keep a smile on my face.

That evening when I got into bed, I thought, *This is no good. Any love I have left for Jack is draining away.*

By then we were about to move into a new home together near Runcorn. It was further from work for me but we still only had one wage coming in and it was the best place we could get for the money we could afford. We were still having to be quite careful about what we spent.

Maybe we shouldn't have gone through with the house move

when the marriage was in such a bad way.

But we limped on together.

If anyone ever asked me to go for a drink after work I didn't even bother to make excuses any more. I'd just say: 'Thanks, but no, I can't come.' And I didn't bother asking Jack if he ever wanted to go to dos with me because I knew what the answer would be.

Work was still really busy and at the end of 2007 I was at the centre of a massive storyline, when it emerged that Michelle's son Ryan had been swapped at birth with another boy, Alex, who was actually her real child. I was averaging twelve or thirteen scenes a day at that point, which meant days lasting at least twelve hours. Then I'd get home at night, see the kids and get on with learning my lines for the next day.

Fortunately learning my lines never bothered me too much. I'd been memorising song lyrics all my life and it was similar to that. Lucky really, or else I'd have been in trouble!

It was hard work but I loved having such dramatic scenes to really get my teeth into. And it took my mind off what was going on with Jack, too.

Then at the start of 2008, Jack got some more work on another theatre tour and was away from home for weeks at a time. He was chuffed to have landed the job and I was happy for him.

One evening I called him as normal. The conversation was fine at first, but then I mentioned that I was going out for dinner the following night with a married couple I had met.

'Why are you going out with them?' he snapped.

'Well, they invited me and I thought it might be nice,' I replied.

'But you don't even know them.'

'But going out with people is how you get to know them,' I said, feeling myself getting a bit pissed off. I was a grown woman, for goodness' sake!

'Well I think it's ridiculous going out with people you hardly know,' he muttered.

And then I just lost it.

'I'm going out,' I shouted. 'So is that all right? Is it all right if I have a life?'

Jack started shouting back at me, and I knew there was no turning back now, even if I'd wanted to. It was too late. The moment had finally come.

I took a deep breath. 'I'm sick of this,' I said. 'I've just had enough of it. I can't cope with this any more.'

There was silence for a beat. 'I agree,' Jack said, finally. 'We can't go on like this.'

Finally we were both admitting our true feelings and as I hung up I knew that was the end of my marriage.

Thing is, this might sound awful but I wasn't even that upset. It just felt like everything had finally come to a head.

I don't want anyone to think that I am blaming Jack for the marriage breakdown. I made plenty of mistakes over the years. I know I was difficult to live with at times and maybe I hadn't always understood how bad Jack was feeling about being out of work or being away from his family. Maybe I wasn't there for him as much as I should have been and I had ignored the many warning signs that we were not compatible.

But at the time I did feel I'd done everything in my power to make the marriage work. I even changed my personality.

We didn't speak for a couple of days, but we exchanged

text messages and agreed to meet at the hotel in London where I was going to be staying while I was down South filming a TV show.

When we sat down and started talking in the hotel, Jack seemed to be saying that he was willing to try again, and then he said, 'I don't want to be part of your team. When we go out everyone just wants to talk to you and I hate that.'

I knew then that it would never work if we got back together. I had been working to build a life for both of us and the kids – *we* were a team! But he seemed to resent me for that, judging from that statement.

It was definitely over. We didn't discuss divorce at that point but we arranged for him to collect his stuff.

When he left I poured myself a large glass of red wine. If I'm honest, my marriage had been over for a long, long time but now it was official. Along with the sadness came a sense of release; I could feel that dead feeling that I'd had inside me lifting away. It was over. There was nothing else I could do now.

When I rang my parents I think they were quietly relieved that we'd come to a decision. As always, they were there to support me in any way they could.

But I dreaded telling the kids. Emily was ten then, but she'd only been three when me and Jack got together and so it was going to be a big shock for her. I decided to tell her first though, because I was worried David was going to be even more upset because he'd had such a close bond with Jack.

'I've got something to tell you, Emily,' I said, putting my arms around her. 'Me and Jack aren't going to be living together any more.'

'Oh,' she said. 'I'm not really bothered, Mum.'

'You're not bothered?'

'No,' she said casually. 'But are you all right, Mum?'

'I'm fine, darling,' I said. 'I'm just fine.'

Next I told David. His reaction shocked me.

'I'm not surprised,' he said.

'Really,' I said. 'Why?'

'Well, you were arguing a lot,' he said. 'And y'know, Jack changed when we moved up North. He always seemed to be in a bad mood. By any chance were you scared of him Mum?'

At that point I realised then that over the years I had become scared – not physically – but over the years I had got to the point where I was always scared of upsetting him. And that's not a healthy way to live. It took my twelve year old to point that out!

Over the years I had become constantly scared of upsetting Jack and putting him in a bad mood.

I felt sad my marriage hadn't worked out, but I felt a real sense of relief too. I had tried to be someone I wasn't for so long because I thought I could make Jack happy that way. But changing myself hadn't made him happy, and I'd ended up feeling trapped and resentful.

Basically, I had to accept that we hadn't been right for each other from the start.

Since Jack was touring we managed to keep the split under wraps until Easter, when I had booked a holiday away for me, the kids and my mum and dad. We were flying to Cyprus to see my good friend called Alexis Galatariotis, whose family own Le Meridien. It's my escapism at all times and the kids love it! I'd talked to the *Coronation Street* press office and they suggested we should wait on putting out a statement until we were just about to leave. That way we would hopefully escape most of the media attention.

So that's what we did. The press statement went out on Good Friday morning and we flew off on holiday that evening. I didn't read any newspapers while I was away and it was brilliant because we were able to totally get away from it all.

It was only when we got back that I saw the way the story had been perceived by people who'd read about it. It seemed again 'Big Bad Kym' had screwed over 'Poor Young Jack'. I knew it wasn't true, but still, it was gutting because the reality of our marriage had been very different. I had made mistakes but we both had. Some people even reckoned I'd dumped Jack because he wasn't working but that couldn't have been further from the truth, and besides, we'd been together for three years after he left *EastEnders*.

Jack was an important part of my life and I really loved the guy. I never wanted him to be unhappy or insecure and I don't think he deserved to be out of work or some of the cards he'd been dealt.

Also, I know I'm no saint myself and I made many mistakes. In fact, I'm sure I was a bloody nightmare to live with at times.

But when we split up, I felt everyone was blaming me. It takes two to tango. I was still being depicted as the manipulative older woman while he was supposed to be this innocent little boy being pushed around all the time. I just hope that by telling my side of the story I can make people understand that things aren't always the way they appear from the outside.

19
NEW LOVE
AND FRESH HEARTBREAK

....

Single life was great. Really great.

I was getting up in the morning, going to work at a job I loved, then coming home and having a great time with the kids. There was no stress, no hassles and I didn't have to answer to anyone.

I was also going out sometimes with my mates from *Coronation Street* – Beverley Callard, Antony Cotton and Ali King – and having a right laugh. I felt like I had my life back.

Jack and I had agreed we would wait for two years and have a 'no fault' divorce, but beyond that we'd had no contact. I'd said he could see David and Emily whenever he wanted and their dad, Dave, had even offered for Jack to see them at his house if that was easier. Jack said he wanted to, but he hasn't really made a huge effort to stay in touch with the kids. There have been a few text messages, the occasional card on their birthdays and Christmas but other than that no attempt to visit them.

I'm not going to lie: that did upset me but more to the point, it upset the children. He was there for seven years of their lives, and now he has no real contact with them and he has not seen them since.

I was enjoying being on my own. I certainly had no intention of getting into another relationship for quite some time.

But then in May of 2008, just three months after I'd split with Jack, I met Jamie Lomas.

We were at the after-show party for the Soap Awards at a hotel in Kensington when he came over and started chatting to me. We'd been talking and giggling for a while when he said 'Ah, Kym Lomas. That's got a nice ring to it.'

If that's not a chat-up line, I don't know what is!

I'd actually met him briefly a year earlier when he'd been on the same train as a gang of us from *Corrie* when we were on our way down to London for another awards do.

He'd come up and introduced himself because he used to work with Alison King on *Dream Team*. I'd thought he was pretty gorgeous then, but I was married at the time.

But when I met him again at the Soap Awards I was very much single. Jamie had been nominated for Best Villain for his role as *Hollyoaks*' bad boy Warren Fox. I had been nominated for Best Actress and Sexiest Female.

I'd gone to the do with my mum but she had gone to bed, so I was standing chatting to my mate from *Saturday Night Fever*, Gerard McCarthy, who was then in *Hollyoaks* with Jamie. Ali King was also there and Jamie's mum and his sister Cassie, who's a successful make-up artist. His other sister

Charley, who plays Debbie Dingle in *Emmerdale*, and is now one of my best friends, had just gone to bed.

We were having a great time and Jamie was really making me laugh. I have no doubt now that he was only trying to get me into bed. He'll even admit it himself!

But by four in the morning I was shattered and said I was going to turn in.

'Oh yeah, me too,' said Jamie, following me up the stairs. 'Do you wanna come back to my room?' he asked, cheekily.

'Yeah, all right,' I said. I really liked him but I knew what I was doing – and what I was not going to do!

We talked for a while and had just started on about tattoos when he casually stripped his top off to show me this gorgeous Indian tattoo on his back. I think he thought one glimpse of his hot body and I'd be falling into bed. Tempting! He was a good-looking fella all right, but I wasn't about to do that.

Not yet, anyway.

I guarantee that if I'd slept with Jamie that night I would never have seen him again. That's how lots of men are. I did show him my panther tattoo on my bum (which he now refers to as my Slaz badge as it's a bit rubbish and resembles a Slazenger logo!), but then we just had a quick kiss and I went back to my own room.

Earlier in the evening I'd had a call from the *Coronation Street* press office saying a story was going in the following day's papers about me and the former footballer Lee Sharpe. We'd been on the judging panel together at the Miss Manchester contest earlier in the week and now the newspapers were saying I'd gone back to his hotel afterwards.

We had been flirting with each other quite a bit that night

and had a bit of a snog, but I was single, so what did it matter? And I had gone back to his hotel – but that was where everyone was staying! And I certainly hadn't slept with him, I was sharing a hotel room with my cousin. But sure enough the story was all over the papers the next day with my picture and the headline: 'Lee Sharpe: Did he Ryder?' Even I had to admit that was quite funny.

I'd told Jamie that evening that the story was appearing and that there was nothing in it. But maybe reading it the next morning had made him think it wasn't worth the hassle of getting involved with me.

When I checked my phone there was a text message from him saying, 'Hi. Nice to see you last night. I've been thinking, maybe better we don't see each other again in that way. Don't really want to be involved in all this newspaper stuff.'

Fair enough, I thought. Nothing had happened between us anyway, so it really wasn't a big deal.

I figured that was going to be my one and only look at that tattoo. Shame! 'OK' I text, 'No problem.'

Mum and I were flying home that day so I turned my phone off and we boarded the plane for Manchester. When we landed and I switched my mobile back on there was another chatty little message from Jamie.

I was a bit surprised – I thought he didn't want to get involved!!

After that we texted each other a few times and we met a couple of times at parties. We tried to meet a couple of times on our own but things kept happening to mess up our plans. Once I was followed from work by some paparazzi guys so rather than drive to meet Jamie I went round and round a roundabout deciding what to do before just heading for home.

So the next time Jamie and I saw each other properly was the following month when we sat at the same table at a charity dinner where I'd been asked to sing in aid of Claire House Children's Hospice in Merseyside.

At first we were a bit wary of setting tongues wagging and were at opposite sides of the table, but by the end Jamie was sitting next to me and we were all over each other, so we were clearly pretty friendly!

That was the night that we really got together properly. For a few months though we were very discreet, because we just weren't ready for everyone to know about us. When you're in the public eye you do have to be a bit careful, because if the papers find out you're dating someone then you break up two months later, the whole thing is so much more awkward. Dating is hard enough without a running commentary from the sidelines!

Most importantly, I wanted to make sure David and Emily were OK about the relationship before everyone else knew. After a few weeks I told them I'd met someone but it was still early days, and if and when the time was right I would introduce them to him. I didn't want to bring Jamie home unless I knew it was serious. I didn't want to cause any more upset in their lives, but they were both so cool about it.

'We just want you to be happy, Mum,' David said. What a sweetheart!

The relationship between me and Jamie became serious really quickly and in the end it wasn't very long before he met my kids and I met his little boy, Billy.

Jamie had split with his ex-girlfriend the year before we met. Billy was two when I first met him, and absolutely gorgeous. Jamie checked with Billy's mum first and she said it was fine for us to meet. I bought him a little toy and then sat and played with him and we got on really well. Seeing Jamie and Billy together I could see what a good dad he was, and I found that incredibly attractive.

Soon afterwards I took Jamie to meet David and Emily at a Pizza Express near our house. Again, they got on brilliantly. The kids were a bit quiet at first but soon they were chattering away like no one's business.

Next, we took all three of the children to the zoo together, so David and Emily could get to know Billy. They absolutely adored him and Billy just thought the sun shone out of David.

David and Emily also have a little brother from their dad's new relationship. It means they're used to having little ones around and they dote on both their kid brothers.

Within a couple of months Jamie and I were at each other's houses almost all the time. It was all pretty quick, coming so soon after the end of my marriage, and I think Mum and Dad were worried I was rushing into things.

But I just wanted to follow my feelings. It seemed mad to put the blockers on this relationship just because the last one had gone wrong. Jamie was an entirely different person from my ex. In fact Jamie and Jack were like chalk and cheese.

Jamie's a real man's man. He loves being with me but he loves seeing his mates too, which is pretty healthy, I reckon. And he's also great fun to be with. We have a real laugh together, which is what I found so attractive in the first place.

Three months after we met, Jamie moved into our house

in Runcorn. It had five bedrooms, which meant Billy could have his own room – he spends three nights a week with Jamie. And we just about managed to squeeze in all Jamie's clothes and trainers too!

We'd only been together for a few months when Jamie announced he was quitting *Hollyoaks*. He'd been fantastic in it, but he'd been thinking about leaving for a while. He felt his character had run its course – after all, he had already murdered three people!

Now Jamie wanted to try other things, which was totally fair. Despite what had happened with Jack I completely supported his decision.

But then in September of that year, just as Jamie was moving in and leaving *Hollyoaks*, we had another major piece of news – I was pregnant!

My doctor had suggested I should come off the Pill for a while to give my body a break from it, so when my period was late, I thought it must just be to do with that. But when it still hadn't come a few days later I decided to do a pregnancy test. It came up negative.

A couple of days later I did another test. Still it was negative.

But deep down I had a feeling that maybe something was going on.

Jamie had gone away on a football trip with some mates, so I'd travelled down to London to go out with Katie and Vince, and Jamie's mum, Helen Webb, came too. I get on so well with Helen and Jamie's sisters that they're more like mates than in-laws. We were all staying in a hotel that evening, but I was spending some time in the afternoon appearing on a kids TV show. On the way to the hotel, I rang my friend Katie Roddy who'd been my dresser on *Saturday Night Fever* and asked her to pick up another test on her way.

As soon as she arrived at the hotel I did the test. This time there was the faintest of faint lines stretching across the tiny window. But I knew any line meant it was positive – the pregnancy must just be at a really early stage.

Oh my God, I thought as I looked at the test. I was excited but pretty scared too. Jamie and I had talked about how nice it would be to have a baby together, but there was a big difference between saying something like that and it actually happening!

During the evening I took Helen to one side and told her the result of the test. I thought she'd be shocked but she was really pleased, for both of us.

I didn't want to break the news to Jamie over the phone, so I waited for him to get back from his trip.

He'd barely walked in the door when I blurted out, 'I'm pregnant.'

He looked at me. 'Right,' he said, really deadpan. That's Jamie, for you.

Neither of us could quite believe it. But once the immediate shock had worn off we were both very happy.

It was strange, but in all the years I'd been with Jack I'd never pushed the issue of having a baby. With Jamie I had to admit that I liked the idea.

We knew we loved each other and I think we both had this little romantic idea that if it happened, it happened, and that would be all good.

I don't think either of us thought *it* would happen quite so quickly, but that didn't stop us being dead chuffed.

I was about five weeks pregnant when I was at work one morning and suddenly felt a sharp pain in the right side of my stomach. Then I started to bleed.

I panicked. Something was obviously horribly wrong.

I hadn't told anyone that I was pregnant at that stage, but I got myself to the medical centre at Granada and told them what was happening. I suddenly felt terrified that I was miscarrying and going to lose the baby.

Our nurse at Granada, a lovely lady called Corin who helped me throughout the pregnancy, sent me straight to the early pregnancy unit at the hospital. There I lay down on a bed and they gave me a blood test. By then the pain had subsided and the bleeding had almost stopped, so I wasn't sure what to think.

A midwife introduced herself to me as Heather and told me she was concerned the pregnancy might be ectopic. She explained I would need another blood test the following day to measure the levels of pregnancy hormone in me. If it had gone up then it was OK. If it hadn't, the pregnancy was over.

The following day Heather came to Granada Studios to carry out the blood test. Later on she called me to say my pregnancy hormone had tripled. I was so relieved I wanted to cry.

I think that scare proved to both me and Jamie how much we wanted our baby. But I still didn't feel confident about the pregnancy. Something inside me always warned that I would never have that baby. Even when I tried really hard I couldn't imagine him or her being there with the rest of us. And the strange thing is that much later Jamie admitted he'd felt the same way, and weirdly so did his sister Charley. But at the time none of us told each other about our fears. We all put a brave face on it.

Over the next few weeks I had more pains and small bleeds that only made me more worried. But each time I was scanned at the early pregnancy unit the baby seemed to be growing. The *Coronation Street* costume department even had to change my costumes because I was showing so soon.

Only when we got a healthy scan at twelve weeks did I feel ready to sit down with David and Emily and tell them the news. I was concerned about how they would feel about it, because it was going to mean a big change to all our lives. But when I told them, Emily screamed, ran across the room and hugged me.

'Nice one,' said David.

From then on Emily would kiss my stomach every night before she went to bed. She was so excited; she just couldn't wait for the baby to come.

The baby was a really lively little thing and from early on I could feel him kicking me ever so hard.

At eighteen weeks I went for another scan and got a DVD to take home of him moving around inside me. I hadn't found out the sex of my other two children in advance, but this time I wanted to know. I thought it would be nice if it was a little girl so that Jamie would have one of each, but I didn't really mind.

'Oh no, it's definitely a boy,' laughed the sonographer, pointing at the scan, 'there's no mistaking that!'

Jamie and I were just happy to know that everything was going well.

But just three weeks later I started getting pain quite low in my stomach. It was a Sunday evening and I was just coming home after a meal out with Mum, Dad, Jamie and the kids, when I felt the baby kick me really hard. The baby could never keep still, but this time it didn't seem right because the kick felt like it was right down in my pelvis. It was surely too low.

Then I started getting this milky fluid leaking out of me. I wasn't sure what it was. I was back in work first thing Monday but at the first possible moment I called the maternity triage at Trafford General Hospital.

'It's probably just an infection,' the midwife said, 'just come down and see us.'

'I need to go to the hospital because I'm not feeling too well,' I told one of the assistant directors I was working with. They were fine about me going but I knew it was massively inconvenient for them because they needed me for a couple of scenes. I felt really guilty dropping them in it like that.

'I guess I can stay,' I said, changing my mind.

I nipped into the loo but then, just as I was making my way back to start filming the scene, I suddenly felt loads of this milky liquid pouring out of me.

I knew something was wrong.

'I'm going,' I said. 'I've got to go. Now.'

One of the floor managers took me to the medical centre and Jamie drove down to pick me up and take me over to Trafford General.

In the car I felt a bit better.

'You're such a drama queen,' Jamie laughed. 'You're worrying about nothing.'

'I know, I know,' I said. 'You're probably right.'

When I got to the hospital they tested the sanitary pad I'd been wearing to see if I had been leaking amniotic fluid, because that would mean that the sac the baby was in had been ruptured.

They came back and said it didn't appear to be amniotic fluid, so that was a relief. It was only later that I was told testing the pad was not always an accurate way of assessing whether I was leaking amniotic fluid.

There were two midwives in the room with us and one of them then said she wanted to examine me. I'll remember what happened next for the rest of my life.

She had just begun when she suddenly turned to her colleague with a look of total horror on her face.

'What's the matter?' I said. 'Tell me. What's going on?'

'Don't worry,' said the nurse, trying to sound reassuring. 'I've just got to get the consultant to come in and have a look.'

By this point I was very scared. The nurse had looked really, really worried.

It seemed to take ages for the consultant to arrive. When she finally got there she examined me and then said quietly, 'Oh dear.'

'What do you mean, "Oh dear"?' I asked.

'Your cervix has dilated by about two centimetres and the amniotic bag that the baby is in is hanging out,' she said.

I still didn't really understand what was going on. All I wanted to know at that point was whether my baby was going to be all right.

'So what does it mean?' I asked. 'Please.'

I was desperate. Suddenly I felt that my baby was slipping away from me and it was all totally out of my control.

'Well,' said the consultant. 'You're in labour as we speak, so we could leave it and see what happens, but the likelihood is you will give birth very soon. Or we could take you into theatre, and try to push the baby back in gently then put a stitch in the neck of your womb and hope that sorts out the problem.'

I started to cry. I knew that twenty-one weeks was far too soon for a baby to be born – he'd have no chance of survival.

Jamie and I were both panicking about what to do.

'But what are the statistics?' I said. 'What are his chances of making it?'

'If you carry on as you are the baby will probably be born very soon,' the consultant said. 'And that, I'm afraid, is too early in the pregnancy for him to survive. If we put the stitch in there's a greater chance he will stay inside you. But I have to warn you, there is the danger we will introduce infection by putting in the stitch and that can cause miscarriage and there's no guarantee it will be successful anyway.

'Don't worry,' she said, when she saw my face. 'We'll give you a low dose of antibiotics afterwards to try to prevent infection.'

But by then I was already showing signs of having an infection in my blood because I had a temperature and tests showed something was wrong. I was feeling very poorly. It may have been the infection which caused the premature labour, but we'll never know now. Either way I still wasn't put on antibiotics until much later on.

Jamie and I agreed we had to have the stitch to give the baby a chance.

As they took me into surgery to put in the stitch I was so nervous that I began shaking violently. Jamie stayed with me as I was wheeled along the corridor to the operating theatre. 'It's going to be all right, babe,' he said.

The next thing I knew I was waking up in a recovery room with my feet higher than my head.

The consultant said the operation had been successful, but the next twenty-four hours were going to be critical. In that time, we'd see if the labour could be stopped. I would have to lie for the entire time with my legs raised.

I lay awake all night. Jamie had gone home so I was all alone. I thought about our baby and willed him to survive. *Please live, please live*, I kept thinking. This baby was so wanted and so loved already. I couldn't let him go.

I could still feel him kicking and moving around inside me. Surely that meant he was still fighting?

I was boiling hot all night and was sure I had a fever, but they never gave me any antibiotics. I even asked if I was supposed to have had them but the nurse said they weren't necessary.

Then, in the early hours of the morning, I could feel myself start to bleed. It was a horrible sensation.

'Don't worry, it's perfectly normal to bleed after you've had a stitch,' one of the doctors told me.

So I still clung on to the hope that our baby might make it, even though deep down I knew he was in real trouble.

First thing the next morning Jamie arrived at the hospital

with a beautiful pair of new pyjamas for me and a teddy bear for our baby. He'd written him a card saying, 'I Love You, from Daddy.' We were both so desperate for our baby to make it.

Jamie had also brought in a flannel and a towel so he washed my face and looked after me as I lay there, unable to move an inch.

Shortly after Jamie, Mum arrived and sat down next to my bed.

The pair of them had been there about an hour and we were chatting quietly when suddenly I felt this gush of water all around my legs. Fluid was pouring out of me.

My waters had broken.

I immediately knew what that meant. The labour was going ahead. There wasn't any hope for our baby now.

I started screaming. 'Somebody help me, somebody help me,' I yelled. I was hysterical. But still the water kept pouring out of me.

Mum was running around trying to get a nurse while Jamie climbed onto the bed and was holding me as I screamed and screamed. 'It's OK, it's OK, it's OK, babe. It's going to be OK,' he was saying over and over again.

But I knew then that it was never going to be OK for our baby. We'd lost him.

After a few minutes the consultant appeared in the room. 'I'm so sorry,' she said.

I looked at Jamie, tears pouring down both our faces. 'It's going to be OK,' he said. 'I love you.'

The fluid kept pouring out. It felt like it would go on for ever. Listening to the sound of it broke my heart because I knew exactly what it meant. Without the amniotic fluid our baby couldn't survive. As that water drained away, so did our baby's life.

All I could think was, *He's gone, he's gone.*

Our baby was gone.

20
LOSING ARCHIE

....

I could feel my baby still kicking away inside me, as if everything in the world was fine.

That was what hurt the most. That he was still there, alive
and thriving. But in the outside world he was just too tiny to
survive. And there was nothing that could be done now to
stop him being born.

It was then that we decided to name the baby. He had a
battle on his hands and we wanted him to have a name rather
than to keep being referred to as 'baby'. Over the past few
months we'd talked about dozens of names but we both loved
Archie. We agreed on Archie Jay Lomas. Jay is what the people
closest to him call Jamie. It sounded good.

'Now your waters have broken, we're going to have to remove
the stitch in your cervix and let the labour proceed,' the
consultant said.

I couldn't answer. I was just sobbing and sobbing.

'Once the stitch is removed it should happen quite quickly,' the consultant went on. 'But I'm afraid we won't try to resuscitate him.'

I'd already known the situation would be hopeless. I was exactly twenty-one weeks and three days pregnant. Medical guidelines state that babies under twenty-two weeks should not be resuscitated at birth or given intensive care treatment, because they're too premature to survive. Even if the doctors had broken all the rules and resuscitated Archie, and by some miracle he'd survived, he would probably still have been extremely handicapped with severe health problems. He just came too soon.

Having the stitch removed was total agony and the only pain relief was gas and air. Afterwards I just had to lie on the bed and wait for Archie to be born, and to die. We were surrounded by all our family who had rushed to the hospital to be with us.

The contractions kept coming although despite being incredibly painful they weren't as strong or as frequent as they should have been. As many mums will tell you, normally you just cope with the agony because you know you'll have a gorgeous baby at the end of it. I didn't have that. Part of me wanted the labour over as quickly as possible in order to end the pain, but another part of me was terrified of that happening because then Archie really would be gone.

Hour after hour it went on like that. Every now and again a nurse would come in, put her monitor against my tummy and listen to the baby's heartbeat. It was like some sick kind of torture hearing the pumping of his little heart, knowing that I was still keeping him alive but that when I gave birth to him he would die.

We barely spoke. There was nothing anyone could do or say as the contractions came and went, hour after hour.

All our family were devastated but trying to be strong for us.

All through the night the contractions kept coming and going, but they weren't getting any stronger or closer together. My mum sat up all night and watched me, her baby. Every time I woke and opened my eyes, she was there, looking at me and making sure I knew she was there for me. By mid-afternoon the following day I was at my wits' end.

The contractions just weren't strong enough or regular enough to get Archie out. The labour was taking ages because Archie was so small that he couldn't really do much of the work of getting out himself.

But as the hours struggled by it was getting more and more distressing.

At this point we all knew that even if I lay there in agony for as long as I could, there'd still be no hope for him once he was born.

As well as the contractions, I had the infection too. My temperature was high and I felt really sick. And I just couldn't get little Archie out of my mind. It was like being in a nightmare where I couldn't wake up.

Dad picked David and Emily up from school and told them what had happened. They both wanted to come in and see me and I said that was OK.

When they came into the room they both came over and cuddled me, but they didn't say too much. I think they were trying to hold it together for my sake.

Afterwards Dad told me that on the way home, Emily just

cried and cried. David said to him: 'Granddad, I know there's no hope for Archie, but I just want Mum to be OK.'

By early evening I felt like I was going mad. 'For f***'s sake, will somebody please help me,' I screamed. Then I started sobbing all over again. I just couldn't cope with it any more. It was like being in hell.

Mum tried her best to calm me down and then the consultant was called. She came in and examined me yet again and as things were progressing too slowly, and the latest tests showed things were getting worse, she made the decision to give me a pessary to speed up the labour.

She gave me the pessary and then I just had to wait. There was a clock on the wall and I watched as another couple of hours slipped by and the contractions became more intense. I didn't want to speak to anyone or hear what any of the nurses had to say. I certainly didn't want anyone else coming in to the room and saying 'I'm sorry.' None of that would change anything.

They started me on antibiotics through a drip to treat the infection but I still felt terrible. And the pain was getting really bad. Mum had seen every single one of her grandchildren born but she said later that she had never witnessed a labour as traumatic as that. The gas and air wasn't working for a while and the pain was horrific. Eventually Charley and Jamie took turns holding on to the pipe to try and make it work. And then to make matters worse, it broke.

Finally, after what seemed like a lifetime, with one final push Archie came out into the world. He tried to take a breath and then he passed away. At the moment I gave birth to him, I looked up and saw Charley's face. She looked horrified, terrified even. I'll never forget her face.

And then there was just silence.

Absolute silence.

It was the silence that haunted me. No baby screaming, no doctors and nurses running around. Just silence.

It was 9.41pm on Wednesday 11 February 2009. Archie hadn't been due to be born until 19 June.

The midwife laid him on my chest and everyone started to cry.

I was in such a state that I was violently sick and started shaking uncontrollably. I handed Archie to Jamie for a cuddle and they put a big tinfoil blanket around me.

He was tiny but perfect. He had died the moment he came into the outside world but he was still warm, so warm. And so beautiful. He had a few strands of hair and tiny eyelashes.

He never opened his eyes and so he looked as if he was asleep with his mouth just slightly open. He was very bruised from the labour but other than that, he was perfect.

That's what made it so traumatic – he was a totally formed baby, but he hadn't made it.

I looked at him for ages and cried and cried. I really thought my heart would break.

I passed Archie to his daddy. Jamie held him and kissed him and then Mum, Dad, Helen, Charley and Cassie all did the same. Everyone was crying.

A nurse came and asked if we would like them to make prints of his hands and feet, which we did.

When she brought him back into the room we asked that he stay with us. Jamie and I couldn't bear the thought of him going to a mortuary.

'He's not going there with all those strangers,' Jamie said.

The nurses dressed him in a tiny little blue hat and yellow cardigan and then I wrapped him in the vest top I'd been wearing during the birth and Jamie put his T-shirt around him too.

That night we laid him in the cot next to my bed and stared at him. We looked after him. We held his tiny hands, and we stared at his perfect nose and his little lips, and cuddled him for hours and hours.

Charley and her fiancé Matthew Wolfenden, who is also in *Emmerdale*, stayed in the room just outside of ours. All the next morning we all took it in turns to hold him and cuddle him.

He was given a lifetime of love in the twelve hours he was with us.

The next morning the funeral director came to the hospital. Very gently he said: 'Hi, we're here to take Archie now.'

Dad asked whether he should carry Archie out.

I just nodded.

We held our baby for the last time and kissed him goodbye. I desperately wanted to keep him. I never, ever wanted to let him go. But I knew I had to.

I handed him to my dad who carried him all the way downstairs to the hearse where he laid Archie into his tiny white coffin. So Dad was the last person to hold Archie.

By then I was a total mess.

Shortly after the doctor said I could go home. Jamie helped me pack my things together and we left the hospital. I'd arrived with my baby but I was going home without him. It seemed so, so unfair. All I had was some leaflets on late miscarriage and how to cope. I hate that word 'miscarriage' – he was a perfect baby and I'd given birth to him.

Back home I just sat on the sofa and cried. My stomach flattened really quickly, as if there had never been a baby there at all. Then the following day my milk came in. My boobs swelled up and I was leaking milk, but I had no baby to give it to.

I felt utterly empty. I didn't think anyone could understand. I didn't even want to talk about it to Jamie or Mum. I didn't want to speak to anyone, I didn't want to be comforted and I didn't want any more 'I'm sorry's. I just wanted my beautiful baby.

We were trying to organise Archie's funeral but I really couldn't think straight. Our friends Robin and Julie Arnold very kindly helped to organise everything. We just couldn't function enough to do it.

I swung between feeling devastated and feeling really angry. I was in a really, really bad place.

Every morning we'd go to the chapel of rest to see Archie. We held his hands, touched his tiny nose and talked to him about how much he was loved and how we would never, ever forget him.

We placed a picture of me and Jamie inside his coffin. It had been taken when I was pregnant on holiday in New York at the New Year. And David wrote him a poem and Emily wrote a letter which were also put in the coffin.

Everyone visited the chapel of rest. David and Emily also came with me to see Archie a couple of times. Emily wasn't scared at all, she just loved being with him. But David found it harder. I was unsure whether to let them go, but I was told by the funeral director that I ought to allow them to express their grief and deal with it how they wished.

'Maybe you shouldn't go every day to see him,' my mum said. I think she was worried about how I'd cope after the funeral, which was set for ten days after his death.

'But I want to be with him,' I said. Being with him was the only thing that made me feel a little better. Letting him go was the hardest part.

In the run-up to the funeral I couldn't think or talk about anything other than Archie and I became bitterly resentful of anyone else who could. I got really mad at Jamie because I felt he was getting on with his life and I was still grieving, when in fact he was just dealing with it in his own way – by not talking about it. Lots of men are like that.

I'm not saying it's not hard for the father, but it is different for the mother. The baby has been growing inside you and then it's gone, and you're left with this awful sense of emptiness.

If I walked into a room and Jamie was watching television, I'd feel really mad. I can see now that Jamie was grieving too, but he dealt with it in a different way. At the time I just felt he was moving on and I didn't want people to be getting on with their lives. It felt as though Archie had never existed.

Coronation Street issued a statement saying Archie had died and the response from the public was amazing. We received hundreds of beautiful cards and someone even started a website which got thousands of beautiful messages, poems and even pieces of music uploaded on it. The support from the public meant a great deal to us, and we were so touched.

We had also got dozens of text messages and phone calls from friends and people I hadn't seen in ages.

One morning my phone rang and it was Myleene. We hadn't really kept in contact very much over the last few years, but being a mother herself by then, I think she could imagine how I was feeling. We cried together on the phone and over the next few days we talked more than we had done since Hear'Say. She was really there for me.

The funeral was held at St Mary's Church in Prestwich, near Jamie's dad's house. Our families were there and lots of friends too. The support we received was amazing and it meant so very much to us. I was really bad with my nerves through the day and I was covered in hives from head to toe, and to be honest I wasn't really there. At the funeral Jamie carried Archie's coffin down the aisle to the front of the church as the Eric Clapton song 'Tears in Heaven' played. It was heart-breaking. At the front there was a big framed picture of me and Jamie holding Archie.

Jamie, Emily and I got up together and Jamie read a poem that had been sent to us and then I got up and read a poem that I chose from the website that had been set up. The words were beautiful and so moving. Then Emily insisted on reading the letter she'd written for Archie. But she was sobbing so much she couldn't finish it and asked me to read the last bit. She'd wanted people to hear what she'd written for her baby brother. Charley read a poem too. It was an incredibly moving service.

Then we went on to the crematorium at Agecroft Cemetery. It was packed and there were loads of flowers there and a beautiful arrangement from Myleene.

Inside, they played me and Jamie's song, 'Chasing Cars',

as the curtains closed on my baby's coffin. I just lost it. I started screaming and my legs buckled beneath me. It's all a bit hazy after that, but I'm told I just kept screaming.

After the ceremony, we drove on to a hotel and had a little wake that Julie and Robin Arnold had organised for us. But although I was there, I wasn't really. I was just blank. People said I was like a different person that day.

The next few days were horrific. I was so angry. I was angry that other people were pregnant and I wasn't. I was angry at people getting on with their lives when I thought they shouldn't. And I was angry at the world.

Mum had lost a baby before I was born and so she, of all people, knew what I was going through, but even she couldn't help me.

The worst thing was that I felt it had changed everything for ever between me and Jamie. We were both grieving in very different ways. He didn't want to talk about it at all. I didn't want to talk about anything else.

I can understand now that Jamie just found it too painful to keep going over and over Archie's death, but I thought he was acting as if nothing had happened, and that made me furious. We had some terrible rows over the weeks that followed. I had so much pent-up anger inside me and a lot of it became directed at Jamie.

I spent day after day sitting on the sofa in a blur. Everyone was being so kind to me but that didn't help at all. I avoided phone calls and talking to anyone.

The whole family had been deeply affected by losing Archie. David had been very quiet at the funeral and every time I looked at him he was staring at the floor. He made sure I knew he was there for me though. And Emily was only 11 at the time. It broke my heart when a few weeks after the funeral I found all these text messages on her mobile that she'd written to Archie. It was just like when I wrote notes to my granddad when he died.

I felt empty and useless. It was like it didn't matter if I was there or not any more. I kept thinking that David and Emily didn't need me.

I was in a very low place. Now I can see that my children will always need me whatever age they are, but at that time I just couldn't see that. I felt like I had nothing to offer anyone. I was at rock bottom and there were days when I didn't want to carry on. I'm not saying I was sitting there thinking how I would kill myself, but I couldn't see any point in it all any more.

Mum was going out of her mind with worry. She'd always fought so hard to protect me and my brothers and sisters, but there was nothing she could do this time.

'I feel so useless,' she kept saying.

But she couldn't help me. No one could.

Everyone tried to lift my spirits, but I didn't want help. My sister Tracey tried to get through to me too, but she couldn't help me either. I didn't want help, I didn't want to heal, I didn't want to move on. I didn't know where to turn so in the end I reluctantly went to see my GP. I told her everything and how devastated I was feeling. I felt like nothing meant anything any more.

'You could have counselling,' she said. 'But I don't know whether it will help. You've got Jamie and your family. Try talking to them.' She didn't give me pills or anything like that, and I'm glad about that now. I wasn't clinically depressed; I was just very, very sad.

My mum had got rid of most of the things we had bought as she felt it would be too painful for me but Ben Thompson, who plays my son Ryan in *Corrie*, had bought Archie a teddy bear before he was born and I kept that with me and would cuddle it every now and then. And we'd also bought Archie a little Adidas tracksuit, which he never got to wear. I'd look at that and try to imagine what it would have been like if he had lived.

We collected Archie's ashes from the funeral director in a tiny box which I have kept on my bedside table ever since. I didn't want to scatter them; I wanted to keep them near to me. We never got the chance to get to know Archie, to see him as a little boy and to find out what his personality would have been like. I wanted him to come home with us some-how. The only thing we have are his ashes and that is why I could never give them up.

We chose a box with a picture of an angel on it, which was engraved with the words 'Your presence we miss, your memo-ries we treasure, loving you always, forgetting you never.'

I still kiss the box every single day. My baby boy.

Three weeks after Archie's death, Kim Crowther, who was then producer of *Corrie*, asked if I would go back in to finish off a few scenes. I didn't really want to face anybody but I didn't want to leave everyone there in the lurch and Mum thought it might do me good.

Everyone at *Corrie* was just amazing and I found it helped

to be busy. But even at work, that feeling of emptiness didn't really go away. I was still sad and very, very angry.

Once those scenes were finished, I took a couple of months off to get my head together.

21

TRYING TO START AGAIN

....

A few months later I decided to go ahead and have a boob job and liposuction. The timing might seem weird but I'd been thinking about having them done for years and I'd had two consultations with a surgeon and planned the operation before I fell pregnant with Archie.

After having David and Emily I'd always had a bit of a belly, and no matter how hard I trained in the gym, I could never get rid of it. And after having had David and Emily I'd become very flat-chested. Certainly being a bit flat up front affected my confidence, and there were lots of clothes that I couldn't wear.

The operation itself wasn't too bad, but the recovery was a nightmare, particularly after the boob job. Because I was adamant that they should look as natural as possible, I had the implant placed under the muscle. That meant three layers of stitching, and it was agony afterwards. When I woke up my boobs were enormous and strangely shaped – they were like two traffic cones or Madonna's bra in the 'Vogue' video!

'Don't worry, it's just swelling,' my surgeon said as I stared at them in horror. I had to hold bags of ice on them and gradually they began to look a bit more normal.

Four days after the op, Jamie was up for Best Actor at the Soap Awards, the do where we had met just a year earlier. I wanted to go along to support him but I was in absolute agony. I wore a lovely Philip Armstrong dress again, but I was in serious pain. I was gutted Jamie didn't get Best Actor that night though, because he should have won hands down.

I was just recovering from the operation when I had to have a post-natal check-up and smear test. I went down to London for it to the gynaecologist I'd had since living down in St Albans.

I didn't hear anything about the results for a month and then I got a phone call from my gynaecologist.

'I'm afraid something has come up abnormal on your smear,' he said.

Oh no, I thought. Surely there couldn't be more bad news.

'It's not cancer,' he said. 'But you may have pre-cancerous cells. I'm going to have to do a biopsy and send some cells away for analysis.'

I felt sick just hearing the word 'cancer'. It was just after Jade Goody passed away. She had been so brave in talking about it and I really think she saved a lot of women by raising awareness.

After weeks of not being able to see any point in life, I immediately realised exactly how much I wanted to be around and just how much David and Emily relied on me.

My gynaecologist was doing everything he could to reassure me, but I still felt scared.

I had the biopsy and then Jamie and I went away for a few days together. We were trying to get things back on track, but it wasn't easy. We were still grieving – but alone, each in our different way.

When we got back, the results of the biopsy were ready. The cells were pre-cancerous and I would have to have them removed.

It was actually a fairly straightforward procedure and they removed the cells. But the whole episode gave me a horrible shock, especially coming so soon after Archie's death

That summer things weren't good between Jamie and I though. Yes, I had the boob job and went back to work, and on the surface it probably seemed like I was coping all right. But inside I was still feeling lost and angry about losing Archie. He should have been born by then but instead all I had was his ashes.

I ached for another baby. I knew getting pregnant again wouldn't replace Archie, but that was what I craved.

I also had quite a few times when I felt very low and found it hard to concentrate at work. Then I'd resent Jamie, because he didn't appear to be suffering in the same way as me at all.

But he was struggling too. He hadn't really talked about Archie's death and I think he bottled a lot of stuff up. We started rowing badly.

By September we had drifted apart. We hadn't stopped loving each other, but we are both fiery people and we were clashing over everything.

'We need to start again,' Jamie said one day.

'What do you mean?' I asked.

He couldn't really explain. What he really wanted was for

us to go back to how it had been when we first started dating and were having fun. Everything had happened so quickly between us, and at a stage when we should have still been going out and having a laugh, we'd been going through this devastating sadness.

Now I know that he was trying to save our relationship. But at the time I thought Jamie had it all wrong.

'I don't want to start again,' I said. 'I want us to get on with what we have got now.'

We couldn't agree on even the most basic things any more.

Eventually Jamie decided he couldn't do it anymore.

Looking back, he was just saying that he wasn't sure how to cope with things between us and he needed time to sort his head out. But at the time all I could hear was him saying he wanted out.

I was so hurt and so angry. After everything we'd been through, I just thought he was bailing on me. Within the space of three days he took all his stuff out of the house. We spoke all the time but that just made me more confused. I didn't know what he wanted. But I certainly wasn't going to hang around while he decided whether he felt he could be with me or not. I needed some kind of certainty and closure. And the press were already sniffing around and had got wind of our separation. So, in the heat of the moment, I decided to take the initiative.

I rang the *Coronation Street* press office and told them to release a statement saying me and Jamie had split.

Putting down the phone, it took a moment for it to hit me: I'd ended it.

Looking back, it was stupid. If I hadn't been so devastated

by Archie's death, I would probably have handled things differently. But at least releasing the statement really brought things to a head between us.

I was heartbroken. After losing Archie and having the cancer scare, it was more than I could deal with. As soon as he left, I missed Jamie terribly.

The children were at their dad's for a few days and I couldn't bear being on my own just then so I spent a few days with my friend Dawn Ward. We've been friends for years after meeting at a charity do. She's married to the former footballer Ashley Ward, and they're successful property developers. They had also been through a terrible time. She'd fallen pregnant at the same time as me and her daughter Aston was born nine weeks prematurely and she had pneumotharax, which meant both lungs collapsed and then later down the line she contracted meningitis. It had been touch and go for a while. It was awful for them. Despite all that, they were still there for me.

A few days after the press statement went out, Jamie and I decided to meet at his mum's where he was staying. We talked and listened to each other properly for the first time in months and gradually I accepted what he was trying to tell me. I realised how much he was still hurting over Archie and how he too was grieving.

'I wasn't trying to hurt you,' he said. 'I was just trying to save the situation. I think we need to start again and to start having fun with each other the way we used to do.'

There was no doubt I still loved him and I did want to save the relationship. It was clear he loved me too.

'OK,' I said. 'So shall we give it another go?'

And that was that. We went back to the beginning, which was all Jamie had wanted. We decided to continue living apart but to start dating again and to have some fun together. I rented a house nearer to Manchester and Jamie rented somewhere too. 'We'll take it slowly this time,' I said. But things rarely seem to happen slowly for me.

22
A NEW BEGINNING

·········

'About your Christmas present,' said Jamie. 'I've had to order it from America, so it won't be coming until January. Is that all right?'

'Yeah, of course,' I said. Obviously it would have been nice to have a surprise on Christmas morning but so long as we were all together and having a good day, nothing else really mattered.

2009 had been such a miserable year that I was determined we'd have a good Christmas.

It was Dave's turn to have David and Emily that year but we had little Billy with us which was lovely. And Jamie was pretty much like a little kid too as he ripped the wrapping paper off all the presents I'd bought him.

Jamie gave me perfume and some sexy underwear (more for him than me), and I really thought that was my lot from Santa that year.

'Er, I think you should look behind the couch,' Jamie said to me.

'Really?' I said, intrigued. I looked behind our leather sofa and there was a piece of paper with a clue on it that led me into the kitchen. In there was another clue that led me into the bathroom. Santa was leading me on a pretty elaborate treasure hunt. I hadn't a clue what was going on.

Then after about five notes I found one that said: 'It's where the magic happens!'

I knew exactly where he meant! So I went upstairs to our bedroom and found another note lying on the duvet cover. It said, 'I love you, baby.' And that was it. No more clues. I thought maybe that was the end of the trail – an 'I love you' note. I was stupidly quite happy with that, as he's so rarely romantic! But Jamie was stood behind me saying: 'Keep looking, keep looking.'

I looked for ages until finally I felt something hard inside the duvet cover. I pulled it out – it was a jewellery box. It was quite big so I still had no inkling what might be inside it – earrings maybe?

I picked it up, opened the box and the most beautiful platinum and diamond ring fell out. My mouth fell open.

I turned round, Jamie was standing behind me. He went down on one knee and said, 'Will you marry me?'

I felt like I couldn't breathe. It was just amazing. I mean, totally amazing.

Only the day before we'd been down town doing some last-minute Christmas shopping and we'd ended up having a massive row because I said he'd never commit – stupid cow that I am! And he already had the ring! He'd even asked my mum and dad for their permission. Of course they agreed, but with a stern warning that he was never to hurt me.

Apparently Jamie had been planning to propose in front of our friends and family on New Year's Eve at our party, but he was so excited about the whole idea that he brought it forward to Christmas Day.

Of course I said yes. I love Jamie with my whole heart and, despite all the sadness we've been through, I know we are good together.

After getting back together at the start of November we had tried to take it slowly, but we just couldn't really keep apart. We'd have fun together, we'd laugh and we'd argue too. Sometimes, Jamie can be a right pain in the arse, but then so can I. And I love him like mad! And because we're both quite fiery there's never a dull moment!

When I had moved into a new rented house with the kids at the beginning of December 2009, Jamie had pretty much moved in too.

But things were on a far more even keel than they had been before. We'd talked more about how we both felt about Archie's death and I think for the first time I realised just how much pain Jamie had been in. Finally we could understand what the other had been through after Archie died. We would never forget Archie, but we were learning how to deal with our heartache over his death together.

Although Jack and I had originally intended to wait two years before divorcing, I brought things forward when I fell pregnant with Archie. I didn't want to give birth to another man's baby when I still had the surname Ryder. It just didn't feel right. I wanted the divorce done with so I could go back to being Kym Marsh. But for the divorce to go through in under two years we had to have some element of blame. I decided to admit adultery as technically Jack and I were still married when I'd got together with Jamie, even though in reality we were separated.

But what should have been quite a simple divorce turned into a nightmare when it came to money.

Jack claimed he hadn't been able to pursue his career because he was looking after my children, but in reality he'd had various different theatre jobs during that time and my parents had done most of the childcare during the time we were together.

And although I didn't have a problem with Jack having his fair share, I felt he was being unreasonable.

Since we couldn't agree on a settlement, lawyers got involved and it dragged on for about a year. I felt that a lot of the problem was with people advising Jack. Even when I suggested meeting for mediation, he refused.

It took months and months but finally we met somewhere in the middle on the financial settlement. I just wanted the divorce over and done with.

We've had no contact since the divorce was finalised and it's been really tough for the children which makes me very sad for them. But our lives are so different now. That chapter of my life is closed.

With the divorce completed, Jamie and I were free to plan our life together. Initially we set a date for the wedding in December 2010.

At the start of the year I took on another big new challenge when Vivien, my agent, called to ask if I'd like to take part in a new primetime Friday-night show called *Popstar to Operastar*.

The show was pretty much what it said on the tin – over a series of six weeks a group of pop singers (or ex-pop singers) would train as opera singers, competing with each other in a live performance every Friday evening.

It sounded really exciting. I'd been offered quite a lot of reality shows over the years but I'd never really fancied doing one before. But this seemed like an amazing challenge. I still loved singing, but I had no idea whether I would be able to perform opera. I decided there was only one way to find out – to give it a try!

The other singers competing included Darius Campbell, who I had first met when we were in *Popstars* together ten years earlier, Bernie Nolan, who was lovely, Danny Jones from McFly and Jimmy Osmond. The show was hosted by Myleene Klass and Alan Titchmarsh, and it was lovely to be working with Myleene again. Over the past few years we had got on really well when we had met at dos and we texted each other and chatted on the phone. The problems we'd had back in Hear'Say were ancient history and I loved seeing her again.

The only problem for me was that I was the last one to come onboard, so by the time I signed up and was assigned a vocal coach I was two weeks behind everyone else.

I thought I'd be able to do the show while filming *Coronation Street* but it quickly turned out to be far harder than I realised. I was squeezing in singing classes before and after work at *Corrie*, which meant incredibly long days. And I felt I was constantly running to catch up. Other contestants would be learning next week's song while I was still labouring over this week's one.

Then I'd have to travel down to London after work on Thursday, rehearse and film recorded sections for the show on Friday, do my live performance on Friday night, then travel back to Manchester again on Saturday. And quite often I would be working again at *Corrie* by Sunday morning. Nightmare!

I felt exhausted but, worse than that, I hardly had any time to spend with Jamie and the kids. I actually loved the opera singing – that was fab. I learnt so much about placing my voice and the technical skills involved. But sadly I couldn't enjoy the whole experience because I was always running around, playing catch-up. Every spare moment I was learning my lines for *Corrie* and words for a song in languages that I couldn't even speak. I can't even speak my own language properly! Sometimes it felt like my head would explode!

By the fourth week I was exhausted. I was given a song called 'Nella Fantasia' to perform, which means 'In My Fantasy'. The lyrics talk about 'souls that are always free' and every time I practised it I would think of Archie. The words just seemed to be all about him. By the time I came to perform on the night I was already quite emotional and when I started singing all I could think about was my baby. It was a struggle getting through it without breaking down, and by the end I was incredibly upset. Myleene was great to me that night though and really helped me through it.

I finally got voted out of the competition in week five and I can honestly say I was pleased to go. Just before I was about to go onstage and sing Katherine Jenkins said in a video clip that I was the weakest singer. I was really annoyed about that, it just felt very unprofessional of her to do that just before someone sings.

I know reality show contestants always say they're happy about being knocked out (to save face, if nothing else!) but I really, really was. I was exhausted doing the show and *Coronation Street*, as well as running a family, and it'd been frustrating not being able to focus on the opera singing as much as I would have liked.

That said, I learnt a lot and I met some fab people. And I really enjoyed learning new skills and having the opportunity to use my voice again.

After *Popstar to Operastar* was over I took a holiday with the kids to recover. Jamie couldn't come because he was rehearsing for a stage show of *A Chorus Line* in Manchester which was a brilliant new challenge for him.

Back home it was a relief to be able to concentrate on *Coronation Street*. At the start of the year my storylines were a bit quiet but I still had to be on-set a lot because working behind the bar in the Rovers means you're in loads of scenes, even if you aren't directly involved in the action.

We also had a new producer, Phil Collinson, who is brilliant and had some incredible plans for the show's fiftieth anniversary in December 2010. It was to be marked with a live episode and also an amazing tram crash with special effects created by the experts who did the film *Gladiator* and also *Dr Who*. I was told I was going to have some great storylines around the anniversary, which was really exciting.

I loved being in big storylines and I will always be grateful to the producer Steve Frost for casting me. I've become good friends with Steve and his wife Hayley over the past couple of years and I once said to him, 'You didn't half take a risk hiring some girl from a pop band to be in *Corrie*.'

'Yes, I did,' he admitted. 'But I knew you'd be good at it. And every producer who comes into a show wants to be remembered for doing good things. For me, one of those things was Kym Marsh.' I thought that was a lovely thing to say.

A lot of 2010 and the first half of 2011 was spent working on this book. It has been really emotional going over my life in such detail. I've spent a lot of time thinking about my childhood and it's been painful reliving the hard times in my life, especially the bullying and the death of my son.

I'm sure some of the bad experiences continue to affect me today. I'm still very conscious of the way I look and I get incredibly anxious if I think someone is talking about me.

But, in general, I count myself as lucky because I came through it all. How many kids do you hear about nowadays who've killed themselves because they've been bullied? And why were they picked on in the first place? Just because they seemed be a bit different. But it's good to be different – it's what makes you special – and if everyone was the same the world would be a very boring place. Kids have got to be given the freedom to be different without being bullied. That's why I support anti-bullying charities to help raise awareness of the problem and work on ways of preventing it.

Being bullied has meant it's always been a struggle for me to make friends. It's almost like part of me is waiting for people to turn on me. I hate that feeling of being let down so much that on some level I've decided it's safer to keep my distance.

I have some good friends at *Corrie*. Then I have my old mate Tracey Shaw whose little girl Grace Kimberly is my goddaughter. Then there's Vince who is one of my closest mates as well as being my hairdresser. Dawn Ward is one of my best friends and has been there so much for me over the past few years. And down in London I have my friend Katie who I met on *Saturday Night Fever*. Since meeting Jamie my other close mates have become his sister Charley who now has a baby boy, Buster, his other sister Cassie who has one-year-old Spike, and his mum, Helen.

But I don't have loads of friends, and sometimes I can feel quite lonely. Now and again I'll look at Jamie, who has loads of mates he's known since he was a kid, and I'll think how great that must be. I just haven't got that.

That's probably why I've always been so close to my family. I'm very close with my sister Tracey and her kids, Trevor, who's now twenty-four, Nathan, who's twenty, Jason, seventeen, and fourteen-year-old Kimberley. Tracey works nights and I work days so it can be hard to find a time to get together, but we talk a lot on the phone and she knows I'm always there for her. Tracey had a tough time when she was married but that ended and now she has a new boyfriend called Ian who is a great guy.

My brother Jon now lives in Rugby with his wife Clare and their son Dylan, who's four. They've also just had another baby called Finley, which is very exciting. My other brother Dave still lives in Ashton-in-Makerfield with his fiancée Faye. Dave also has a twenty-year-old son, Scott, from an earlier relationship.

Sometimes now we can go for months on end without all seeing each other, which is a real shame, but we try to keep in touch on the phone.

But of course I still see Mum and Dad all the time and really they are my closest friends. They live in Runcorn which is about twenty-five miles away from our house in Manchester and still help look after David and Emily on the days I'm working. They're an incredible support to me, just as they always have been. And now Emily is my dad's shadow in the same way as I was his shadow when I was her age.

There is no way I would have achieved anything if they hadn't been there encouraging me, helping me and picking me up whenever things went wrong. They're my inspiration too. They've been married forty-five years now and are still as in love as they have ever been. I think that's an incredible achievement and I can only hope that me and Jamie have the same kind of marriage.

Emily is at the age now where she is more interested in her friends than anything else and she's not so bothered about hanging out with her family. When she is with us she's constantly texting her mates because they probably seem a lot more interesting. But I try to explain to her how important family is. Friends will come and go but your family are for ever. When things go wrong and life is crap, it'll be your family who're always there for you.

In the course of writing this book, it's also been quite painful going back to the years before I auditioned for Hear'Say, when me and the kids were living hand-to-mouth, and it looked like my singing career was never going to come to anything.

That was so bloody tough. But leaving David and Emily to join the band was even harder. I hated being away from them. But hard as it was, I'm glad I did it. Mum was absolutely right that day when she told me that sometimes you have to make short-term sacrifices for the sake of long-term gain. All our lives would be so different now if I hadn't taken that chance. We don't live an extravagant lifestyle, but we're comfortable, secure and happy and that's enough for me.

I keep in touch with Myleene and Danny from Hear'Say, but sadly I don't have any contact with Noel and Suzanne. I try not to dwell on the past, and just concentrate on looking forward.

When I started this book, I wasn't quite sure how it was going to end. In all honesty, I didn't think it was going to be a totally happy ending. Because although I had Jamie, two fantastic kids and a brilliant job, there was still something missing.

I longed for another baby. It was a physical ache inside me.

Nothing was ever going to replace Archie; no one ever could. But I was still desperate to have a child with Jamie. I turned thirty-four in June 2010, and I felt like I shouldn't wait around. As I'm at risk of complications, I at least wanted to have age on my side.

Jamie and I talked about having another baby but I was adamant if we did try again we should plan things meticulously to do everything in our power to prevent us going through another loss.

Even though Jamie was keen on the idea of trying again, I think he was also pretty scared about how I would cope if things went wrong again.

So there we were, all ready to plan and organise the conception in fine detail this time. And then we were a bit careless one night and the pregnancy came out of the blue again!

It's funny how life turns out that way sometimes.

I was two days late when I decided to do a pregnancy test. As soon as I looked at the plastic kit a little blue line had formed. I felt so excited – but terrified too.

Jamie was away doing a personal appearance so again I had to wait for him to come home before breaking the news.

'I've got some news,' I said, within minutes of him stepping in the front door. 'I'm pregnant,' I said.

Jamie was delighted, but just like me he was also very nervous. We both so wanted this pregnancy to go well.

David and Emily were so excited about the new baby too. But they never forget about Archie either.

'Just because he isn't here doesn't mean he's not my brother,' Emily said to me earlier in the year. And when we went on holiday in the summer David was walking along one evening when he stopped and said to me: 'Look Mum, there's Archie.'

'What do you mean?' I said.

'Look, up there. It's the brightest star in the sky.'

I could feel tears in my eyes when he said it, but it was lovely. It showed me that despite how I felt when he first died, I had never been grieving for Archie on my own. We were all in it together.

I have a great relationship with Jamie's son Billy too. He calls me 'my Kym' and he's very, very cute. He's five now and stays with us three nights a week. He wanders around the house after his older brother and we call him 'David's shadow'.

I'm so proud of the way David and Emily have turned out. David has his GCSEs this year and Emily reached her teens in November 2010.

David is thinking about staying on at school because there aren't many jobs around right now, and he still isn't sure what he wants to do. He's such a good kid. While I was a nightmare at his age, he's never caused me any trouble at all. He's very protective of me and hates it if I get hassled when we're out. But over the years he's learnt to handle the kids at school who take the mickey out of him for having a mum on the telly.

He'll get lads coming up and saying, 'David, your mum's a MILF.'

'Whatever,' is his standard response.

And when I had to do a scene where I was seen getting out of a bath naked (but covered in strategically placed bubbles!) he had a kid say: 'Phwoar. Saw your mum in the bath last night, David!'

'I saw your mum in a magazine,' he replied, dead cool.

'Oh, what magazine?' the kid asked.

'RSPCA!'

I think he gets the lip from me!

Emily and I are very similar, so I guess there is bound to be a bit of trouble ahead there! Emily is very bubbly and as soon as she walks into a room you know she's there. She really reminds me of myself at her age, except she is much more popular than I ever was. She's feisty and fiery and she loves singing and acting and goes to theatre classes on a Saturday morning. She's very talented. And she's gorgeous-looking – which I'm sure is going to give me a whole pile of things to worry about in the next few years. If she does choose to go into show business though, at least I'll be able to help her make decisions along the way.

Me, David and Emily are still incredibly close, and I like to think we can talk about anything; we have a very open relationship with each other. I guess we grew up together really as I was only 18 when I became a mum. When I think back to the days when we were living in that house with the flying ants, I know that it was David and Emily who got me through it. It was them that gave me something to smile about every day, however bad things seemed. And it was for all of us that I entered *Popstars* and life changed for ever.

By the summer of 2010 Jamie and I had decided to push our wedding back. Although we really want to be married one day, we started wondering why we were putting ourselves under too much pressure. We decided to just relax and enjoy ourselves, rather than piling on more stress with months of wedding planning. I'm sure we'll get married one day, but at the moment it's not a priority. We're good as we are. I love him, he loves me – it's that simple. Oh, of course we still have some right blazing rows from time to time. But that's just us! I wouldn't have it any other way.

In the autumn of 2010, Jamie was invited back to *Hollyoaks*, which was amazing, particularly as everyone thought his character Warren Fox had been killed in a fire! But he was such a popular baddie that they wanted him back and Jamie agreed.

He had done a few short films, some theatre and appeared in BBC1's *Casualty* but acting work had been really hard to come by in the time he'd been away from the show and Jamie likes to be busy. He'd still like to do other things one day, maybe try out for shows in LA, and hopefully he'll do that when the industry picks up a bit again.

I'm still ambitious, and who knows what other challenges might be out there too. But I'll always be proud to be in *Coronation Street*. It's a national institution, for God's sake!

God willing though, my biggest role is still yet to come – as a mum to a new baby and two teenagers!

It's been a long old slog from being a single mum too skint to pay the leccy to where I am today. But we got there. And I do mean 'we'.

My family. My life.

23
MY HAPPY ENDING

....

From the moment I discovered I was pregnant I knew I had to do everything in my power to keep this baby safe.

Losing Archie had been horrific and I couldn't imagine how Jamie, the kids or I could go through that all over again. It was a scary time, knowing we were facing the same worries and uncertainties we'd been through before, and I'd lost all confidence in the medical profession.

But I wanted this baby so much. It mattered more to me than anything.

I decided to make an appointment with a private consultant who was recommended to me by my gynaecologist. In November 2009, I'd presented a documentary for *Tonight with Trevor McDonald* called *Born Too Soon*, which looked at the shocking numbers of babies born prematurely in Britain. There are about 50,000 preemie babies born in this country each year, one of the highest rates in Europe, and it is still on the increase. But many of the experts I spoke to in making that programme said that maternity services still remain the 'Cinderella' section of the NHS – starved of resources and attention, even though they do the most incredible work.

At the moment, women in Britain aren't even scanned again after twenty weeks.

It seems terrible that you have to pay if you want a better service than what you can get on the NHS, but I knew that's what I had to do. It was very important to me that I would be taken care of by a doctor throughout this pregnancy and I wanted to know that there would be a medical expert on the other end of a phone if I ever needed them. I wanted everything to be different to the way it had been when I had Archie. I had to have that peace of mind.

From the start of this pregnancy I was classed as a high-risk patient as I had lost Archie and David was also born prematurely, and at thirty-four years old I wasn't exactly the youngest mother in the world. On top of that, I'd also had pre-cancerous cells removed from my cervix.

My first meeting with my consultant at about twelve weeks into the pregnancy was an eye-opener.

I asked him whether he thought this pregnancy would be OK.

'I'm not going to lie to you,' he said, looking me straight in the eye. 'There's a lot stacked against you.'

'I understand,' I said quietly.

What I'd wanted him to say was, 'Yeah, it's all going to be OK, kid. Don't worry about a thing.' But of course he couldn't. If he'd said that he would have been lying and he couldn't do that.

He was totally straight with me from the start and I really appreciated it.

We discussed whether he should put a stitch in straight

away to prevent my cervix from opening too early but he was reluctant to do that. No one had been able to tell me exactly what had gone wrong with Archie's pregnancy – whether an infection had caused the cervix to open or whether it was the cervix opening that had caused the infection. Because of this uncertainty, my doctor didn't want to dive straight in with a stitch, as there is a danger that having a stitch can introduce infection or even cause miscarriage.

Instead, he said he would carry out a cervical scan every week from sixteen weeks. That way he'd be able to tell if there were any changes in the cervix and labour was about to start prematurely.

It was around then that a scan showed that I was carrying a baby girl. Jamie and I were delighted. Even though we were both very nervous about how the pregnancy would progress, we wanted our baby to have a name right from the start.

'What about Polly?' Jamie suggested one day. 'I just kind of like it.'

I liked it too. It was incredibly straightforward but it just felt right. Now all we had to do was give Polly the best chance of survival.

The first scan went fine but I was only seventeen weeks gone when I got some bad news. It was the first time I'd gone for an appointment at the Bridgewater Hospital in Manchester on my own, as neither Mum nor Jamie could come with me that day.

I felt perfectly normal and didn't think anything had changed at all so when I laid down for the scan I was feeling quite confident. But within moments the consultant had spotted a problem. He could see that the cervix was changing ever so slightly and beginning to open.

'I think we are going to need to put in a stitch to prevent the cervix from opening further,' he told me.

I could barely hear what he said from that point on. The minute I left the room I started to cry. 'Here we go again,' I thought. It seemed that everything was happening just the way it had with Archie. The doctors had put a stitch in to prevent Archie being born so early and that hadn't worked. Why would it work this time?

A familiar feeling of dread washed over me. All those terrible memories came flooding back and I couldn't fight them. 'I'm going to lose this baby too,' I thought. 'It's all happening again.'

My doctor was lovely and tried to reassure me but I was utterly distraught. He told me I'd have to be admitted to hospital in two days' time to put in the stitch. He said the cervix opening was a gradual process so nothing was going to happen in the next few days, but he did want to carry out the op soon.

I went home and told Jamie the news. I was crying and so upset – we were so worried. For the next two days, until I had to go into hospital for the op, I couldn't think about anything else.

I kept torturing myself with thoughts about how the stitch hadn't worked last time so why should I trust that it would on this occasion. Friends kept trying to reassure me, saying that the stitch had been put in too late with Archie when nothing could be done to save him. They tried to persuade me there was much more chance of success this time but I wasn't convinced.

I also knew what was involved with having the stitch – the risk of introducing infection, causing miscarriage and all sorts of other complications.

But if I didn't have the stitch then nothing was more certain than the fact that I was going to lose Polly. Without the stitch, this baby was going to arrive way too early.

I had absolutely no option. Whatever my concerns, I had to have that stitch. It was the only hope our baby had of surviving.

I couldn't help but think that things were happening in exactly the same way as they had done when I was pregnant with Archie. If my cervix had started opening at seventeen weeks in that pregnancy then I may have been about two centimetres dilated at twenty-one weeks, which is when he was born.

No one was quite sure why this was happening. David had been born almost seven weeks premature but back then I hadn't even asked the doctors why they thought that might be. I was just happy to have my baby. Now, though, it puzzles me and I wish I'd questioned it at the time. But Emily I carried to full term and I'm not sure why that pregnancy should have been so different.

All of us – me, Jamie, David and Emily – were really nervous during those two days before I had the stitch. We all knew there was no alternative but we were still very, very worried.

When I went in to the hospital for the stitch, Jamie stayed by my side the whole time. I was given a spinal anaesthetic, which completely numbed my legs and torso, but I was fully conscious so I could keep talking to Jamie throughout the operation. At first the doctors hadn't been sure whether Jamie would be able to stay with me during the procedure but I desperately wanted him to be there so finally they allowed him to stay and he got all gowned up. He stood by the head of the bed and held my hand all the way through. It certainly isn't a pleasant procedure but Jamie was brilliant. He was an unbelievable help and I really needed his support after what happened with Archie.

I had to stay in the hospital overnight because if there were going to be any problems or complications they normally happen in the first twenty-four hours. I had a catheter fitted so I didn't need to use the toilet, which meant I basically did not move at all. I just lay on the bed wearing a particularly attractive pair of bed socks to prevent blood clots from forming!

After twenty-four hours they took the catheter out and I should have been allowed to go home but there'd been a complication. During the procedure they'd had to move my bladder to be able to put the stitch into my cervix. The bladder had become very swollen and bruised, which meant I couldn't pass urine, so I had to stay in for another day until that healed.

It was while I was in hospital that my doctor came in to see me.

'Look, we need to have a chat,' he said, really seriously. 'I'm concerned about the amount of hours that you're working. With all the difficulties you are having in this pregnancy you need to be resting as much as you can. Working is not going to help you. Obviously it is your decision but my advice would be that you should take some time off and rest.'

I didn't need to think about it for a second. 'OK,' I said.

I absolutely love my job at *Corrie* and I hate being away from the Street and all my mates there, but when it came to having my baby, there was no contest. I had to do everything I could for Polly and if that meant taking time off work, then that is what I would do.

I was certain everyone at *Corrie* would be fine about me taking time off because they have always been incredibly supportive to me through everything that has happened while I've been there. But I was still overwhelmed when they were so kind.

I was still in hospital then, so Vivien my agent called and asked if it would be all right for me to have some more time off work. Everyone she spoke to on set was brilliant. There were no arguments, no quibbles, just total support. They said I should take off as much time as I needed. It must have been a real pain for them because they had to completely rewrite a storyline I was in but they were fantastic about it.

I felt bad about causing disruption to so many other people in the cast but I felt that this was my only chance to have the baby and I had to do everything in my power to keep her.

When I got home from hospital I was told I had to spend most of my time resting, although I could occasionally potter around the house, cook dinner or maybe nip to the shops for an hour occasionally, so long as I didn't overdo things.

'That's fine with me,' I thought. 'I can deal with that.'

And at first it was fine. It was the run-up to Christmas and I was able to get David and Emily's presents and sort out all my shopping. We were also preparing to move house so I was able to oversee the packing up while Jamie was at work. I wasn't allowed to lift boxes or do anything strenuous but my mum and Jamie's mum came round to help. They were brilliant.

We moved into our lovely new house on the outskirts of Manchester on 21 December 2010. Jamie and I both loved it – it felt like a proper family home.

The day after we moved in I was due back to see my doctor for my weekly internal scan and examination. Jamie was working and Mum couldn't come with me either so Jamie's mum came instead.

As usual I lay down on the bed and he started the examination but within minutes of looking at the monitor I could tell something was wrong. I could see my cervix had opened right up all the way down to the stitch. The only thing holding the cervix in place and keeping the baby inside me was the stitch.

This was serious. I started to cry.

By then I was twenty weeks and a few days. It was almost exactly the same time as when I had lost Archie. Again it just felt like everything was happening exactly the same as before.

'I'm sorry, Kym, but we're going to have to admit you immediately,' my doctor said. 'We really can't ignore this. There are drugs we can give you that might be able to stop this continuing and to prevent labour from starting.'

'OK,' I mumbled but I could barely speak.

It was three days before Christmas and it felt like it was going to be the worst one ever.

I was utterly distraught. It was like I was in a nightmare

and I couldn't wake up. I was crying and as much as Jamie's mum tried to comfort me there was nothing anyone could do to make me feel better.

I spent the next few days in hospital while they gave me anti-inflammatory drugs to help prevent the cervix from opening. But the doctors will only let you have them for a period of forty-eight hours at most in case they harm the baby. So I knew I only had forty-eight hours for the drugs to work. It was still way too early for my baby to be born.

While I was in hospital the doctors noticed I had another problem too – as if I didn't have enough already! Basically, they realised my uterus wanted to expel anything within it, which is why I had been having minor contractions since about nineteen weeks. The baby was still so small that I couldn't even feel the contractions but that was what was happening. So the problem with my uterus, combined with what they called an incompetent cervix, was what was causing my body to keep trying to give birth to the baby when it was still unable to survive on its own.

On Christmas Eve my doctor came to visit me again.

'We'll scan you again first thing in the morning,' he said. 'If anything has changed and the situation is looking better than you can go home. If it hasn't, then I'm afraid you will have to stay here for Christmas.'

I nodded and tried to smile but it was tough.

That night I stayed in my hospital bed all on my own. Jamie was at home with the kids, trying to get everything ready for the following day. I felt so alone and I'm not ashamed to say that I did have a little weep. I knew I had to do whatever I could to give the baby the best chance I could and I'd made my peace with that but the worry and the separation from Jamie and the kids was just horrific.

My family and Jamie's family were brilliant trying to make Christmas as much fun as they could for David and Emily but it was tough for them too. There were still boxes everywhere from the move but everyone rallied round; Jamie's dad got us a tree and my mum emptied enough boxes of kitchen equipment to be able to start preparing the turkey.

First thing on Christmas morning Jamie came to the hospital with David and Emily. I was so overwhelmed to see them, it was just brilliant – even if Emily was still in her pyjamas! That was hilarious.

Jamie came with me for the scan and we were both so nervous when they started checking to see whether the drugs I'd been given had been able to stop labour progressing.

In the end a doctor said he was happy that things appeared to have calmed down and I could go home so long as I had complete bed rest. But if I didn't do that then I'd have to be readmitted again.

I was delighted to be going home for Christmas but I was still consumed with worry about the baby. What on earth would happen to her next?

Back home I couldn't do anything. And I was terrified of moving in case I harmed the baby. Even when the rest of my family were at the table eating their Christmas dinner, I lay on the sofa in the other room on my own with my feet up. I tried to make Christmas as much fun as I could for David and Emily but it was a difficult time for all of us.

The next few days were much the same. I couldn't relax for a moment, I was so very frightened. I didn't know whether this baby would make it or not. I just took each day as it came and didn't make any plans for the future at all. I certainly didn't consider buying any baby clothes or a buggy or anything.

The situation remained the same over the next few weeks. I had to stay indoors on total bed rest. I was only allowed out of bed to go to the toilet and I certainly wasn't allowed out of the house. There were times when I got really down. Sometimes friends would joke: 'Oh, lucky you being able to stay in bed all day, watching telly.' But it was incredibly boring. I watched daytime TV endlessly and read dozens of magazines. Mum and Dad would visit every day and Jamie and the kids sat with me whenever they could but it was still tough. There were times when I got very down and low. I'm so used to being on the go all the time that I really struggled with not being able to do anything. And on top of all that I still had the worry about whether our baby would make it.

David and Emily were brilliant in those weeks. It was hard for them too. I couldn't run them around to places they wanted to go, I missed a parents' evening and I couldn't even cook their tea. David often cooked dinner and he grew up a lot during that time. It certainly made me realise how lucky I am to have such grounded, sensible, amazing kids.

The weekly scans continued and a few weeks into the New Year I was readmitted to hospital for the same forty-eight-hour course of anti-inflammatory drugs. It seemed that my cervix had opened further.

I was constantly hoping and praying I'd reach different milestones. For a while, my main goal was to reach 'viability', which is twenty-four weeks' gestation when a baby is able to cope on its own outside of the womb. Obviously, the baby can still have a lot of problems to deal with but there is a chance of survival then, so that was a big milestone for me.

'OK, we've made it to twenty-four weeks, lets get to twenty-six,' I said hopefully to Jamie when we hit that marker. 'At least Polly will be a bit bigger then.'

But before I even made that – at twenty-five weeks – things looked pretty grim again and after a scan my doctor thought it was unlikely I'd be able to hold out much longer.

'This baby could be coming at any point now,' he said.

I was readmitted into hospital to be given two shots of steroids twenty-four hours apart, which were intended to build up the baby's lungs so that if she was born early they would be more capable of working on their own.

It was the same steroids I'd had to have when David was about to be born prematurely, to help his lungs.

Obviously Polly had got a chance of surviving if she was born at twenty-five weeks. It wasn't a good chance, but it was a chance.

Some babies go on to lead perfectly normal lives after being born at twenty-four or twenty-five weeks but for others they can have a range of disabilities to cope with. So we not only had the worry about whether Polly would survive, there was also the concern that she might be born with severe disabilities, and we worried what her quality of life might be in that situation.

Jamie and I talked about how we'd cope if she was born with special needs. I decided I would give up work and be a full-time mum. We were well aware that everyone's lives in the family would change.

We both realised that looking after a child with a disability is very, very hard and we knew the future could be tough but we knew we'd just have to be strong and get through it together. She was our daughter and whatever happened, happened. We would deal with what was thrown at us and do whatever it took to look after her.

We didn't talk about those worries all the time but I know we both thought about them a lot. We still did not know what to expect.

At that time, I was kept in hospital for two weeks with more drugs that the doctors hoped would stop me from going into full labour. And I was still on total bed rest too, which also meant I was on blood thinning drugs to prevent my blood from clotting.

All the drugs made me feel pretty rubbish but it was a case of gritting my teeth and getting on with it.

Then, at twenty-six weeks, I was lying in bed in the hospital one night when I suddenly started getting contractions. I called a nurse and was immediately taken to the labour ward. This time it really did seem like the baby was on its way. It was still very early and as they wheeled me down the corridor I was crying my eyes out. I phoned Jamie and told him what was happening but he was at home with Billy so I told him to stay there and I'd call him later when I had a better idea what was happening.

That was such a bad night. I was on my own and all I wanted was for someone to remove me from this absolute nightmare and make it all better. For months and months I'd been in fear for my baby's life and it felt there was never going to be any let up from it.

In the labour ward they gave me an extra tablet aimed at stopping labour. I was then on the maximum dosage – that was my last hope. And, incredibly, over the next hour or so the contractions seemed to subside and everything calmed down. It was amazing. I'd come extremely close to having the baby but somehow it had passed.

After a few hours I was taken back to my normal ward. It was brilliant. I rang Jamie and told him what had happened. We were both thrilled to bits.

And then we got to twenty-seven weeks and still nothing had happened. And although it looked on the scan like the baby could come at any moment, she still hadn't appeared.

'Well, I can't keep you in hospital any longer,' my doctor said one day. 'So far the baby hasn't arrived and we have just got to hope she stays inside for a bit longer. We've thrown absolutely everything we can at you to keep this pregnancy going but now it's basically a waiting game. If you can just get to twenty-eight weeks then everything will be a lot better.'

So that was it. I was off home again.

As much as I'd hated being cooped up on a hospital ward for two weeks I'd felt safe there. If anything happened, I was surrounded by experts who could react at a moment's notice. But the thought of going home scared me. I kept thinking, 'What happens if I go into labour on my own? How long will the labour take? Will I get to hospital in time?' I was terrified about leaving hospital.

But after a few days back home with Jamie and the kids I was able to relax. Things seemed to have finally calmed down a bit so I simply focused on getting to twenty-eight weeks.

My doctor had said from the beginning that if I made it to twenty-eight weeks he would be absolutely thrilled, although he wasn't really expecting it.

'You made it,' he smiled, when I went in for my scan and check up that week.

'Yes,' I laughed. 'We made it.'

And then twenty-nine weeks came and my consultant was really, really pleased with me, although he still thought I could go into labour at any moment. 'I don't know how this baby is still hanging on,' he said, looking at the scan.

Even I could see that Polly was literally hanging in there by a thread – the stitch that had been put in all those weeks earlier.

'Well, whatever you're doing, you're doing it right,' he said. 'So just carry on relaxing.'

Then thirty weeks came and went and that was amazing. Every time I saw my doctor he was scratching his head about how Polly still hadn't come but it was all good news – the longer she stayed in me, the more her vital organs were developing and she was putting on weight.

By thirty-one weeks I had quite a big bump and I was beginning to feel uncomfortable in the way you do towards the end of a pregnancy. Most women would still have nine weeks – more than two months – to go at this point but I felt Polly really couldn't hang on much longer now.

I was feeling a lot of pressure low down and the baby's head had been pretty much engaged since about twenty-two weeks.

At thirty-two weeks my doctor said I could stop taking the pessaries that I'd been on since seventeen weeks to tighten the cervix because they no longer had any effect.

Then he looked at me and said, 'Right, well, you are now past the danger point. I can book your next appointment as a normal ante-natal check-up.'

At that moment I could have kissed him. For the first time in the entire pregnancy I felt normal. I suddenly felt like I'd turned a corner and I could finally look forward to having my baby. Little did I know I only had another week to go – but at least for that week I was really happy.

Up until that point I hadn't bought anything for the baby at all but at last I thought, right, it's OK now, I need to go and get stuff and start getting myself organised.

So one day I went out to Mothercare and bought all the bits I needed.

Earlier that morning I'd felt like I had a bit of an upset stomach. 'Oh, maybe that's a sign,' Mum said. But I'd had so many false alarms that this time I just put it out of my mind.

By late afternoon, though, I was getting contractions. I still didn't think this was the real thing, but when Jamie got home from work at *Hollyoaks* the pains were coming every five to eight minutes.

'Maybe we should go and get this checked out,' I said.

We drove to the hospital where they put me on a monitor.

'Yes, you are definitely having regular contractions,' the nurse said. 'We're going to take you to the labour ward.'

My consultant was called who advised that my stitch should be removed because if the baby really was coming this time then it would have to be taken out or it might rupture. Removing the stitch was pretty painful but I had gas and air for relief and Jamie was there again, holding my hand.

Then Mum came to the hospital, as well as Jamie's sister Charley.

I knew this time that it was really happening.

The contractions continued coming every five to three minutes throughout the night but by the morning I was still only two centimetres dilated. It carried on all through the next day too and the pain was horrendous but the labour was so different to when I'd given birth to Archie.

Although it was painful there was a sense of excitement in the room. With Archie I'd known throughout the labour that there would be no chance that he might live.

This time we'd all been waiting for Polly for so long and it had been such a worrying time that we were just desperate to see her.

Finally, after twenty-three hours in labour, Polly was born at 5.21p.m. on 23 March 2011.

She had managed to stay inside my womb for thirty-three weeks and one day and weighed four pounds and one ounce. David had been born at almost exactly the same time, although he had been heavier, four pounds and sixteen ounces.

The moment she popped out Jamie was watching and he just started crying. Then Mum started crying, too.

I was just totally out of it because they'd given me a spinal injection and diamorphine for the pain. But I also think I was in shock.

I remember hearing Jamie say, 'Is she breathing, Is she

breathing? Is she breathing?' and the nurses telling him it was all OK.

Then Jamie cut the cord and Polly was placed on my chest. It was incredible. My baby was here. At last. And she was healthy.

Within minutes she'd been whisked away and taken down to the Special Care Baby Unit to be properly checked out as she was very small. But she was breathing on her own, which was brilliant, and she looked fab.

I think it was then that I started to cry. It seemed that finally the constant fear of the past seven months was over.

But after about an hour we were told Polly had started struggling to breathe on her own and had had to be ventilated.

'Oh no,' I thought. 'Please God, not again.'

We rushed down to the Special Care Baby Unit but, thank goodness, when we got there, she was already much better. Apparently she'd got a little mucus in her lungs during the birth but that was soon taken care of and she only needed to be on the ventilator for a few hours.

The following day I was able to hold Polly properly for the first time. It was just wonderful. She still had a feeding tube and other tubes attached but it was amazing just to be able to pick her up.

Since then she has made incredible progress.

She was kept in hospital for three weeks but she grew stronger and stronger. I went to the hospital twice a day. I dressed her, changed her nappies, helped her take a bottle and bathed her, which was lovely. It's strange remembering how to do all those thing again after so long. But brilliant.

She lost a few ounces of her birth weight at first, as all babies do, but then came back to four pounds five ounces and the doctors were all very pleased with her progress.

Like a lot of premature babies it was hard for her to suck properly from a bottle and so for a while she had to take some of her feeds from a nasal tube, but once that came off we were allowed to take her home.

The whole family were so excited. The day we bought her home was one of the happiest days of my life. We feel so incredibly fortunate to have her because we know it could all have been so much worse.

I think she looks like Jamie and not at all like me although some of my friends reckon they can see a resemblance.

Polly is a real little fighter. She has been through so much already because whatever I went through during the pregnancy, she went through it too. But she made it.

David and Emily absolutely adore her and used to come up to the hospital with me to visit her all the time. Now she's home they can't get enough of her! So many cuddles. They've both been amazing through it all.

I know there is no way I could have got through the past year without Jamie, David, Emily and all our family to support me. It was very tough for everyone but we were very much a team and that was what got us through. And it was all so, so worth it.

And so, after all the fear, the pain and the worry, we have finally got a lovely, happy ending.

PICTURE ACKNOWLEDGEMENTS

© Alamy/United Archives: 10 above. Author's collection: 1, 2, 3, 4, 5, 6, 7, 12, 13 left, 15 below left and right. © Newspics: 16. © Getty Images: 10 below right, 13 below right. © PA Photos: 11 above. © Rex Features: 10 below left, 14 above. © Rex Features/ITV: 8, 9, 11 below, 13 above right, 14 below. © John Swannell/Camera Press, London: 15 above.

Every reasonable effort has been made to trace copyright holders, but if there are any errors or omissions, Hodder & Stoughton will be pleased to insert the appropriate acknowledgement in any subsequent printing of this book.